The Green Literacy HANDBOOK

Inspire Environmental Stewardship Through Critical Thinking, Reading, and Writing, Grades K–5

JEN CULLERTON JOHNSON
MARY K. GOVE

Solution Tree | Press

a division of
Solution Tree

555 North Morton Street
Bloomington, IN 47404
800.733.6786 (toll free) / 812.336.7700
FAX: 812.336.7790

email: info@SolutionTree.com
SolutionTree.com

Visit **go.SolutionTree.com/literacy** to download the free reproducibles in this book.

Printed in the United States of America

FSC
www.fsc.org
MIX
Paper | Supporting
responsible forestry
FSC® C008955

Library of Congress Cataloging-in-Publication Data
Names: Johnson, Jen Cullerton, author. | Gove, Mary K., author.
Title: The green literacy handbook : inspire environmental stewardship
   through critical thinking, reading, and writing, grades k-5 / Jen
   Cullerton Johnson, Mary K. Gove.
Description: Bloomington, IN : Solution Tree Press, [2025] | Includes
   bibliographical references and index.
Identifiers: LCCN 2024054016 (print) | LCCN 2024054017 (ebook) | ISBN
   9781960574480 (paperback) | ISBN 9781960574497 (ebook)
Subjects: LCSH: Environmental economics--Study and teaching (Elementary)
Classification: LCC HC79.E5 J65156 2025 (print) | LCC HC79.E5 (ebook) |
   DDC 372.8--dc23/eng/20250219
LC record available at https://lccn.loc.gov/2024054016
LC ebook record available at https://lccn.loc.gov/2024054017

Solution Tree
Jeffrey C. Jones, CEO
Edmund M. Ackerman, President

Solution Tree Press
Publisher: Kendra Slayton
Associate Publisher: Todd Brakke
Acquisitions Director: Hilary Goff
Editorial Director: Laurel Hecker
Art Director: Rian Anderson
Managing Editor: Sarah Ludwig
Copy Chief: Jessi Finn
Developmental Editor: Kate St. Ives
Senior Production Editor: Miranda Addonizio
Proofreader: Anne Marie Watkins
Text Designer: Rian Anderson
Cover Designer: Fabiana Cochran
Content Development Specialist: Amy Rubenstein
Associate Editor: Elijah Oates
Editorial Assistant: Madison Chartier

Always for Fernando. With love for my son,
Nico, and my goddaughter, Mica.

—JCJ

I dedicate this book to Alec Zenil, my grandson.
May the Earth be a better place for him to live.

—MKG

Acknowledgments

I'm grateful to God for all things. Thank you to Mary Gove for being a mentor and friend. For my Chicago family: Fernando, Nico, Colleen, Brian, Jack, Amy, John, Deb, Jim, and all my cousins. To my family in Argentina: Patricia, Silvina, Lorena, Walter, Ariel, Marianna, Lucia, Leo, Gina, Mateo, Mica, and Malena. In memory of my parents, grandparents, and father-in-law. Thank you to my fellow writers and friends: Bridget Joyce, Carol Moran, Amy Judt, Danielle Wynn, and Jane Gangi. To the work of Dr. Wangari Maathai and the Green Belt Movement (GBM); Lisa Merton and the GBM board; and Jennifer Seydel of the Green Schools Network, Andrea Holbrook, and Al Stenstrup, which planted many seeds. To Jim Cummings and Kijana Schools, Barbara Koenen and the CCRx team. Thanks to all my colleagues at Chicago Public Schools, Chicago Teachers Union, Cook County Juvenile Detention Center, and Wright College: Walter Taylor, Tara Whitehair, Susan Grace, Mr. Ward, Dr. Leonard Harris, Dianne Johnson, Regina Hanks, Steve Hyman, Mojisola Gray, Saleha Banu, Ms. Branch, Ms. Carlos, and Mr. Washington. A round of applause for our editor, Kate St. Ives, with support from Miranda Addonizio. Thank you to Dr. Lisa Ravindra, Dr. Jo Hayes, Richard Leonard, and Susan Temple. Very special thanks to Dr. Patty Dean for her friendship and support for all things reading—you are a light! To teachers, students, readers, and champions of Green Literacy—past, present, and future—you give it life. Thank you.

—JCJ

I would like to acknowledge that the genesis of Green Literacy occurred with inspiration from Dennis Sebian, whose environmentalism opened my eyes to the degradation of our natural world caused by industrialization and globalism. Over seventeen years ago, Dennis and I began giving talks about "ecological critical literacy" using children's books as springboards. In 2008, Dennis passed away. In 2010, Jen and I met at a Green Schools conference, where the conference organizers put us together. Meeting Jen and working with her on this Green Literacy journey have enriched my life; I am grateful for our work and the fun we have had together. Thanks to the teachers in our professional development programs with whom we have shared experiences and from whom we have learned. Thanks also to Kate St. Ives, our editor, for her insightful questions and nudges. Finally, I would like to acknowledge the many supportive people in my life: my husband, George; my daughter, Jessica; and countless friends in Cleveland and in Gainesville Cohousing.

—MKG

Solution Tree Press would like to thank the following reviewers:

Tonya Alexander
English Teacher (NBCT)
Owego Free Academy
Owego, New York

Ian Landy
Regional Principal of PIE
School District 47
Powell River, British Columbia, Canada

Shanna Martin
Middle School Teacher & Instructional
    Coach
School District of Lomira
Lomira, Wisconsin

Christie Shealy
Director of Testing and Accountability
Anderson School District One
Williamston, South Carolina

Sheryl Walters
Senior School Assistant Principal
Calgary, Alberta, Canada

Visit **go.SolutionTree.com/literacy**
to download the free reproducibles in this book.

Table of Contents

Reproducibles are in italics.

PART 2
TEACHING OF GREEN LITERACY 55

CHAPTER 3
Creation of the Green Literacy Model 57

CHAPTER 4
Thematic Unit Design and Customization With Twelve
Insights Into Green Literacy Teaching 79

PART 3
SUPPORT TO DESIGN YOUR OWN GREEN
LITERACY THEMATIC UNITS 105

CHAPTER 5
How Landscapes Shape Us 107

About the Authors

Jen Cullerton Johnson is an award-winning children's author, educator, and environmental advocate. She teaches at Chicago Public Schools and has been an adjunct instructor at Wilbur Wright College, City Colleges of Chicago. Jen has nearly two decades of teaching experience. Her educational career has spanned diverse settings, including working with incarcerated youth and in urban classrooms; teaching abroad in Japan, Ecuador, and Argentina; and leading nature-writing workshops in outdoor settings.

A champion for trees and environmental education, Jen is a certified TreeKeeper for the city of Chicago, where she volunteers to care for and advocate for urban trees. Her passion for trees has taken her across the globe. She has planted trees in Kenya with the Green Belt Movement, and in 2025, begins a Forest Therapy guide training. Her short stories and essays have been recognized with numerous awards and honors, including grants from the Illinois Arts Council; an ambassador's award to study writing in San Miguel de Allende, Mexico; and a teacher travel study with other educators from the Morton Arboretum in 2025 to further her studies on trees and biodiversity in Mexico.

Jen is the author of *The Story of Environmentalist Wangari Maathai* (2019) and its forthcoming Spanish translation in 2025. Her award-winning picture book *Seeds of Change* (2010) has been a bestseller for over a decade and is now available in Spanish (*Semillas de cambio*, 2024). She is an experienced presenter, sharing her expertise at conferences and professional development workshops across the United States and abroad, including presentations for the Association for the Study of Literature and Environment (ASLE), the Children's Literature Association (ChLA), the Green Schools National Network, and the North American Association for Environmental Education (NAAEE).

Jen earned a bachelor's degree in English literature and Spanish language from Indiana University, a master's degree in education from Loyola University Chicago, and a master of fine arts in creative writing from the University of New Orleans.

Mary K. Gove, PhD, is professor emerita at Cleveland State University, as well as a coauthor of *Reading and Learning to Read*, which promotes a balanced approach to literacy education and has been used in undergraduate and graduate literacy education programs since the early 2000s. Her award-winning dissertation, "Beliefs About Reading," continues to be a cornerstone of textbooks.

Before teaching at Cleveland State, Mary taught grades K–6 in public schools, was a reading specialist for grades 1–6, and worked in an urban district as a full-time professional developer. She won various awards for several professional development programs she spearheaded during the 1990s as she worked as an urban school district's professional developer.

She has published many articles in professional journals as well as written book chapters. In 2021, she and Jen Cullerton Johnson published the chapter "Green Literacy K–5: Nurturing a Scientific Mindset" in *Age of Inference: Cultivating a Scientific Mindset*.

Mary has presented at numerous conferences, such as those of the International Literacy Association, the National Council of Teachers of English, the Association for the Study of Literature and Environment, and the Green Schools National Network. Before and during her work at Cleveland State University, she wrote and led many grant efforts toward professional development, most of them organized around action research. While teaching at Cleveland State, she focused on critical literacy, professional development centered on action research, and ecological awareness and Green Literacy.

Mary attained a teaching degree from Drury College in Springfield, Missouri, and a master's degree and doctorate from Kent State University. She now resides in Gainesville Cohousing in Gainesville, Florida, where she and her husband, George, have a private house and share common spaces, including a common house, a swimming pool, a garden, and a workshop, as well as lots of fun.

To book Jen Cullerton Johnson or Mary K. Gove for professional development, contact pd@SolutionTree.com.

"I teach fourth grade. This year, I am all about getting ready for standardized testing. I see the need for my students to get involved with environmental issues beyond Earth Day, but I need to focus on literacy and math."

—Rachel

"I teach second grade in the city. The neighborhood is a little dangerous, so our school doesn't have a garden. We don't go outside much. I need ways to engage my urban students on environmental issues in the classroom and relate to their city life."

—Nick

"Environmental issues are enormous and scary, and they are messy. I don't even know how to bring up something like climate change except in a superficial way. My students recycle, and my students turn off the lights, but really, how do you start a deeper conversation? It would be more doable to use something familiar to my fifth-grade students and me."

—Sharia

"I've got a big concern. I want to talk about environmental problems with my students. But the environment and problems like fracking have become so politicized in the news that I am a bit afraid to do so. Is there a way I can start this conversation so that it won't push the buttons of parents who have economic concerns?"

—Henry

"So many demands are placed on me as a classroom teacher. I believe in my third graders' thinking about the environment. We created a classroom garden last year, and that's great, but I want to start something where my students think deeper. I don't know if I have the time or know how to do it. If there was a way to add to what I am doing now, I might be interested in trying it."

—Aziza

What Is Green Literacy?

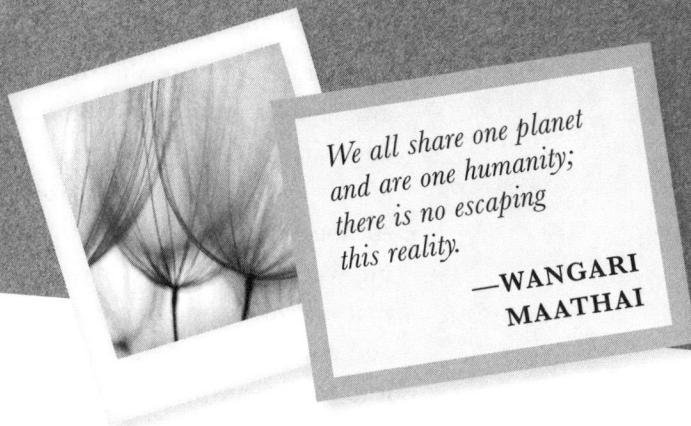

We all share one planet and are one humanity; there is no escaping this reality.

—WANGARI MAATHAI

While at a districtwide summer meeting on core curriculum in 2012, we presented ways to bring environmental awareness into K–5 classrooms. Teachers discussed two "big idea" questions.

1. How do we, as educators, bring critical environmental issues into our classrooms?

2. What holds us back from adding deep discussions about environmental challenges?

After we requested their permission to record them, the teachers shared their thoughts and feelings. Many teachers expressed they were willing to raise young people's environmental consciousness but were uncertain how to proceed when challenges arose. During this presentation, what struck us was these teachers' intention to take care of the living world and, in our case, a sincere willingness to facilitate similar connections for students.

Later, as we culled the recorded dialogue, we found that despite their support for student environmental awareness, teachers face concerns, reasonable doubts, and significant challenges in trying to birth those connections. Here, we've reconstructed what these teachers shared in a roundtable discussion about the challenges of teaching environmental issues in their classrooms.

Talking with these teachers, we recognized their thoughts and feelings. We felt them too. We've often grappled with fears, concerns, and doubts about teaching controversial environmental issues. Some years, our students made great strides. In other years, we made mistakes that hindered environmental awareness. Throughout our experiences, we've valued providing young people with classroom time to develop their voices and visions on complex environmental situations in which we have hope they will become future environmental leaders.

From this place of shared concern, we explored formal ways of bridging environmental awareness in students with the academic learning they must do in classrooms. We acknowledge that this work is ongoing and extensive. We see a growing demand from teachers locally and globally to incorporate more environmental awareness into their classrooms. Although we acknowledge the need for students to learn scientific principles, in our ongoing work and in this book, we seek to empower teachers and students through dialogue that considers environmental justice by making connections between the power of stories and environmental challenges. We believe sincere interactions with the living world often lead to student-initiated earth stewardship.

After a decade-long process of working with teachers and students of various subjects and backgrounds in both rural and urban areas and public and private spaces, community associations, and religious organizations, we coined the term and concept of Green Literacy. *Green Literacy* is a literacy-based practice anchored in our relationship with the Earth and humanity, rooted in environmental justice, and stemming from critical pedagogy. *Critical pedagogy* aims to empower students by encouraging them to question established knowledge, actively participate in their learning, and become agents of change. Questioning established knowledge often invites students to think critically about power dynamics within environmental issues. Green Literacy is a teaching practice that develops in-depth thinking, dialogues, and responses to the complexities of our relationship with the environment. Green Literacy uses multiple texts and digital media as catalysts for shifting perspectives with critical conversations. It is fixed in critical pedagogy so that students examine the social context of environmental justice issues, which includes but is not limited to race, class, and gender. Rooting Green Literacy in critical pedagogy empowers students to scrutinize the intricate matrix of environmental justice.

We support a transformative approach to teaching that weaves environmental awareness into every moment of learning every day of the year. Green Literacy disrupts traditional thinking and reveals how social and environmental challenges are profoundly connected. Green Literacy helps you empower students to uncover dynamics in texts that expose connections to environmental justice. You lead students to question narratives, uncover deeper meanings, and challenge how messages shape their understanding of the world. Together, you and your students confront these questions boldly and purposefully. Green Literacy reimagines how we all think, learn, and act about environmental issues. It connects social and environmental challenges, sparking critical thinking and inspiring action.

During Green Literacy professional development sessions, we often share the picture book *Duck! Rabbit!* by Amy Krouse Rosenthal (2009). We invite teachers to decide whether the image on the page depicts a duck or a rabbit. The optical illusion sparks curiosity: Is it a duck? Or is it a rabbit? Some teachers can see only a rabbit, while others see only a duck, seemingly stuck in their own perspectives. It isn't until near the end of the book that a shift in perspective occurs, and the image is seen differently. Suddenly, a duck becomes a rabbit, and a rabbit becomes a duck. When the reader steps back, they can see both a duck and a rabbit simultaneously. The set perspective followed by the moment of realization mirrors the way people often approach environmental issues. For example, take the issue of deforestation. Some people might focus on the economic benefits, like job creation and the use of timber, while others might just see the environmental harm, such as the loss of forests and wildlife. When we step back and look at the bigger picture, we can see the two sides are connected. When we reach sustainable solutions, like responsible logging or reforestation, we can meet economic needs while protecting the environment. Like in *Duck! Rabbit!*, shifting perspectives helps us see the whole story and find better ways to address challenges.

Our goal in writing and publishing *The Green Literacy Handbook* is to influence your and your students' perspectives on environmental and social issues. By this, we mean that you and your students will broaden your perspectives. As classroom teachers in the urban areas of Chicago and Cleveland, we have witnessed how Green Literacy practices help students develop a deeper understanding of diverse perspectives (to see both the duck and the rabbit) and articulate and amplify their voices on critical topics related to environmental justice. Further, we have observed that as Green Literacy practices help students find their voices and express their perspectives on environmental issues, they are empowered to advocate for sustainability and justice in their communities.

Our Vision for Green Literacy

We see you and your students developing continuous shifts in perspective, a magnification of thought, more compassion for the natural world, and an ability to grasp and respect our connections to each other and all living things. We believe future generations will need to be able to see many sides and the big picture if they want to solve environmental justice challenges.

We envision The Green Literacy Handbook as a tool for all teachers and students who want to engage with environmental challenges presented in the familiar formats of children's books and digital media, which act as springboards for critical thinking and critical dialogue.

We view the practices found within these chapters as a portal of empowerment for young people to cultivate their own voices, articulate the voices of others, and, through this process, create their own critical stance on social justice and environmental issues that affect the world they live in.

We believe that the state of our planet depends on how people, especially young people and their teachers, as part of a global society of concerned citizens, shift perspectives. Through student-initiated projects, small and large, teachers and their students can contribute to sustainability through systemic change.

We stand for a certain type of teaching, one that facilitates an open and nonauthoritarian stance among teachers and their students and questions power relations. Through this, we recognize the classroom as a microcosm of society where power dynamics reflect broader societal issues. By questioning and analyzing these power relations, both you and your students can understand and address the uneven distribution of power and privilege that influences environmental decisions and policies. To bring about systemic change, first, we must have a safe space and abundant time to connect with others so all voices are valued and examined creatively over time. Creating safe spaces allows for the nurturing of critical dialogue where every student feels heard. Deep understanding and meaningful connections develop not in haste but through sustained, thoughtful conversations. Over time, this process can cultivate a community of learners equipped to collaboratively work toward systemic change.

We hope that you will draw from our Green Literacy model to create your own thematic units and that this will lead to shifts in perspectives and actions around stewardship of the planet.

We call our book *The Green Literacy Handbook* because, like a trusted guidebook for explorers, it's designed to be a practical, flexible resource that supports your unique journey as an educator. A handbook, unlike a traditional textbook, invites you to chart your own course—whether that means diving into specific sections when the need arises, revisiting ideas as your teaching evolves, or using the reproducible "Green Literacy Thematic Unit Planning Template" (appendix A, page 193; also available at **go.SolutionTree.com /literacy**) to design your own Green Literacy unit. Because every teacher has their own experiences, interests, and classroom dynamics, this handbook honors those differences, offering tools and insights to meet you where you are and help you on your way.

We envision you, whether as an individual or as part of a teaching team, returning to these pages time and again, much like a gardener references a manual to cultivate a thriving landscape. Teaching Green Literacy is challenging yet deeply rewarding, and this handbook is here to nurture your growth, helping you expand your perspective, deepen your skills, and empower young people to critically engage with the world around them. That's why the book's introduction advises you on how to use this handbook—to ensure this resource feels approachable and adaptable to your needs.

Finally, we thank our teachers, past, present, and future, who work to protect our natural world. We thank them for engaging in practices within this handbook so that young people can think critically and have dialogues in their communities. We are grateful for compassionate teachers who guide young people so that community and inquiry arise, making way for empowering acts of environmental stewardship. Our young people are the gatekeepers of our living world, so we offer you, their teachers, practices to help them engage in environmental conversations that will be at the heart of their adult lives.

How to Use *The Green Literacy Handbook*

> *We have the choice to use the gift of our life to make the world a better place— or not to bother.*
>
> **—JANE GOODALL**

Welcome to *The Green Literacy Handbook*. You've found a go-to guide for deepening your practice of empowering young people to critically think, read, and write about urgent environmental issues.

Green Literacy is a teaching practice that develops in-depth thinking, dialoguing, and responding to our relationship with the environment, using multiple texts and digital media as catalysts. We created Green Literacy to help address the gaps between environmental education and its impact on young people's thinking. We offer a theoretical framework and teaching process to help make meaning and spark critical conversations about urgent environmental issues.

The Green Literacy Handbook is for any educator who wants to facilitate opportunities for their students to take a stand for the natural world, advocate for sustainable and equitable environmental change, and champion systems thinking to solve complicated environmental issues like e-waste, energy overconsumption, pollution, and loss of biodiversity. The primary audience for *The Green Literacy Handbook* includes K–5 educators such as classroom teachers, curriculum developers, program directors for nature-based community centers

1

or museums, outdoor educators, and homeschooling parents who are passionate about integrating environmental awareness into their various curricula.

Your commitment to empowering young people surely predates holding your copy of *The Green Literacy Handbook*. We know the handbook may not be the beginning of your pursuit. We offer it as a companion to the important work you are already doing. We see you, the teacher, standing at the crossroads with us. Together, we mark our stance as a place where education meets the Earth, showing others that becoming environmentally conscious is our way forward if we want to live in a viable and sustainable future. Whether you are a classroom teacher in traditional or nontraditional spaces, a homeschooler, a community organizer, a college professor, a steward of nature, or an advocate for critical thinking, we acknowledge you for your time, energy, heart, and resources you've poured into helping young people face complicated environmental hurdles with resilience. What you do matters—and what we do together transforms.

HOW *THE GREEN LITERACY HANDBOOK* IS ORGANIZED

The Green Literacy Handbook is divided into three parts: (1) "Foundations of Green Literacy," (2) "Teaching of Green Literacy," and (3) "Support to Design Your Own Green Literacy Thematic Units."

Part 1 contains two chapters. Chapter 1, "Green Literacy's Theoretical Foundations," offers descriptions and classroom vignettes that illustrate the theoretical foundations of Green Literacy, highlighting its connection to critical pedagogy. This chapter introduces Green Literacy ideals, which are agreed-on values that a teacher and students collaboratively create on an environmental issue. Chapter 2, "Green Literacy's Practical Foundations," lays the groundwork for Green Literacy by focusing on five essential components organized into three phases that reflect the natural process of deeply engaging with an idea. The first phase, *engage*, emphasizes developing thematic questions and fostering critical thinking through commentary. The second phase, *empower*, focuses on curating Green Reads and Views (carefully selected books, articles, videos, and other media that explore human and animal relationships with the natural world) and selecting Green Literacy strategies using the three cycles of comprehension. The last phase, *shift*, guides students to develop Green Literacy ideals. We provide support for adopting the actions of these three phases through guided use of the Green Literacy Thematic Unit Planning Template.

Part 2 includes chapters 3 and 4. Chapter 3, "Creation of the Green Literacy Model," chronicles our work with teachers in both long (yearlong) and shorter professional development sessions. Our model is rooted in our collaborative experiences, in which we work closely with teachers to explore, refine, and implement Green Literacy. The chapter includes rich examples centered on the thematic question, "How do you become an environmental leader?" It walks readers step by step through the process of developing a thematic question, curating Green Reads and Views, and applying the three cycles of comprehension with

Green Literacy strategies. The chapter provides guidance for cocreating Green Literacy ideals and offers a focus on K–2 learners, showcasing specific adaptations used by K–2 teachers.

In chapter 4, "Thematic Unit Design and Customization With Twelve Insights Into Green Literacy Teaching," we reflect on how our conception of Green Literacy thematic units has evolved from what we created with teachers who participated in our Green Literacy professional development sessions, offering readers a sense of the variability of design for thematic units. We also present practical insights, strategies, and reflections to help teachers adapt Green Literacy to meet the diverse needs of their students. The chapters in part 2 collectively aim to empower you with the tools and confidence to seamlessly integrate Green Literacy into your teaching.

In part 3, we introduce and guide teachers through three thematic units, starting with personal connection and expanding to broader communal and global perspectives. We organize chapters 5, 6, and 7 based on the engage, empower, and shift phases initially introduced in chapter 2. Chapter 5, "How Landscapes Shape Us," is the starting point, focusing on personal connections. This chapter explores how the landscapes around students shape their identities and how these connections—or the lack of them—affect their relationships with nature and their communities. Chapter 6, "How Extreme Weather Events Connect Our Communities," transitions from personal to communal themes, examining the impacts of extreme weather events, the plight of weather refugees, and the effects of climate anxiety on young people. Finally, chapter 7, "How Systems Thinking Changes Our World," brings students to explore how systems thinking can transform their understanding of interconnectedness and the power structures that sustain or disrupt ecological balance.

The chapters in part 3 offer thoughtful, intentional, and supportive units with suggestions and choices to show you how you might explore these big-picture environmental questions with your students. We include in each chapter completed segments of the thematic unit planning template (full completed templates for the part 3 units may be found at **go.SolutionTree.com/literacy**) along with commentary, a curated Green Reads list, suggested Green Literacy strategies, and space to develop Green Literacy ideals. While the units in chapters 5–7 are ready to use as they are, they are meant to be customizable to fit the unique needs of your students or your specific teaching context, or they can serve as inspiration to create something entirely new. To further support you in this process, the planning template can help you develop or customize a unit, guiding you to brainstorm and build your ideas through the Green Literacy process. The engage, empower, and shift phases include steps to develop a thematic question, foster your learning through commentary, curate Green Reads and Views, select Green Literacy strategies, and develop Green Literacy ideals. A blank planning template is available in appendix A (page 193). Completed examples in chapters 5–7 reflect a variety of teaching environments and perspectives.

In the epilogue, we emphasize professional development for teachers and school communities, such as through workshops and collaboration, while offering ways to embed Green Literacy into school culture with an eye toward future sustainable, student-led actions.

In *The Green Literacy Handbook*, we follow an arc of learning that builds from the personal to the global so that you may be aware of this as you plan for your classroom.

- We start with chapter 3's question: "How do you become an environmental leader?" To inspire students with their unique and personal connections, we ask them to consider the question, "What can I do?"

- In chapter 5, the question, "How do landscapes shape us?" expands students' awareness of the land around them.

- Chapter 6's question, "How does extreme weather connect our communities?," connects students to larger community contexts.

- Finally, chapter 7 asks, "How does systems thinking change our world?" to make students aware of how systems and environmental challenges and solutions interconnect in our world.

We have intentionally structured this progression—personal, communal, and then global—to reflect how people naturally develop care and responsibility for the environment (Reilly, 2021). We hope this helps you understand our reasoning for selecting these themes and see how they work together to guide students toward deeper environmental awareness and action.

Repeating Chapter Features

While *The Green Literacy Handbook* is divided into four thematic movements—foundations in part 1, teaching in part 2, design in part 3, and future steps in the epilogue—repeating features in chapters 1–7 help support you. They are as follows.

- **Chapter Snapshot—What You'll Explore:** This feature at the start of each chapter gives you a quick, bullet-point reference to what the chapter is about and what it contains.

- **Conclusion:** Each chapter concludes with a recap of the chapter's key concepts or central points.

- **Teacher's Corner:** At the end of each chapter, we offer a reproducible space to journal, reflect, and consider the chapter's learning through questions that can be used individually, in pairs, or in teams.

A Design for Flexibility

The Green Literacy Handbook is an at-your-fingertips reference that should be used as support. It is designed to be flexible, acknowledging that there are different ways and reasons to use it. This emboldens you as an educator to adapt the handbook to your unique teaching style and classroom needs.

As you peruse *The Green Literacy Handbook*, please keep in mind that there is no right way or wrong way to engage. Choose the chapter that might be best for you and your situation. Here, we do offer some guidance on where you might begin depending on your circumstances. Consider where you might be, and then start with the corresponding chapter.

- If you are a classroom teacher, preservice teacher, or member of a teaching team, you may want to start Green Literacy in the classroom and go to part 2, focusing on chapter 3. As quickly as you feel comfortable, you may then move into the Green Literacy thematic units (chapters 5, 6, and 7).

- If you are a college professor or graduate student interested in literature-based teaching methods or some other related class, you may begin with part 1, chapters 1 and 2.

- If you are a curriculum director or staff developer for Green Literacy, you may want to ground yourself in theory by starting in part 1, chapter 2, but move quickly into part 2 with a focus on chapter 3.

- If you are a homeschooler, you might want to speed-read the entire book and then decide which Green Literacy thematic unit to focus on.

- If you work as an environmental community organizer at a nature center and want to begin designing your own thematic units, you may consider starting with chapter 5.

- If you work with refugees or newcomers to your country, you may consider starting with chapter 6.

- If you work in a STEM or STEAM school, you may consider beginning with chapter 7.

TRANSFORMATIVE RIPPLES

However you choose to engage with *The Green Literacy Handbook*, we ask you to hold this close: All good—and green—things take time and space to grow. Rest in that truth, for it is within that patience that your insights will deepen, empowering your students to take a critical stance on the pressing environmental issues we face. We often yearn for success, for change to come swiftly, but like systems thinking, it requires persistence and grace. As you move through these chapters, be gentle with yourself and your students. Trust that in time, your students will find their voices, becoming able to speak critically and thoughtfully about environmental issues.

Nelson Mandela (1990), one of our most enduring lights of education and freedom, once said, "Education is the most powerful weapon which you can use to change the world." His words resonate with us, echoing our belief in the transformative power of education. In the context of Green Literacy, each lesson holds the potential to ripple outward, contributing to a future that is sustainable and just for all living things.

May your path through Green Literacy be one of discovery and growth for you and your students alike.

PART 1

FOUNDATIONS OF GREEN LITERACY

In part 1, "Foundations of Green Literacy," we lay the groundwork for understanding and implementing Green Literacy. These foundations offer you the essential support and structure needed to cultivate environmental awareness and critical thinking in your students. We establish strong theoretical and practical underpinnings to create fertile ground for seminal discussions, creative exploration, and actionable learning about pressing environmental issues.

Part 1 equips you with both the conceptual clarity and the actionable strategies needed to transform Green Literacy into a dynamic and impactful force in your classroom. With these foundations in place, you'll be ready to move into part 2, where we'll guide you step by step through implementing Green Literacy thematic units using real-world examples and collaborative strategies.

CHAPTER 1

Green Literacy's Theoretical Foundations

In the end, we will conserve only what we love; we will love only what we understand and we will understand only what we are taught.

—BABA DIOUM

This chapter explores the underlying theories and principles that form the basis of Green Literacy. Drawing inspiration from critical pedagogy and other educational frameworks, this chapter provides a theoretical lens for understanding how Green Literacy empowers educators and students to critically engage with environmental issues.

UNDERSTAND THE GREEN LITERACY FRAMEWORK

Green Literacy teaches young people to understand and engage with environmental issues through critical thinking, reading, writing, discussion, and, in time, the possibility of action. It helps young people see how ecological systems connect to their own lives and empowers them to take steps toward sustainability.

Green Literacy also develops in young people the ability to critically analyze power dynamics, particularly as they pertain to environmental issues. As we noted previously, Green Literacy builds on critical pedagogy by encouraging students to question dominant ideas,

---

Chapter Snapshot— What You'll Explore

In this chapter, we share with you how to:

- Work from the shared premise of the Green Literacy framework's four agreements, which provide for in-depth dialogues

- Develop Green Literacy ideals—a set of agreed-on, shared values about the environment and our interactions with it

- Engage in the three cycles of comprehension, which move readers from literal criteria to supporting criteria and to critical thinking, including systems thinking about environmental issues within texts or digital media

- Incorporate read-alouds, silent reads, and digital media as springboards to critical conversations about environmental stewardship

- Create in-depth Green Literacy dialogues supported by research

think critically, and take action. Just as critical pedagogy challenges traditional education, Green Literacy asks students to examine environmental myths, like the notion that natural resources are limitless, and connect what they learn to real-world solutions. As such, we consider Green Literacy a branch of critical pedagogy, sometimes called *critical literacy*, in which teachers encourage young people to consider power issues and think systematically. In the domain of Green Literacy, students and educators collaboratively probe into the societal forces shaping environmental policies and practices, fostering a critical consciousness toward ecological issues. Table 1.1 compares the specific key elements of critical literacy with Green Literacy.

Table 1.1: Critical Literacy and Green Literacy

Similarity	Critical Literacy	Green Literacy
Focuses on power dynamics	Analyzes how language and media can perpetuate power imbalances	Considers that power dynamics affect environmental decision making and policies
Uses critical analysis	Encourages questioning the status quo and looking for underlying meanings in texts	Promotes critical examination of environmental information and how it's presented
Ensures social justice and equity	Aims to reveal and challenge social inequalities	Addresses the intersection of environmental issues with social inequity
Follows a learner-centric approach	Centers on the learner's perspective, encouraging them to relate texts to their own life	Places the student's relationship with the environment at the heart of learning
Engages collaborative discussions	Promotes dialogue and understanding through group discussion and debate	Facilitates group conversations about collective solutions to environmental problems
Engages with contemporary issues	Relates the skills of literacy to current real-world issues	Ties literacy to current and emerging ecological challenges
Spurs advocacy and activism	Cultivates students' abilities to advocate for societal change	Encourages active participation in environmental advocacy

The Green Literacy framework, guided by the intentions of critical literacy, consists of four agreements that help create a classroom culture where you and your students can explore environmental topics, make personal connections, and take action. These agreements support you in making Green Literacy an active, significant part of teaching and learning, and they shape classroom interactions.

- **Agreement 1: Background knowledge advances reading success (Freire, 1970)—** Green Literacy students' knowledge of the world, especially power relationships, advances their comprehension skills. These students consider a depth of meaning and the significance of ecosocial context on themes that matter.

- **Agreement 2: Generating themes from personal connections to various texts and other media is critical**—Green Literacy students generate environmental themes from personal connections to books and digital media to promote critical discussions that examine dominant myths. For example, a student who has experienced a clean water shortage in their community might therefore question the idea that natural resources are limitless. Another student might reflect on the use of oil in their daily life—like fuel for cars or plastic manufacturing—and realize that oil is a finite resource that will eventually run out. These personal connections can spark valuable discussions about the importance of conserving resources and the global impact of relying on limited natural resources. With real and relatable examples, students can better understand why the idea of limitless resources isn't true and think critically about how to address these challenges. Discussions about generative themes in Green Literacy promote students' holding of many perspectives, coming up with the whole story rather than fragments.

- **Agreement 3: Facilitating an open and nonauthoritarian stance allows for sharing of power and responsibility (Shannon, 1990)**—Green Literacy students share power and responsibility with the Green Literacy teacher. These students exchange ideas and opinions, which fuels more expressions and ultimately leads the class to pursue their ideas for classroom or school projects and activities. The Green Literacy student takes initiative within constraints of time, resources, school policy, and common sense.

- **Agreement 4: Questioning power relationships opens awareness to enlarge perspective (Shor, 1992)**—Green Literacy students and teachers realize that society comprises contending forces and interests. These students and teachers advance questions to examine characters' and authors' viewpoints, which leads to analysis of which voices are present or excluded, whose perspective is credible, who has power in the situation, and what that power entails (that is, skills and competence, physical strength, money, or position).

We designed the agreements as a framework to nurture a rich educational environment where both you and your students can explore the complexities of environmental issues. When you adhere to these tenets, the learning space becomes a dynamic arena for examining ecological issues, and it encourages your students to think critically and engage fully as they dissect and discuss the facets of environmental care and ethics. The four agreements support the process and practice of Green Literacy teaching that then develop in-depth thinking, dialoguing, and responding to our relationship with the environment using multiple texts and digital media as catalysts. While we have delineated process and practice into separate chapters (chapter 1 and chapter 2) for clarity and focus, we recognize that they are intrinsically interwoven, with each element enriching and informing the other within the learning journey.

DEVELOP GREEN LITERACY IDEALS

Green Literacy ideals are a set of agreed-on, shared values developed through teacher and student collaboration and consensus on an environmental issue. These values emerge when you and your students engage in meaningful dialogue, reflect on your experiences, and work together to address environmental issues.

We developed our list of Green Literacy ideals through our own process of collaboration and consensus as authors when developing this handbook. By reflecting on our shared experiences and diverse perspectives, we identified the following Green Literacy ideals.

- We believe humans are interdependent and interconnected with other animals and plants on the Earth.

- We believe humans must protect nature's diversity, including human nature.

- We believe individual species of animals and plants need a suitable ecological system large enough to survive and thrive.

- Natural resources need to be used carefully and wisely, allowing room for the commons and circular economies.

- We believe in solving problems systematically.

As you develop Green Literacy ideals with your students, the process unfolds as a structured and evolving journey (Vasquez, Tate, & Harste, 2013). It often begins with introducing critical concepts related to environmental issues and laying the groundwork for deeper exploration. Students then engage in collaborative brainstorming sessions, capturing their personal and collective ideals. This collaborative phase typically progresses from paired discussions (using a strategy such as think-pair-share) to small-group discussions and eventually to larger group discussions, encouraging students to explore multiple perspectives and refine their thoughts (Green, 2012). Together, you and your students can draft, display, and discuss the ideals to ensure they remain a central focus in your classroom and serve as a living guide for ongoing learning. For example, a third-grade class learning about the decline of pollinators might agree on shared values like recognizing that every living being has a role in nature, understanding that small actions can support ecosystems, and emphasizing the importance of working together to nurture the environment. A fourth-grade class addressing plastic waste could prioritize values such as making mindful choices about consumption, taking responsibility for reducing waste, and fostering cleaner, healthier spaces for all living things. These agreed-on, shared values are Green Literacy ideals, and the collaborative process to reach them helps your students understand environmental challenges and motivates them to work collectively and take meaningful action, fostering critical thinking and teamwork skills.

Reflection is a critical component of the Green Literacy ideals process; it helps students relate their ideals to their personal lives and broader community engagement (Marcinkowski, 2010). This reflective practice energizes students to take a stand on environmental and social justice issues to drive meaningful change (UNESCO, 1977).

Importantly, the process is dynamic—Green Literacy ideals are revisited and revised over time to incorporate new insights and experiences and to ensure they remain relevant and actionable. This cycle often extends beyond the classroom, as students share their experiences and projects with the broader community, reinforcing their commitment to real-world environmental action.

As you guide your students in your classroom, it's essential to observe patterns and shifts in their thinking as they grapple with environmental issues. For instance, students may initially assume all neighborhoods are as safe as their own. After reading books like *No Bad News* by Kenneth Cole (2001), they may realize that safety is not universal and begin to question how everyone can have access to safe neighborhoods. Through discussions, students might arrive at the shared value that "everyone deserves a safe neighborhood," which becomes a Green Literacy ideal. This example illustrates how introducing diverse perspectives can lead to significant shifts in understanding and the development of shared values (Vasquez et al., 2013).

While you and your students create and display Green Literacy ideals in the classroom, you'll likely notice stronger student buy-in and an enhanced ability to articulate these ideals in their thinking. It's crucial to remain open to revising these ideals as new insights emerge. We want to emphasize that reaching a critical stance takes time, practice, and opportunities to wrestle with ideas and values (Green, 2012). With your guidance, your students will navigate these complexities, evolving their opinions and values as they read, view, and dialogue about environmental and social justice issues. At times, competing ideas may initially seem equally valid. Over time, some perspectives will prove more robust or explanatory, leading your students to refine their understanding and adopt more nuanced views (Marcinkowski, 2010).

While the time commitment required to develop and revise Green Literacy ideals can be substantial, it is time well spent. An approach that includes investigating and balancing multiple perspectives leads to the creation of substantive, thoughtful ideals and discourages easy, oversimplified answers to complex problems. Fostering this reflective and iterative process helps your students build a deeper understanding of environmental and social justice issues, and it uplifts them to become thoughtful, engaged citizens prepared to address the challenges of their world. In chapter 2 (page 31), we further explore the development of Green Literacy ideals with your students.

The following vignette about Patty, a teacher who participated in a professional development project we led, and her second-grade students offers a nuanced look at how the process of developing Green Literacy ideals might unfold in practice. It highlights the open-ended and adaptable nature of the journey, showing how each class brings its unique insights, challenges, and opportunities to the creation of meaningful Green Literacy ideals.

Second-grade teacher Patty chooses to read the picture book <u>where the Forest Meets the sea</u> by Jeannie Baker (1988) with a class of somali English learners. In Baker's book, a boy and his father explore a primeval forest threatened by commercial development. The father journeys with his son to a remote island that is reached by boat. The boy begins to investigate the forest by following a creek as it winds through the trees; he observes many trees, plants, and animals that all peacefully coexist within the forest. When the boy returns, his father is resting by a fire, cooking a freshly caught fish for their evening meal. In the last pages, the boy and his father build a sandcastle by the shore. A mirage of a hotel-like resort is partially drawn on the landscape, prompting the reader to consider the future of the primeval forest—a natural resource for the community and a special place for father and son.

After reading the book aloud, Patty points to one page where it says, "My father says there has been a forest there for over a hundred million years" (Baker, 1987, p. 5).

"That sure is a long time this forest has been standing," Patty says. "I want to tell you a word that means a very old forest such as this; it is primeval. Let's write it here on our whiteboard."

Patty continues, asking, "What do you think the author wants us to consider when the boy asks his father, 'But will the forest still be here when we come back'?" (Baker, 1987, p. 28).

Maahir raises his hand. "People cut trees to build hotels and parks. Maybe when they come back, it will be gone. I hope it's not gone."

"Why do you hope the forest is not gone?" Patty prods.

"There would be no place for them to go," Maahir answers. "And that's sad."

"Look!" Amir says, pointing to the illustration of the mirage at the edge of the page. "What is that?"

"A hotel," Marie says. "And in hotels, you can have a job."

"My mother says people make a lot of money when they build big buildings," Dhuuxo says.

"But if more buildings are builded, can the boy and his father get to come back there to camp?" wonders Maahir.

"Good question," Patty says. "Do we all need a place in nature to go as the boy and his father do?"

Several students agree and then speak about their special nature places.

"I like to play on the beach."

"My auntie brings me to the park where I can climb a tree."

At the end of the class discussion, Patty writes two sentences on the board: "We need jobs" and "We need a special place in nature." The students then write about those two contrasting ideas. Many of the students write about their special nature places. A few write about their fathers' and mothers' jobs. A couple of students attempt to find a solution between nature preservation and economic growth.

Fartuum suggests, "We can have jobs at the beach and enjoy being on the beach doing our jobs."

"Good work! Do you think we should make a Green Literacy ideal about special places in nature?" Patty asks. "What should we say?"

Several students hesitate and wait for more cues from Patty.

"Let's see," Patty says, walking to the classroom's displayed Green Literacy ideals. "We already believe 'Everyone should respect nature. We believe we are all connected to all living things.' What can we add?"

"How about 'We believe everyone should have a special place to go to in nature'?" Amir says.

In the preceding example, the students dialogued about a dilemma that many of us likely feel or have felt. Each student voiced the desire for material comfort, even luxury, yet at the same time, they wanted special places to go in nature (indeed, special places in nature may themselves offer people comfort and a kind of luxury). Though children and adults want to be materially secure, many want to protect and preserve the natural environment.

The vignette of these second graders and their teacher demonstrates engagement with the Green Literacy framework in four ways.

1. The teacher understood that social relationships increase students' ability to read words; for example, Patty focused on the meaning of the word *primeval*. (Agreement 1)

2. The students and their teacher generated ideas from the connections they made to the book—for example, the students' ideas about the need for jobs and the need for unique places in nature. (Agreement 2)

3. The students worked with the teacher as a facilitator; that is, the joint work unfolded in a nonauthoritarian manner. (Agreement 3)

4. The students and their teacher discussed and questioned power relationships. They covered how some people make a lot of money, which equals power, by building resort hotels in beautiful places of nature instead of preserving such places. (Agreement 4)

In sum, the vignette illustrates the Green Literacy framework in action, and the action within that framework leads to the creation of Green Literacy ideals. Through the construction of meaningful social interactions, connections to text, collaborative learning, and critical questioning, Patty and her students engaged with environmental and social issues. This approach encouraged critical thinking, amplified student voices, and explored the complexities of balancing human needs with environmental preservation. Through these efforts, Patty and her students built both understanding and environmental awareness, and they began the process of creating guiding ideals.

Tips for Teachers to Create Green Literacy Ideals

- **Choose relevant texts:** Select books and digital media that address environmental themes and resonate with students' experiences, like the texts we suggest throughout *The Green Literacy Handbook*, on our companion website (**www.greenliteracy.org**), and at **go.SolutionTree.com/literacy**.

- **Facilitate guided discussions:** Lead conversations that help students articulate and reconcile complex ideas about urgent environmental issues. Ask open-ended questions that allow students to become aware of multiple perspectives.

- **Encourage personal connections:** Prompt students to relate the story to their own lives, which enhances their depth of understanding.

- **Balance critical thinking and empathy:** Help students explore practical solutions that reflect both critical thinking about development and empathy for natural spaces.

- **Extend learning with writing:** Ask students to express their thoughts in writing, which fosters literacy skills and personal expression.

- **Develop classroom ideals collectively:** Work with students to create and evolve class ideals based on discussions, ensuring the ideals are meaningful and jointly owned.

- **Remain open to student ideas:** Listen to students' suggestions to foster a sense of agency and ownership over the learning process.

USE THE THREE CYCLES OF COMPREHENSION

The *three cycles of comprehension* is a system of comprehension we developed to explore concepts in texts and media. Cycle 1, *simple comprehension*, occurs when students retell or summarize the story, nonfiction text, or digital media, including when they make inferences about what the author wrote. Cycle 2, *criteria comprehension*, occurs when students support their thinking about the story, nonfiction text, or digital media with criteria either prompted by their teacher or thought of on their own. Cycle 3, *perspective comprehension*, occurs when students engage in the story, nonfiction text, or digital media in a way that involves exploring the social world and their relationship to it. This includes engaging with explicit and implicit perspectives, debating different sides of issues, and valuing and developing assumptions and beliefs that make sense to students. Perspective comprehension includes *systems thinking*—that is, thinking that concerns how one event is related to or caused by other events and how complex problems are solved. We advocate using the three cycles of comprehension to explore the ideas in texts and digital media within Green Literacy thematic units. Use of the three cycles of comprehension ultimately leads students into critical thinking, reading, speaking, and writing. See figure 1.1 for a visual representation of how the three cycles of comprehension are interconnected and support one another in a nonhierarchical fashion, ultimately leading to the creation of Green Literacy ideals, which for us is an action in and of itself.

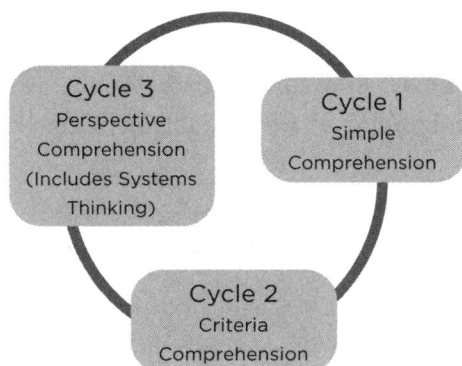

Figure 1.1: The three cycles of comprehension.

While one cycle of comprehension supports the next, as we all know, comprehension is a dynamic, fluid process where students can shift back and forth between different levels of understanding, hence the emphasis on *nonhierarchical*. The circle in the figure is whole, emphasizing that comprehension is not always linear. Your students may alternate between simple comprehension, such as identification of facts, and more complex forms, such as critical analysis or perspective taking, depending on the context and their cognitive engagement (Kintsch, 1998; van den Broek & Espin, 2012). This flexibility highlights the importance of fostering opportunities for your students to engage with texts at varying depths, which supports their ability to navigate and interpret meaning across multiple dimensions.

To honor the fluidity of comprehension, we use the word *cycles* because it reflects the natural back-and-forth movement of both learning and nature. In Green Literacy, cycles capture how ideas are revisited, refined, and built on over time, making the process dynamic and adaptable. Similarly, in nature, patterns like the water and carbon cycles demonstrate how things connect and repeat to create balance. Unlike *layers*, for example, which feel fixed, cycles highlight growth and change.

In the following sections, we discuss each cycle in greater detail.

Cycle 1: Simple Comprehension

In simple comprehension, the first cycle, your Green Literacy students focus on understanding the text—that is, they restate or summarize the story, including making inferences about what the author wrote. Your students identify literary devices used in a fiction or nonfiction book they are talking about, such as scene, character, plot, climax, and theme, as well as identify the text's central idea and supporting details. In many comprehension-assessment schemes, simple comprehension is the beginning of the close reading needed for college and career readiness. In Green Literacy's practice, simple comprehension focuses on understanding rather than agreement, since understanding what the author says does not require the reader's agreement.

A study by Peggy Albers, Jerome C. Harste, Sarah Vander Zanden, and Carol Felderman (2008) illustrates simple comprehension and shows the needed ability to move from simple comprehension into the next two cycles of comprehension. Albers and colleagues (2008) found that preservice teachers and fifth graders are able to read and achieve simple comprehension but have little success at identifying the tacit messages encountered in consumer culture. Investigators showed both groups a Walmart ad that introduced a new Barbie clothing collection. The Walmart ad displayed three smiling girls dressed in various shades of pink confidently marching down a fashion runway. Barbie doll clothing and complementary accessories lined the margins of the ad. Both the preservice teachers and the fifth graders talked about fashion, which was what the designers of this ad portrayed. From a Green Literacy perspective, both the preservice teachers and the fifth graders reached simple comprehension of the ad, including making inferences about what the producers of the ad portrayed.

Neither group attempted to unpack the larger messages about a consumerist culture that the ad's numerous elements connected and communicated to the viewer—namely that possessing material objects like a Barbie doll is associated with happiness and social standing. The fact that neither group went beyond simple comprehension leads us to consider how ingrained the messages of advertising and consumerist lifestyles are in citizens of wealthy countries—even at a young age (Albers et al., 2008). We advocate developing students' awareness of how people's habits maintain the systems that drastically endanger the world's limited natural resource base. Our experience indicates that as you and your students work with the Green Literacy process, this kind of eco-awareness grows. This example shows the need to advance students from simple comprehension to the following two cycles of comprehension (criteria comprehension and perspective comprehension), which allow students to engage in critical and systemic thinking and create sustainable solutions to urgent environmental issues. It's important to guide students, especially ones in grades K–5, through cycle 1 to help them understand the basics of a story or concept. These young students may need more support to grasp the fundamentals. Taking time to explore key ideas is essential. Once students have a solid foundation, moving into deeper exploration and critical thinking in the later cycles allows them to connect ideas, ask questions, and engage meaningfully with the material.

Following is a list of what simple comprehension does.

- **Aids in understanding of text:** Grasping and retelling the text, which include summarizing the narrative and making inferences about the author's intentions, further understanding.

- **Serves as a basis for close reading:** Establishing simple comprehension forms the groundwork for the close reading skills essential for higher education and professional success.

- **Focuses on comprehension over agreement:** Emphasizing understanding of the author's message doesn't necessarily require concurrence from the reader.

Cycle 2: Criteria Comprehension

We define criteria comprehension as supporting one's thinking about the story, nonfiction text, or digital media with criteria. Students support their ideas by drawing from their background knowledge and from the text or media they read or view.

Here, we look at a classic critical literacy study by Josephine Shotka (1960) to illustrate how criteria comprehension could work. Shotka, an educator and researcher, provides valuable insights in her work from 1960, offering a perspective rooted in critical pedagogy. Shotka asked first graders to consider two central questions: (1) What is a home? and (2) What is a community? Through a series of lessons, the students compared their home experiences with the experiences of children in their textbooks. They recognized similarities: The textbook children played with one another and attended school, and their families had people who helped them, such as doctors and mail carriers. The students pointed out some differences, such as the textbook children always looked clean and happy, and their houses were bigger and prettier than their own. Prompted to explain these distinctions, the students revealed the author and illustrator "couldn't think of making the children look dirty" and they "[wanted] the pictures and the stories to be happy [because] children didn't like sad stories" (Shotka, 1960, p. 301). Thus, when invited to read critically to support their thinking with criteria on how their lives differed from what they saw in the pictures, these students explained why authors and illustrators choose certain representations of the world. The first graders were asked to support their ideas or give criteria for them, engaging in what Green Literacy calls the second cycle of comprehension.

In fostering criteria comprehension, you, the teacher, encourage your students to substantiate their thoughts by integrating their own experiences with insights gleaned from texts or media. This process of correlating personal understanding with external information deepens their analytic skills and enriches their capacity to critically engage with content. It enables students to construct informed opinions, reinforcing the learning experience through the synthesis of personal and textual knowledge.

The skill of supporting ideas from texts read and media viewed is emphasized in many state standards and in the Common Core State Standards (CCSS); this skill is also emphasized in college coursework. This is how young people expand their schemas or knowledge.

Following is a list of what criteria comprehension does.

- **Defines comprehension:** Students back their interpretations of texts and digital media with specific, well-thought-out criteria.
- **Includes sources of support:** Students use both prior knowledge and specific information from texts or digital media to support their points.
- **Activates knowledge expansion:** Students develop schemas, broadening their cognitive frameworks.

Cycle 3: Perspective Comprehension

We define cycle 3, perspective comprehension, as engaging in the story, nonfiction text, or digital media in ways that allow students to explore the world and their relationship to it. Perspective comprehension includes both explicit and implicit perspectives, characters debating different sides of issues, and the development of assumptions and beliefs that make sense to young people. Developing Green Literacy ideals can be part of this process of examining assumptions and beliefs.

Here, we offer an example that altered students' focus, allowing them to enter perspective comprehension. In their study, critical pedagogy researchers Allan Luke, Barbara Comber, and Jennifer O'Brien (1996) describe a first-grade teacher who invited her class to analyze how catalogs promoting and selling Mother's Day gifts portray mothers. These students examined the catalogs and interviewed each other using the following questions: How are the mothers in the catalogs like and different from other mothers? What mothers are not included in the catalogs? Where do children get the money to buy presents? and Why do the catalog producers go through all this trouble to ensure people know what is available? The teacher-directed dialogue led the young students to realize that their mothers of differing cultural and social-class perspectives were not represented in the catalogs. The students then interviewed their own mothers and other mothers in their community about what Mother's Day meant to them. As a result, students revised their conceptions of Mother's Day. They perceived that Mother's Day was less about buying gifts and more about sharing time with or helping their mothers. In this way, they considered the social context of Mother's Day by questioning mothers, and in doing so recognized the difference between media and real-life portrayals of Mother's Day.

Thus, in this perspective comprehension example (Luke et al., 1996), the teacher initiated a discussion about the catalogs (the text). Then the students interviewed their own and others' mothers. Their findings impelled them to perceive a point of view that contrasted with the perspective of mothers that the consumer catalogs portrayed. Investigating topics or issues with perspective comprehension is particularly important for young people to become invigorated to act on their beliefs. We include in the teaching of cycle 3 instances where young people and their teacher consider how they *value*, or see as ideal, certain characteristics of a text, character or person, or point of view. In the preceding example, the students realized that some mothers tend to value restful time and time together more than physical objects.

Since cycle 3 includes systems thinking, students may be guided to consider structural fixes that involve changes to a system to solve complex environmental issues.

Perspective comprehension proves advantageous for 21st century students because they must realize that each author presents a belief and wants readers to believe it. Critical literacy theorist Patrick Shannon (1995) advocates that educators develop a language of critique with their students to shift their thinking beyond commonplace understandings. One way to develop such a language of critique is by asking students to consider differing perspectives. Cognitive linguist George Lakoff's (2005) work calls for a precise kind of language study that interrogates texts in terms of frames, or what linguist James Paul Gee (1996) calls *cultural models*. These frames position readers in specified ways and endow them with certain identities while reading and analyzing a text. Lakoff (2005) defines *frames* as "mental structures that shape the way we see the world . . . the goals we seek, the plans we make, the way we act" (p. xv).

Thus, cycle 3 of Green Literacy, perspective comprehension, goes beyond having different opinions or recognizing different points of view. It involves the ability to coordinate multiple layers of complexity, including thinking systemically and determining a stance that is *credible* (Sensoy & DiAngelo, 2012). A credible stance built by understanding of established knowledge brings new evidence to the issues at hand. From the perspective of comprehension, soldering connections with their lives and other texts intensifies students' comprehension of the material and such correlations' journey to opinions. From an academic perspective, knowledge claims must stand up to review by peers and scrutiny by specialists in the subject.

Following is a list of what perspective comprehension does.

- **Goes beyond the text:** Students' thinking goes deeper, using texts or media as gateways to explore broad ecosocial issues.

- **Engages with content:** Students actively engage with diverse perspectives and debates within the narrative.

- **Values student perspectives:** Students validate and cultivate their own assumptions and beliefs.

- **Incorporates systems thinking:** Students gain understanding of the interconnections between events, emphasizing the cause and effect within systems.

EMPLOY PERSPECTIVE COMPREHENSION TO INCLUDE SYSTEMS THINKING

In Green Literacy classrooms, K–5 and beyond, young people wrestle with the process of critical comprehension, supporting their thinking with evidence and considering multiple points of view and systems thinking. You and your students reflect on, clarify, articulate, and discuss an issue with intellectual humility, curiosity, and generosity. The goal is to expand both your (the teacher's) and your students' knowledge bases and critical thinking, not to protect preexisting opinions. You and your students can flourish intellectually by critically dialoguing at the start about your personal opinions, drawing on multiple perspectives, and conversing about them.

To facilitate deep conversations, multiple texts from many genres are needed. You and your students can examine various voices and points of view, which is unlikely to happen through reading only one text. Some texts are more profound or provocative than others. Learning through a critical stance includes using texts whose themes concern vital issues. Extending these ideas through discussion leads your students into an area of thinking called *systems thinking*, where action toward the environment is often made through structural fixes.

Green Literacy perceives a system as composed of interrelated parts that affect one another. Natural systems include plants and animals, ocean currents, the climate, the solar system, and ecosystems. Designed systems include machines of all kinds, government agencies, and businesses. The word *system* then refers to many disparate factors that affect each other's outcomes. Environmentalists apply systems thinking by viewing a "problem" as part of an overall system, rather than analyzing specific parts, outcomes, or events. You will find that systems thinking and determination of structural fixes are parts of the Green Literacy process. In chapter 7 (page 159), teachers can involve students in systemic ways by thinking about how much "stuff" we have and what we do with it.

When young people work with Green Literacy, they quickly realize that environmental challenges are complex and multifaceted. There are no easy solutions to fix issues such as global warming, dependence on fossil fuels, deforestation, bioengineered foods, air pollution, and more without considering the human factor and without realizing such issues are interconnected. We begin to examine how we interact both advantageously and adversely with the environment under established systems of law, education, government, medicine, family, and religion. When systemic changes are enacted over time, we come to understand they can be sustainable. Thomas A. Heberlein (2012) writes in *Navigating Environmental Attitudes* that connecting environmental problems with their complexities and structural fixes is most likely to offer sustainable solutions because the changes are systemic and often address cognitive and technological aspects. In effect, these problems demand a reworking of an entire system, including people's attitudes.

You and your students will need time to absorb and understand how systemic changes or structural fixes can be helpful. One example we highlight is the institution of corporate average fuel economy (CAFE) standards in 1975 following the Arab oil embargo, which were then extended by Congress in 2006, increased in 2011, and extended to 2025. The CAFE standards dictate that automakers must build cars and light trucks with higher gas mileages—that is, they can drive farther using less gas. Since cars built under these standards burn less gas, they put less global warming pollution into the air. Having U.S. car manufacturers build cars within the CAFE standards is systemic change because this affects every car owner within the United States and thus has a massive effect on the amount of global warming pollution that the United States produces. Systemic changes usually require support from and decisions made by gatekeepers—in this case, Congress and the president. As the example of raising the CAFE standards shows, systemic changes often involve political will—and Green Literacy has your students consider power relationships concerning environmental issues that may lead to creating political will. A more recent example is support of electric cars to move us away from fossil-fuel use.

In summary, the three cycles of comprehension—simple, criteria, and perspective—work together to build young people's engagement in systems thinking and ultimately environmental awareness. Teachers move students from understanding specific texts and digital media they, the teachers, have chosen to analyzing them and connecting them to real-world environmental issues. This cycle will support you and your students in articulating critical stances and later developing Green Literacy ideals.

In the following vignette, we'll look at how David and his fifth-grade students enact the comprehension cycle, using perspective comprehension especially, to reach systems thinking, which leads to their creation of new Green Literacy ideals. We offer this vignette to demonstrate, in tandem with our previous vignette example, the progression and depth of thinking, talking, and responding that students display when the Green Literacy framework and the three cycles of comprehension are incorporated into classroom discussions at differing grade levels. In the previous vignette, Patty and her second-grade students understand and use the three cycles of comprehension. While teachers of this age group may not explicitly teach the cycles to their students, they focus on building foundational comprehension skills in age-appropriate ways. In contrast, this vignette of a fifth-grade class highlights how older students and their teacher actively discuss and engage with the three cycles of comprehension, making them a central, explicit part of their learning process.

David is a Green Literacy teacher at a school where grades are looped. As their fourth-grade (and now their fifth-grade) teacher, he has given his students experience working in critical thinking groups. He uses the biography The Boy Who Harnessed the Wind (Kamkwamba & Mealer, 2009) with his students. In this remarkable biography, William Kamkwamba, a fourteen-year-old Malawian boy, engineers a windmill based on what he reads and learns in library books. The biography is divided into three parts: (1) village life of subsistence farming through child William's eyes, (2) a famine and how William studies elementary physics textbooks in a local library and uses scrap materials to build his first windmill, and (3) the outside world's discovery of William, which leads him to give a TED Talk and eventually go to Dartmouth College.

David has selected this biography to explain how technology can impact developing countries. He wants his students to consider how the internet enables people to get information they want and to connect with helpful people beyond the local village or city. William builds his first windmill with only the help of an old textbook and without international monetary support. After William makes friends at a TED conference, he is able to obtain the resources to go to school and eventually build more windmills for his village. David wants his students to dialogue about how the best international assistance may be rooted in local connections rather than top-down efforts through foreign governments.

As a prereading activity and an introduction to simple comprehension, students watch and respond to William Kamkwamba's (2007) first TED Talk. They develop questions to use as they read the biography. Example student questions include the following.

- So, he didn't go to school. Why not? Did he ever get to go to school?

- How did he make this windmill? Did anyone help him?

- Did he make the second windmill?

- How did the TED people help him?

- What happened to William after he did the first TED Talk?

These questions set the stage for close reading, which is cycle 1 (simple comprehension), moving to cycle 2 (criteria comprehension). David encourages his students to read while they work with partners to cite precisely what happens in the three parts of the book, and the partners develop a timeline of events for each part.

Afterward, David starts the first of three whole-group discussions. During the first of these discussions, he focuses on simple comprehension and stresses, "Let's discuss what happened before we jump to the big ideas." The students share their timelines and reach consensus as they make a master timeline for all three parts in the biography.

Once the students have read the entire book, they've worked on the timelines as partners, and David is sure all students have mastered cycle 1, he shows Kamkwamba's (2009) second TED Talk, made two years after his first. Afterward, the students are impressed with William's improved English and confidence. The class likes his final message: "I tried and I made it. . . . Trust yourself and believe."

David then moves the students into cycle 2, where they find support in the text for their ideas. The partners combine to form foursomes of experts, and with their timelines, the groups each choose events in the book that demonstrate the value of or need for one of the following: science, technology (particularly the internet), or social justice. A week later, when the student groups present, the listeners use a spider map graphic organizer to link the different areas of expertise.

Moving into cycle 3 (perspective comprehension), David asks, "Can anyone share connections between the perspectives? And I dare you to refer to a page in the book."

Ronald from the science group raises his hand and says, "I see social justice and science connected. Before William made the windmill, his family lived on subsistence farming and went through a terrible famine where they had one scoop of maize porridge daily. I take the dare. Page 74."

Tamara says, "I see technology and activism connected. The activism came from people William met at the TED conference. Plus, after the village realized the windmill could bring them electricity, and people from outside came to see the windmill, the whole village was proud of William's accomplishment."

"How was that activism?" David pushes.

"Well, William met activists from the U.S. at the TED conference, and they helped him get money by communicating through the internet for William's ideas of getting electricity to others in his village, and for William and his friends to be able to go to school, things like that," Tamara answers.

"Why do you think the village people changed their minds about William? How did their perspective change?" David says. "I double-dog dare you to connect the page to your idea."

James, a shy student, offers, "They wanted to have electricity too. They saw good things can happen in the village and other villages. On page 251, William's mother said when she was asked about having lights in her house from her son's work, 'We're proud. We thought he was going mad.'"

Skillfully guiding the class toward creating Green Literacy ideals, David says to James, "Good thinking," and to the class, "Remember when we talked about different kinds of power? The people William met at the TED community set up a website so that people could learn about William's goals and give money to his projects if they wanted to. I think this could fit into our Green Literacy ideals. As we talk, let's consider what thoughts we should write as our Green Literacy ideals."

After a brief discussion about the classroom's Green Literacy ideals, one student adds, "We believe fuel sources, especially alternative energy, should be shared with developing countries."

"Wow," says David. "This idea is a breakthrough Green Literacy ideal. Class, do you agree?" The classmates all raise their hands in agreement.

The discussion continues when Julie says, paraphrasing from the book, "I think that activism from the developing world can help African countries to have more wind and solar power. On page 214, William's father says he enjoys his lights more than a city person because he paid nothing to the power company and has no power outages like people in the city. So maybe helping small communities in Africa make windmills for their town like William did might be better than everybody getting electricity from one big giant power plant like how we do here in Chicago."

"Yeah," adds Tamara. "Remember what happened to William's town when the grain supplies were sold off by the president's friends? Most people starved, and only a few people had grain to eat."

"So," says Michael, changing the subject, "wind and solar power are called alternative sources of energy because they are not traditional sources of energy, which are mostly from fossil fuels like coal and oil."

"Good use of words, Michael," David says. "Alternative energy is a term on our Green Literacy word wall."

David refers back to what Julie said earlier. "Julie and class, I like our discussion about local forms of energy and how they helped William's town grow, rather than having big companies or governments come in and take over the energy supply. Maybe this idea might be turned into one of our Green Literacy ideals. What do you think, class? Do we believe that local energy sources like wind and solar are tools to bring energy with some control over it for local people? Is this idea important enough to be one of our Green Literacy ideals?"

After more discussion, the class agrees, and David places this Green Literacy ideal on the list on their wall: "Small-scale, local alternative energy sources are extremely helpful to small villages in developing countries because they can acquire them more easily than large-scale energy sources."

Before the bell rings, Ronald asks, "What can we do here in Chicago? We've got electricity and rarely have power outages. What can we do to be like William?"

Looking at this vignette through the lens of the Green Literacy framework and its four agreements, you can see that the young people understood social relationships as they increased their ability to read words. For example, displaying *alternative energy* on the class word wall made the concept part of the community's thinking and reasoning together. Second, the students generated ideas from the connections they made between the book and their values pertaining to science, technology, and social justice. Third, they collaborated with David, a facilitator who worked with his class in a nonauthoritarian manner. Fourth, they discussed and questioned power relationships—in this case, the power William had with his persistence and skill in making a windmill even though his fellow villagers sneered at him and he had few resources. Also, the students discussed the power of the people William met at the TED conference to use the internet to make his dreams come true—that is, William wanted his family and villagers to be more connected to others and have more resources, particularly to be able to go to school.

David supported his students' thinking by progressing them through the three cycles of comprehension. The students mastered cycle 1 (simple comprehension) when they first determined what the author wrote through reading and working with partners to develop a timeline of what happened in each part of the biography. The students progressed into cycle 2 (criteria comprehension) when they defended their ideas with information in the text as they worked in expert groups, considering the value of or need for science, technology (particularly the internet), and social justice. We noted the complexity of thought and interpretation in cycle 3 (perspective comprehension) when the class articulated differing perspectives concerning alternative energy, particularly wind, in developing countries. Finally, David incorporated the Green Literacy process into his classroom so that students' thinking and in-depth discussion concerned the whys and hows of alternative energy used in developing countries. In fact, the class came up with and agreed on two Green Literacy ideals.

As a way of summarizing what students do as they work through Green Literacy's three cycles of comprehension, we developed the following characteristics of Green Literacy thinkers and readers in grades K–5, which we call *comprehenders*.

- They interact or engage with certain books and digital media that function as springboards for vital discussions about environmental stewardship. These discussions probably would not occur otherwise, since environmental issues are complex, interconnected, and often cloaked in another problem.

- They increase their awareness of environmental and social justice unfairness and of their part in the system that perpetuates environmental and social justice unfairness.

- They appreciate that facts and points of view will be accumulated through reading, viewing, and discussing.

- They recognize that diverging sources of information reinforce certain facts and points of view, and thus, they actively apply how to check the credibility of sources.

- They respect that everyone has a right to their opinion; they value multiple perspectives on an environmental issue, supporting critical thinking.

- They realize how complex systems interact and ways to change them systemically, including the power dynamics needed to make systemic changes. They recognize how students can work with others to make needed changes.

As students build their skills as comprehenders, they naturally progress toward more meaningful discussions. In the following section, we share research-based strategies to help you create and support these in-depth discussions in your classroom.

CREATE IN-DEPTH GREEN LITERACY DISCUSSIONS

Green Literacy thematic units innovatively draw from research on read-aloud discussions that support critical thinking and reading comprehension. For example, interactive read-alouds have been shown to help children build deeper understanding by modeling inferential thinking, teaching vocabulary in context, and scaffolding comprehension skills (Wasik & Bond, 2001). Research highlights how engaging students in discussions during read-alouds encourages critical analysis and interpretation of texts, making their reading experience more meaningful (Fisher, Frey, & Hattie, 2016). These strategies support the goals of Green Literacy by embedding analytic thinking into the exploration of environmental themes.

The Green Literacy teacher is a facilitator who applies the research to read-alouds, silent reads, and digital media discussions. To promote critical thinking, we suggest that you minimize giving your students directives and asking them single-answer questions. As the discussion progresses, you invigorate your students to respond to each other's views, not to the teacher's point of view. Finally, as you invite discussion, you and your students become aware that the common classroom pattern of teacher question, student answer, teacher evaluation (Cazden, 2001; Eeds & Wells, 1989; McGee, 1995) tends not to support critical response.

Here are some strategies Green Literacy teachers use to enhance high-level comprehension discussions.

- They choose high-quality literature with complex stories and issues of humans' impact on the environment that warrant critical discussion (Hoffman, Roser, & Battle, 1993; Keene & Zimmermann, 2007; Santoro, Chard, Howard, & Baker, 2008; Sipe, 1998).

- They preread the children's literature or digital media they choose, as well as related commentaries, and consider thematic connections.

- They determine where in the text or digital media they should stop to talk, what strategies they should use as they read aloud to engage students in critical dialogue and response, and what suggestions they should utilize as models for future lessons.

- They read texts aloud at least twice to allow higher-level thinking to percolate among the class in the second read. In the first read, they make sure everyone is on the same page and knows what the author wrote—that is, Green Literacy's simple comprehension (Dennis & Walter, 1995; Martinez & Roser, 1985; McGee & Schickedanz, 2007).

- They engage students in critical dialogue by returning to the idea that, "consciously or unconsciously, when writers write and artists create, they include certain values and perspectives on the world and exclude others" (Crafton, Brennan, & Silvers, 2007, p. 513). Also, they focus critical discussion on what determines "fair" and "unjust" in stories read and how situations could be changed (Vasquez, 2010).

- They advocate cooperative learning strategies such as think-pair-share or turn-and-talk (Kagan, 1990; Keene & Zimmermann, 2007; Lyman, 1981) to provide each student a chance to explore their ideas on the issue at hand. This enriches the whole-group talk. When students simultaneously share ideas due to the excitement generated by the conversation, the teacher can refocus on the significant idea in the discussion by saying, "John and Jim, each of you take turns sharing what you said," rather than controlling communication with raised hands (Hoffman, 2011, p. 188).

- They build on student responses by repeating and affirming confirmations, and when there is extensive agreement, they act as the devil's advocate to voice alternative points of view that the young people don't. In this way, the discussion focuses on the interpretive points related to the theme of the text. Green Literacy students build on each other's ideas, rather than presenting unrelated topics (Hoffman, 2011).

CONCLUSION

Green Literacy, rooted in critical pedagogy, fortifies teachers and students to engage in meaningful, in-depth dialogues about urgent environmental issues through the lens of thematic, big-picture questions on environmental stewardship. These dialogues are guided by a framework of four foundational agreements that shape classroom interactions and create a collaborative environment where transformative ideas can flourish.

As a teacher, you have a pivotal role in cocreating Green Literacy ideals with your students. These ideals naturally arise through reflective conversations and shared experiences, and they influence how you and they act individually and collectively. This dynamic and evolving process places students' voices, experiences, and critical thinking at the forefront, fostering a sense of ownership and engagement.

To support the development of these ideals, the three cycles of comprehension provide a practical, structured approach to deepen understanding and encourage exploration. The simple comprehension cycle helps students grasp the author's core message to ensure foundational comprehension. The criteria comprehension cycle emphasizes the importance of supporting ideas with evidence, whether from texts or personal experiences, to reinforce critical thinking. The perspective comprehension cycle challenges students to consider diverse viewpoints and practice systems thinking, pushing them to see beyond immediate contexts. Together, these cycles offer a versatile approach that supports both structured learning and creative exploration, enabling students to connect ideas and think critically about complex issues.

At the heart of this chapter—and every chapter in *The Green Literacy Handbook*—is the principle of trust. We trust you, the teacher, because we are teachers ourselves. Decades of experience have taught us that no one knows your classroom or students better than you. Your ability to adapt strategies—whether through read-alouds, silent reading, or multimedia discussions—ensures that every student can meaningfully participate in and grow through the Green Literacy process. Your expertise is essential in creating a space where students recognize words and think critically, collaborate creatively, and develop as thoughtful stewards of our shared environment.

Now, consider how this chapter has impacted your learning as a teacher. We offer a dedicated space for you to do so in the following "Teacher's Corner" reproducible tool (also available at **go.SolutionTree.com/literacy**). Whether you're working on your own, with a teaching partner, or within a schoolwide learning network, after exploring chapter 1, we encourage you to reflect on what you've learned.

Teacher's Corner

Here are some questions to support your reflection.

- Reflect on a meaningful personal experience in nature that has shaped your approach to teaching about the environment. How has that experience influenced your classroom?

- How did the vignettes from the chapter resonate with you, and why?

Here are prompts for journaling.

- Write about your process for teaching about nature or an environmentally related theme. How might Green Literacy ideals help enhance your process?

- What insights have you gleaned from the chapter that could transform the way you teach your students as you incorporate Green Literacy into your curriculum?

Here are discussion guidelines.

- Discuss the impact of personal nature experiences on your teaching. How can you and your colleagues share your stories to foster a deeper connection with the environment among your students?

- Share and discuss a section of vignette from the chapter that affirmed or made you rethink your teaching approach. What lessons can you draw from it?

Green Literacy's Practical Foundations

The more clearly we can focus our attention on the wonders and realities of the universe about us, the less taste we shall have for destruction.

—RACHEL CARSON

In chapter 1, we explored the theoretical foundations of Green Literacy: the four agreements that form the Green Literacy framework and provide for in-depth dialogues; Green Literacy ideals; the three cycles of comprehension; and finally, research supports for incorporating read-alouds, silent reads, and digital media as springboards to critical conversations about environmental stewardship as well as in-depth Green Literacy dialogues. In contrast, here in chapter 2, we move to practical aspects of Green Literacy: its themes and questions for thematic units and how to foster thinking through commentary in relation to the thematic questions that support teachers and students in taking a critical stance. We offer complete example commentaries throughout. The purpose of this is to increase the teacher's background knowledge and to build their confidence in navigating complex environmental issues as they design their thematic units and work with their students.

Also, in this chapter, we present examples of Green Reads and Views (books and digital media) as well as describe Green Literacy teaching strategies and illustrate how the Green Literacy units are organized around themes and are multigrade. We briefly explore academic standards. As we do throughout the handbook, we

Chapter Snapshot— What You'll Explore

In this chapter, we share with you how to:

- Discuss Green Literacy themes

- Develop a thematic question and foster thinking through commentary to support taking a critical stance

- Synthesize Green Reads and Views (books and digital media) suggestions

- Use Green Literacy strategies

- Organize multigrade Green Literacy units around themes

- Explore academic standards with Green Literacy in mind

provide an example of how K–2 teachers engage in Green Literacy teaching to illustrate how K–2 students respond differently than students in grades 3–5 and beyond.

This chapter outlines five core components of organizing an effective Green Literacy thematic unit: (1) developing thematic questions, (2) fostering reflection through commentary, (3) curating impactful Green Reads and Views, (4) selecting tailored teaching strategies, and (5) guiding students in creating Green Literacy ideals. We pair these components with completed sample segments of the Green Literacy Thematic Unit Planning Template (available as a reproducible in appendix A, page 193, and at **go.SolutionTree.com /literacy**). With practical examples and clear guidance, this chapter helps educators bring Green Literacy into their classrooms in meaningful and engaging ways.

DESIGN GREEN LITERACY UNITS

Each Green Literacy thematic unit is a cluster of several lessons that conceptually fit together around an environmental theme. They are multigrade, with specific books and media recommended for different grade levels. The thematic units draw on multiple texts and digital media with the same theme; they creatively use reading and writing strategies that lead to environmental and social critique in recommended grade-level ranges. We support a thematic approach that connects different subjects through big ideas or concepts, similar to the approach you'll find in the International Baccalaureate program and numerous other contemporary curricula. This thematic approach helps students see the bigger picture by linking their learning to real-world themes like sustainability, identity, or global citizenship. It's a way to encourage creativity, critical thinking, and collaboration while making learning more meaningful and engaging.

Green Literacy thematic units can be easily aligned with any academic standards, including state standards, the Common Core State Standards, or others. We model how teachers and students can use these texts and digital media as catalysts for critical dialogues and, hopefully, action toward earth stewardship. You and your students may reflect that taking effective action includes finding solutions that work to change systems, including unjust systems with regard to race, class, and gender and the use of natural resources.

As shown in figure 2.1, Green Literacy units are organized around theme and incorporate the following steps: (1) develop your thematic question, (2) foster your thinking through commentary, (3) cultivate a list of Green Reads and Views, (4) select Green Literacy strategies, and (5) develop Green Literacy ideals.

These five essential design components are organized into three phases or acts: (1) engage, (2) empower, and (3) shift. *Engaging* emphasizes developing thematic questions and fostering your critical thinking through commentary. *Empowering* focuses on curating Green Reads and Views and selecting Green Literacy strategies using the three cycles of comprehension. *Shifting* incorporates guiding students toward shared and agreed-on values in Green Literacy ideals.

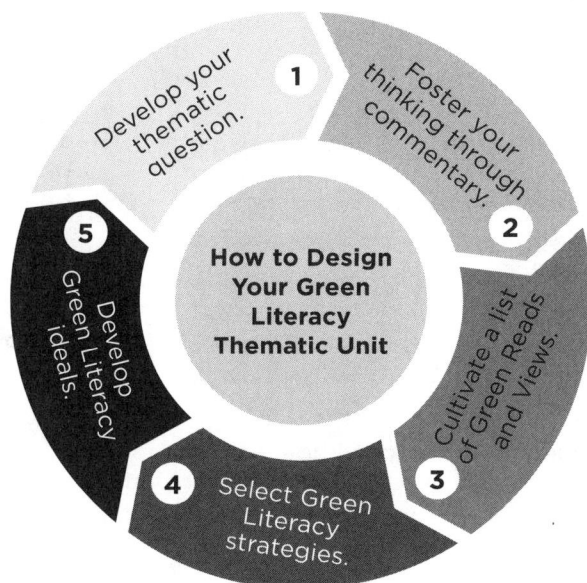

Figure 2.1: How to design your Green Literacy thematic unit.

We chose to structure the five elements of Green Literacy through the actions of engage, empower, and shift because they mirror the natural progression of human thought and action. We think of it as tending a community garden: First, you prepare the soil, inviting curiosity and observation (engage). Then, you plant seeds, nurturing growth through exploration and understanding (empower). Finally, you watch the garden flourish, transforming the space and the people who care for it (shift). This metaphor reflects how we guide students and ourselves to connect with environmental issues—starting with curiosity; growing through reading, writing, and action; and culminating in meaningful change. We will talk more about the engage, empower, and shift organization throughout chapters 4–7 when referring to organization and the thematic unit planning template.

We created the Green Literacy Thematic Unit Planning Template in figure 2.2 (page 34) to guide you in building meaningful, sustainability-focused lessons using the Green Literacy model. The template centers on the five essential elements of a Green Literacy thematic unit. These elements work together to provide you with a clear and adaptable framework for bringing environmental learning into your classroom.

While we offer guidelines for how to use the thematic unit planning template, we envision flexibility and teachers using it in various ways. You can follow along with what we wrote and implement some or all of the model lessons developed by Green Literacy teachers in a professional development series (chapter 3, page 57), you can implement just the thematic questions from our model lessons and customize the template, or you can use the Green Literacy model and this planning template to create entirely unique units to meet your students' needs. The template is meant to serve as a practical tool for whichever way you decide to use it, and it is *not* meant to bog you down with extra paperwork. It may help you streamline your process and energize you to focus on creating and teaching meaningful, engaging learning experiences.

Name:

Grade level:

School context (for example, urban, rural, public, or private):

PHASE 1: ENGAGE

Develop Your Thematic Question

Here are some guiding questions to consider as you develop your thematic question. Reflect on these prompts to clarify your focus.

1. Brainstorm

   • What issue that could lead to a big idea about the environment are you most passionate about exploring with your students?

   • What current events or real-world examples resonate with you and can help bring environmental issues to life for your students?

2. Prioritize

You might have more than one environmental issue you'd like to explore with your students. Now, think about which one will create the most meaningful conversations and learning.

Through this brainstorming and prioritization process, write your thematic question. Some stems that might be useful are:

   • How can/do . . . ?

   • What might . . . ?

Write your thematic question here.

See page 38 in the book for more information on creating thematic questions.

The process of developing a thematic question is the heart of unit planning. A big, open-ended question such as, "How can we live in harmony with nature?" serves as the foundation for your unit, helping to focus your students' learning and inspire their thinking. A strong thematic question encourages curiosity and connects lessons to larger, real-world challenges.

Consider what your students already know about the environmental issue and how your school community might respond to the topic. Think, too, about the ways your administration can support you as you teach this lesson. How can you shape your question so it encourages collaboration and reduces any challenges? What is your willingness to engage with the environmental issue?

Foster Your Thinking Through Commentary

First, review the following questions and respond to a few or all of them. Use a list or brainstorm freely to capture your ideas.

- Whose voices or stories do you need to hear to understand this issue, and why are they important to you?

- What unfair systems or problems do you want your students to think about when learning about this issue, and how can you help them ask questions and find ways to make things better?

- Whose experiences or ideas are sometimes left out when this issue is talked about, and how can you share those voices in your classroom to help everyone learn more?

From your responses, begin to find springboards that will help you develop commentary that deepens your thematic exploration.

Springboards to Support Commentary

- Springboard 1:

  - Title or source:

  - Key insights:

- Springboard 2:

  - Title or source:

  - Key insights:

- Springboard 3:

  - Title or source:

  - Key insights:

See page 40 in the book for more information on developing springboards for commentary.

Commentaries, both those developed by you and those developed by us (pages 110, 136, and 162), offer opportunities for you to facilitate student discussions, encourage debate, and help students connect their learning to their own experiences. Whether through class discussions, journaling, or creative projects, commentaries foster critical thinking and communication in a way that makes lessons resonate.

Figure 2.2: Green Literacy Thematic Unit Planning Template. Continued ▶

PHASE 2: EMPOWER

Cultivate a List of Green Reads and Views

Consider the three cycles of comprehension as you choose your strategies: simple comprehension (retell and summarize), criteria comprehension (support thinking), and perspective comprehension (investigate explicit and implicit perspectives and move to systems thinking).

Select texts and digital media that flow from your thematic question and your commentary research. If you need help finding texts or digital media, consult **go.SolutionTree.com/literacy**, our companion website (www.greenliteracy.org), or your school or local librarian.

What types of texts or stories (fiction, nonfiction, poetry, or multimedia) can you use to help your students connect emotionally and critically to this environmental issue? What is the author's message?

Green Reads
Title: Author's message:
Title: Author's message:
Title: Author's message:
Title: Author's message:
Title: Author's message:

The inclusion of Green Reads and Views in the Green Literacy model ensures that you can introduce your students to high-quality books and media that inspire and challenge them as they consider environmental issues. These resources act as gateways for understanding complex environmental topics, offering diverse perspectives, and sparking meaningful conversations. The template helps you identify and organize the best Green Reads and Views for your lessons, ensuring a rich and engaging learning experience.

Select Green Literacy Strategies

What reading, writing, and drama strategies will encourage your students to express their thoughts, analyze the issue, and explore solutions? Reading, Writing, and Drama Strategies:	How can you support all your students—no matter their reading level or background—to engage deeply with the issue and build their understanding? Immersive Strategies:

See page 45 in the book for more information on selecting Green Literacy strategies.

See page 16 in the book for more information on the three cycles of comprehension.

PHASE 3: SHIFT

Develop Green Literacy Ideals

As you work with your students to create their Green Literacy ideals, remember this is something that happens naturally during your teaching. You can plan all the other steps ahead of time, but for this last part, you'll need to pause and observe how your students respond.

Reflection 1

As you plan how to guide your students in creating their Green Literacy ideals, take a moment to think about the lessons you've already taught. How did your students respond during these activities? What really stood out to you? Write down some notes or free-write about what you noticed happening in your classroom.

Reflection 2

In your free-writing, think about what stood out to you during class discussions about the books. What were some interesting things your students said about using the reading and writing strategies?

See page 47 in the book for more information on how to facilitate the Green Literacy ideals discussion.

In the following sections, we detail the elements of the thematic unit planning template, which encompass creating a thematic unit and developing Green Literacy ideals with your students.

Develop Your Thematic Question

To start exploring how to develop a thematic question, we'll consider Green Literacy themes. As you may recall, a Green Literacy theme is a big idea or concept related to humans' impact on the environment and environmental social justice that helps students explore and connect with real-world issues. These themes encourage critical thinking about our relationship with the planet and inspire action for sustainability. Green Literacy themes highlight concerns within the environmental movement with a focus on humanity's interaction with nature. We believe the following definition provided by the U.S. Environmental Protection Agency (EPA, 2013) concerning environmental justice aligns with Green Literacy:

> Environmental justice is the fair treatment and meaningful involvement of all people regardless of race, color, national origin, or income with respect to the development, implementation, and enforcement of environmental laws, regulations, and policies. EPA has this goal for all communities and persons across this Nation. It will be achieved when everyone enjoys the same degree of protection from environmental and health hazards and equal access to the decision-making process to have a healthy environment in which to live, learn, and work. (p. 1)

We see you as embracing the EPA's definition of environmental justice—that everyone should enjoy "the same degree of protection from environmental and health hazards and equal access to the decision-making process to have a healthy environment in which to live, learn, and work." Issues such as pollution, deterioration of the physical condition of communities, and access to natural resources and renewable energy are part of public discourse. As that discourse grows, young people become increasingly aware of large-scale environmental problems and their connection to social justice. We hope you and your students can connect with and find your voices in the conversation through engaging in Green Literacy's themes.

Here are some more examples of themes that may help foster those connections and voices; the themes can be adapted across different ages and grade levels.

- Cycles of growth and renewal
- Connections between living things
- The power of place in local and global ecosystems
- Water as a life source
- Resilience in nature and communities
- The role of light in ecosystems and creativity

We've intentionally left the listed themes broad to allow for exploration through various age-appropriate activities, readings, and discussions, while encouraging students to make connections to their personal experiences and the world around them. Themes can also be more narrowly defined if needed.

Themes act as the overarching lens for exploring ideas in Green Literacy, while Green Literacy ideals serve as the personal and collective values that emerge through engagement with those themes. This is where the theoretical and practical merge. For example, a theme like "cycles of growth and renewal" might invite students to explore how natural systems and personal growth are interconnected. This might lead to a Green Literacy ideal about resilience, as students reflect on how systems recover and adapt over time. The cyclical nature of this theme reinforces the idea that change is constant and essential, helping students connect their learning to real-world processes and personal development.

Each Green Literacy thematic unit begins with a thematic question—a spark to inspire curiosity and guide meaningful exploration. A good thematic question is open-ended and thought-provoking, and it encourages students to critically examine the connections between people and the environment. Teachers create their thematic question before they engage with commentary. The chosen thematic question guides the commentary. The commentary is for the teacher's background knowledge and confidence in navigating complex environmental issues as they work with their students. We invite you to begin by using our thematic questions and then move into creating your own, aided by the sense of what makes a strong thematic question.

- **A strong thematic question:** How do environmental challenges impact different communities around the world, and what can we do to help?

- **A weaker thematic question:** What are the effects of deforestation? (This is too narrow and doesn't invite deeper, connected thinking.)

In chapters 3 and 5–7, we provide specific thematic questions to help guide learning. As you gain confidence in designing your own units through using the Green Literacy Thematic Unit Planning Template, you may want to develop thematic questions that align with your students' interests and community context. Some questions on the planning template ask you to brainstorm: (1) What issue that could lead to a big idea about the environment are you most passionate about exploring with your students? and (2) What current events or real-world examples resonate with you and can help bring environmental issues to life for your students? If you are having trouble brainstorming, we offer the following list of environmentally focused thematic questions that include a human element and emphasize social and environmental justice to spark your curiosity.

- How do changes in nature affect the health and happiness of different people?

- What's the connection between poverty and problems like pollution or damaged environments?

- How can we work together to make the world a fairer and healthier place for everyone?

- What can we learn from people and cultures that live peacefully with nature?

- How do natural disasters show unfairness in the world, and how can we fix this?

- How do the things we buy and use affect the planet and other people around the world?

- Why is having clean water important, and how is it a basic right for everyone?

- How can people in our community take action to fight climate change and protect the future?

- Do environmental rules and laws treat everyone fairly, or do they sometimes fail to do so?

- How can we make sure everyone has safe parks, green spaces, and healthy places to live?

This list is a starting point to help you craft questions that connect the environment to broader human experiences and issues of justice. These kinds of questions inspire curiosity, critical thinking, and action, helping students see their role in building a fairer, healthier world.

Foster Your Thinking Through Commentary

Commentaries in Green Literacy function as thoughtful annotations or analyses of a text, focusing on its connection to environmental themes. In practice, a commentary is a series of interpretations of an environmental theme that pose questions, which often disrupt what is commonly assumed. For example, a commentary might explore the theme of renewable energy and the issue that increasing solar panel production also creates new environmental challenges, such as mining for rare materials. This disrupts the common assumption that renewable energy solutions are always environmentally harmless and encourages critical thinking about the complexities of sustainable practices. We use commentaries to examine power relationships, leadership issues, and solutions that advocate systems thinking; commentaries reflect critical stances, which can include ecocriticism and the study of literature and the environment from an interdisciplinary point of view. The commentaries in *The Green Literacy Handbook* were written by us. When teachers begin to develop their own commentaries through interrogating their chosen thematic question, they gather sources, critically evaluate them, and consider different understandings of the environmental issue. Engaging in commentaries helps a teacher decide which Green Reads and Views to use in their thematic unit. Using or creating commentaries also positively influences the teacher's confidence in teaching the environmental issue.

Our intention is for commentaries to push your critical thinking as well as instill confidence to launch into critical conversations with young people. Through commentaries, we aim to widen the context so that chosen texts are meaningful to students (Knapp, 1995). While the commentary will ultimately support you in engaging with your students in the three cycles of comprehension and traveling beyond what the author conveys to consider points of view not mentioned in the text (Luke et al., 1996), you will use the commentary to guide your own thinking as you plan for critical discussions. Commentaries *inform* the work you and your students do by creating the possibility of transformation toward a more just, equitable, and tolerant society. They empower first you and then, through your guidance, your students, motivating them to acquire and apply reading and writing skills to articulate their ideas.

The decision to include already-designed, completed commentaries in chapters 3 and 5–7 was guided by teacher feedback from our Green Literacy professional development before we started writing this book. Some teachers expressed uncertainty about the environmental issues featured in texts, while others demonstrated a general understanding and sought deeper insights to enrich their teaching. Our completed commentaries bridge the gap, equipping you with structured thematic analyses that build confidence and provide clarity. Please note these commentaries act not as rigid instructions but rather as a gentle compass, pointing the way toward understanding and encouraging you to chart your own course. We believe that by using these examples as models, you can build confidence, fostering a deeper relationship with environmental themes. We encourage you to use the provided commentaries as a starting point for developing your own. Then, when creating your own commentaries, take ownership of the process, deepen your connection to the material, and tailor it to your students' needs.

The thematic unit planning template guides you through crafting commentaries by prompting reflection on the following critical questions, which frame your teaching.

- Whose voices or stories do you need to hear to understand this issue, and why are they important to you?

- What unfair systems or problems do you want your students to think about when learning about this issue, and how can you help them ask questions and find ways to make things better?

- Whose experiences or ideas are sometimes left out when this issue is talked about, and how can you share those voices in your classroom to help everyone learn more?

As you begin to explore texts, you might ask yourself questions like these.

- What environmental issue or theme is central to the text?

- How does the text portray interconnected systems (for example, ecosystems or human communities)?

- How do the characters' actions reflect or challenge environmental problems?

Using these questions and the planning template, you can begin to develop your own commentary. For example, when working with the book *One Well: The Story of Water on Earth* by Rochelle Strauss (2007), you might ask yourself whose voices are represented and whose are missing. The text highlights global water issues; it might not explore the lived experiences of communities most affected by water scarcity. This could provide an entry point for a discussion about inclusion and equity with your students, and it could encourage you to bring in additional resources, such as articles or videos featuring firsthand accounts from individuals in regions where access to clean water is a daily challenge.

Here are three ways you can engage with commentaries.

1. **Use the provided commentaries as they are:** If you're short on time, new to the unit, or unfamiliar with the environmental topic, you can directly use the commentaries provided in this book. Many teachers find this approach helpful when starting out or building confidence in a new area.

2. **Adapt and expand the provided commentaries:** Feel free to adapt commentaries to suit your needs. Something we've provided might spark your curiosity, prompting you to explore further. As you follow your interests, remember to return to the thematic question to connect your ideas and maintain focus.

3. **Create your own path:** You may choose to take a different direction entirely, using the thematic question as a starting point for your own learning and connections. This approach allows you the freedom to explore topics in a way that resonates with you.

Whichever approach you choose, we encourage you to keep the thematic question at the forefront and allow yourself the freedom to explore and learn in a way that feels authentic and meaningful.

Our provided commentaries can help support teachers. One example of this is a commentary we created for a group of educators who engaged in long-term Green Literacy professional development. The reproducible "Illustration of How Green Literacy Commentaries Support Teachers" is available online at **go.SolutionTree.com/literacy** and includes a commentary on the book *Common Ground* by Molly Bang (1997) and a description of how Albert, a third-grade teacher, used the commentary's insights in teaching his class.

Cultivate a List of Green Reads and Views

Green Reads and Views bring the theme and thematic question of the unit to life. The process of thinking within commentary development, either by us or by you, supports you in choosing Green Reads and Views for your students. These texts and media help build background knowledge, offer multiple perspectives on an environmental issue, and increase teachers' confidence.

Our master list of Green Reads and Views (available at **go.SolutionTree.com/literacy**) is a compilation of children's books and digital media resources whose themes draw on human interactions with the natural world and reflect human and animal relationships with the natural world. These resources help bring thematic questions to life, connecting big ideas to relatable stories and real-world examples. This handbook offers a starting point, and your personally curated list can draw from it while incorporating books or media from your own research or experience that resonate with your students and support their environmental themes.

As you complete the planning template, use its Foster Your Thinking Through Commentary section to reflect on key questions that identify relevant environmental issues. Your responses will shape your approach and guide your selection of Green Reads and Views for your students.

The following four questions are the basis for choosing Green Reads and Views for students to read about, think about, and discuss complex environmental themes.

1. Does the text or media source express a connection to humanity and the environment?

2. Does the text or media source require students to use critical thinking when reading or viewing the environmental justice–themed story?

3. Does the text or media source enable students to provide multiple answers and perspectives on the situation in the environmental justice–themed story?

4. Does the text or media source offer the possibility of students personally connecting the environmental justice–themed story to their local or global landscape in hopes of eventual action toward earth stewardship?

In addition to using these questions as guiding criteria, you can add your own criteria if desired. As more environmental justice–themed books and digital media are published, your options for readings and viewings will grow, and the four questions will help guide what you choose from the growing pool of possibilities.

You and your students will find that many of the suggested Green Reads and Views already have prominent places in classrooms, schools, and neighborhood libraries. Some classics like *The Giving Tree* by Shel Silverstein (1964) and *The Lorax* by Dr. Seuss (1971) remain in print. Some newer picture books, such as *We Are Water Protectors* by Carole Lindstrom (2020), focus on how humans work with nature, which inspires young people to consider their role in protecting natural resources. Similarly, *The Wisdom of Trees: How Trees Work Together to Form a Natural Kingdom* by Lita Judge (2021) invites discussions on the interconnectedness of ecosystems and human responsibility in caring for the environment. These books spark conversations about real-world experiences, such as preparing for extreme weather, conserving water, or planting trees to restore habitats. Other suggested Green Literacy readings are Laurie Lawlor's (2012) biography titled *Rachel Carson and Her Book That Changed the World* and Lynne Cherry's (2004) illustrated *The Sea, the Storm, and the Mangrove Tangle*, a hybrid book that contains ecology information within a fictional story. These books correspond with our four questions by emphasizing human interaction with nature and the threat posed to nature by human activity; *Rachel Carson and Her Book That Changed the World* covers the threat of chemicals to birdlife, and *The Sea, the Storm, and the Mangrove Tangle* features the impact of pollution and development on mangrove ecology. Lawlor (2012) mentions how chemical companies protected their interests and tried to discredit Rachel Carson (1962) and her pioneering book, *Silent Spring*.

We acknowledge the importance of informational science texts. Nonfiction books are essential to young people's interpretation of the natural world, and they are an important part of the science curriculum. Such books include Anne Rockwell's (2006) *Why Are the Ice Caps Melting?*, which introduces young readers to the facts about climate change rather than the human interactions around it. Another example of an informational science text is *If Sharks Disappeared* by Lily Williams (2017), which explores the role of sharks in marine ecosystems and the consequences of their extinction. While this book presents scientific data, it also fosters a deeper human connection by emphasizing how the health of the ocean impacts our well-being and future. However, these books do not answer our four questions. In effect, they do not address the human factor within complex environmental issues, which is the reason we developed Green Literacy.

In Green Literacy, digital media offer engaging ways to introduce environmental concepts and encourage critical thinking while leveling the playing field. What we mean by this is students at low reading levels can connect with a visual rendering of information and story to enrich their background knowledge so that when they see similar material in written form, they have a greater capacity for comprehension. Also important, these same students can contribute to a classroom dialogue based on their viewing, which serves to increase confidence and create a critical stance.

A useful Green View that makes an important but complex activity easily understandable to viewers is the YouTube video "How to Take Care of the Environment," which emphasizes the essential practices of reuse, recycle, and reduce (Fun World For Kids, 2021). This video serves as an accessible starting point for conversations about everyday actions students can take to care for the planet. Another valuable resource is "What Is Biofuel? Biomass and Biofuels for Kids" (Learn Bright, 2020). This YouTube video introduces students to renewable energy, explaining how scientists and engineers are developing biofuels as cleaner alternatives to traditional fuels. The video invites students to think critically about energy sustainability and its role in environmental protection. Both videos align with Green Literacy's aims in selecting texts or media, adhering to the four guiding questions that spark critical dialogue. These resources help students explore environmental issues, ask meaningful questions, and develop a thoughtful, critical stance.

When selecting either reads or views for Green Literacy learning, focus on texts and media that are engaging, accessible, and aligned with your unit's environmental goals. Look for materials that build comprehension, spark curiosity, and encourage students to think critically about the issue presented. Along with using the curated list of reads and views provided online, you can explore local libraries, consult research librarians, view children's publishing houses' reading lists (like Lee & Low Books' STEM and STEAM reading lists), and browse online educational platforms for additional selection ideas. Partnering with environmental organizations, like The Nature Generation, or seeking input from community groups can uncover valuable resources. These resources help connect your classroom content to the real world, thereby inspiring deeper engagement through critical reading, writing, and speaking.

Utilize the section for Green Reads and Views in the planning template. After you select the texts you want to use, we suggest noting the author's message for each one. This practice helps you better understand the purpose of the text and organize your teaching strategies effectively. Here's an example for a fourth-grade thematic unit on exploring connections to nature.

1. **Title:** *Have You Ever Seen a Flower?* by Shawn Harris (2021)
   - **Author's message:** This book encourages readers to observe and connect with nature. It highlights the sensory and emotional experiences of interacting with the natural world.

2. **Title:** *The Hike* by Alison Farrell (2019)
   - **Author's message:** This story inspires exploration and appreciation of the natural world. It shows the joy and discovery found in outdoor adventures with friends.

By noting the author's message for each book, you can align your teaching strategies with the themes presented. For example, *Have You Ever Seen a Flower?* could be paired with a Wonder Walk activity (page 122), where students closely observe flowers in their local environment and write sensory-rich descriptions of what they see, hear, and feel. Similarly, *The Hike* could inspire students to create illustrated maps of their own outdoor adventures, document their observations, and reflect on their connection to nature. In the following section, we look more closely at the process of selecting Green Literacy strategies and how to use the template to do so.

Select Green Literacy Strategies

The strategies presented in this section build directly on the foundation of Green Reads and Views, providing thoughtful, insightful, and practical ways to engage students with the theme and resources of the unit. By connecting stories, visuals, and media to teaching methods, these strategies help bring the thematic question to life and encourage students to explore, reflect, and act on their learning in meaningful ways.

We define a *Green Literacy strategy* as a teaching strategy that helps young people develop critical thinking. Many of these come from best-practice literacy strategies, such as readers' theater (students read scripts aloud with expression to bring the story to life) and directed reading (students engage in the text by predicting what will happen based on prior knowledge, then reading sections to confirm or refute those predictions). These strategies also include free response (students engage with the text by asking open-ended questions, making connections to personal experiences, and providing detailed written responses that go beyond simple, factual responses) and connection making (students make connections to the text from their lives or from other readings).

When you are in the planning stages, use the section of the planning template called Select Green Literacy Strategies. This is a space for you to brainstorm strategies that will work best for your class. To guide your brainstorming, we provide two key questions.

1. What reading, writing, and drama strategies will encourage your students to express their thoughts, analyze the issue, and explore solutions?

2. How can you support all your students—no matter their reading level or background—to engage deeply with the issue and build their understanding?

For the second question, we recommend using an immersive strategy, which involves creating hands-on, engaging experiences that allow students to explore a topic profoundly and personally. Immersive strategies help students connect with the material in meaningful ways, fostering curiosity and active participation. As stated, one example in chapter 5 is a Wonder Walk, where students explore their local environment—such as a nearby park, schoolyard, or neighborhood—and reflect on how natural and human-made systems interact. This strategy encourages students to ask questions, make observations, and think critically about their surroundings, which builds a foundation for deeper discussions and learning. In chapters 5–7, we outline additional immersive strategies that can be adapted to fit your students' needs and support critical thinking and creativity.

In chapters 5, 6, and 7, we offer support to design your own thematic unit, and we outline various Green Literacy strategies for you to explore. We recognize that as an educator, you are adept at identifying what will effectively engage your students. Whether you experiment with new methods or stay within the comfort of proven techniques, you can adapt these strategies to your classroom's specific needs. When embracing these methods, remember the transformative power of drama strategies and role play. These approaches can unlock students' imagination and empathy, often leading to profound understanding and retention. Encourage students who might be hesitant—these interactive tools can be incredibly impactful for those who struggle with conventional learning because the tools offer them a dynamic and inclusive way to connect with the material.

Here are some choices.

- Use the Green Literacy strategies as written within each thematic unit chapter (chapters 5–7) with the suggested books.

- Pick and choose among these strategies and the suggested books within each thematic unit chapter.

- Use tried-and-true strategies that you know would lead your students to simple comprehension (understanding the text), criteria comprehension (supporting ideas by drawing from the text), and perspective comprehension (seeing perspectives different from one's own as well as thinking systemically).

- Use the suggested books within each thematic unit chapter or ones of your own that probe into the thematic question.

Green Literacy strategies offer students opportunities to think about environmental issues in meaningful ways. They are also opportunities to connect to academic standards in a way that works for your classroom. Thematic units are designed to engage students with big environmental ideas while aligning with the goals and benchmarks set by your school or district.

The important work of thinking critically, discussing, and citing evidence within the text and within digital media occurs in the Green Literacy classroom through thematic units. Green Literacy teachers know that the process of Green Literacy and its thematic units support academic standards, including the CCSS. This intermix of different subjects allows teachers to facilitate real-world connections. For example, in a unit about ocean pollution, students might read *All the Way to the Ocean* (Harper, 2006; making a connection to an academic standard in English language arts), investigate the effects of plastic waste on marine life (making a connection to science), and analyze how interconnected systems—such as manufacturing, waste management, and ocean ecosystems—contribute to and are impacted by pollution (making a connection to social studies and systems thinking). This interdisciplinary approach helps students make real-world connections while meeting academic standards. Equally important, the units are arranged thematically, which allows teachers to plunge into several subjects while adhering to the overarching goal of the CCSS, which combine language arts standards with those of science and social studies. Thus, Green Literacy lends itself well to teaching standards such as the CCSS. It is thematically organized and interdisciplinary in its approach.

Develop Green Literacy Ideals

Engaging your students in critical dialogues sets the stage for your class to come together and collaboratively develop Green Literacy ideals. These ideals, which we first discussed in the introduction and in chapter 1, represent the shared and agreed-on values that emerge after critical conversations and through consensus as students explore environmental themes. We encourage you to revisit chapter 1 (page 9) to reflect on the foundational concepts and how they connect to the work in action.

Green Literacy ideals often emerge most powerfully at the end of a unit, when students have had time to synthesize their knowledge, experiences, and reflections. These ideals are not rigidly planned. Rather, they are cultivated through meaningful reflection, shared dialogue, and an organic exploration of the unit's themes. We have observed that many teachers conclude their units by collaboratively developing Green Literacy ideals with their students, fostering a sense of ownership and empowerment.

Teachers often ask whether Green Literacy ideals can be developed at the beginning or middle of a unit. Our response is that as the teacher, you are the expert in guiding your class discussions and determining what works best for your students. The consideration we emphasize is that critical discussions about environmental issues require time and cannot be fully explored in one or two conversations. Shifting perspectives and fostering meaningful engagement necessitate providing students with ample opportunities for reflection, dialogue, and inquiry throughout the unit.

If you are using the Green Literacy Thematic Unit Planning Template, you'll find there a dedicated space to brainstorm and document these moments. Use that space to reflect on the teaching you have done throughout the unit and to consider how your students responded. What stands out for you? What moments of insight, curiosity, or passion surfaced during discussions, readings, and creative activities? Take notes or free-write about what happened in your classroom—capture the highlights, surprises, and meaningful exchanges that unfolded.

As you reflect, pay particular attention to how your students' perspectives may have shifted during the unit. Look for moments where they moved from seeing environmental issues as distant or abstract to understanding their relevance and urgency in their own lives. These shifts often signal the development of Green Literacy ideals.

For example, a student might begin a unit thinking of deforestation as something happening far away in rainforests they've never seen. However, after reading *The Great Kapok Tree* (Cherry, 1990) and discussing the interconnectedness of ecosystems, they might realize how local tree loss affects their own community's air quality, wildlife, and climate.

Intentionally, we have not provided a fixed space in the template to write these ideals. You will find that they are personal to each class and should reflect the unique journey of your students. Use your reflections and observations to capture these moments and honor the growth that occurred during the unit.

When teachers follow the five core components of an effective Green Literacy thematic unit—(1) developing thematic questions, (2) fostering reflection through commentary, (3) curating impactful Green Reads and Views, (4) selecting tailored teaching strategies, and (5) guiding students in creating Green Literacy ideals—they lead their students to enact the flow of empower, engage, shift while being immersed in a complex environmental topic. This then leads to a critical stance.

TAKE A CRITICAL STANCE THROUGH GREEN LITERACY

As we discussed in chapter 1, Green Literacy is part of critical pedagogy, which emphasizes that you and your students take a critical stance toward any texts—from fairy tales to newspaper articles and everything in between—and look at power relationships. To be clear, taking a critical stance means looking closely at information, asking questions about its purpose, and considering different viewpoints to understand its deeper meaning. In critical literacy, it encourages readers to think beyond the words on the page, ask why the author wrote the text, and consider how it connects to the world around them (Freebody & Luke, 1990). In Green Literacy, taking a critical stance involves examining environmental issues to understand their root causes and questioning the systems and decisions that contribute to these problems. In this way, a Green Literacy critical stance goes further by encouraging students to think critically about solutions and take meaningful action to address issues like climate change and pollution. It helps learners connect what they read with real-world challenges and empowers them to make a difference (Freebody & Luke, 1990).

For example, fourth graders could read the story of Cinderella, take a critical stance, and ask who has power over Cinderella's life at the beginning of the story. Why do the stepmother and her daughters order Cinderella around and make her into a servant rather than treat her as a respected member of the household? The fourth graders may talk about experiences in their blended families to understand the plight of Cinderella and the family dynamics at the beginning. With the Cinderella story, the teacher would focus on family power issues, while in Green Literacy teaching, the power issues considered are related to human impact on the Earth.

In Green Literacy practice, you and your students take a critical stance in multiple ways by bearing in mind power relationships and their connection to environmental justice themes. Power entails different forms: position, physical strength or control, money, and skills and competence, including literacy abilities. You and your students take a critical stance when you ask questions that lead to an analysis of perspectives both present and excluded in the text; when you consider whose perspective is credible and support your reasoning; and when you reflect on who has power in the situation and how others may be empowered.

Ira Shor (1992), a leading proponent of critical pedagogy, states that the information, research, and analysis of environmental themes (which you and your students will undertake in chapters 3 and 5–7) achieve what he calls:

> habits of thought, reading, writing, and speaking which go beneath surface meaning, first impressions, dominant myths, official pronouncements, traditional clichés, received wisdom, and mere opinions, to understand the deep meaning, root causes, social context, ideology, and personal consequences of any action, event, object, process, organization, experience, text, subject matter, policy, mass media, or discourse. (p. 129)

Through the themes found in Green Literacy thematic units, you and your students come to realize that our natural resources are limited and that a sense of valuing place and earth stewardship is as important to our identity as human beings as race, class, and gender. You and your students will begin to formulate a critical stance when you grasp that there are clear winners and losers in the old ways of mining, polluting, and using up the global commons of air, water, fossil fuels, and forests, and in not realizing that we depend on nature for our lives. Teaching Green Literacy themes within our thematic units supports your students to take a critical stance by determining the local and global consequences of resource use and of our relationship with the natural world.

TEACH COMPREHENSION IN GRADES K–2

We single out K–2 teaching because students in this grade range are typically at an emergent reading level, so they need supports to develop the comprehension skills that, with continued guidance, become the ability to think critically about texts and multimedia.

A skillful Green Literacy teacher of kindergarten through grade 2 begins the process of teaching comprehension by avoiding a focus on single correct answers to questions. They encourage their students to share what they are thinking and feeling in relation to texts and multimedia. K–2 Green Literacy teachers are aware of the three cycles of comprehension. They emphasize that students speak up in classroom discussions with their observations, connections, wonderings, and ideas about illustrations and the ways books and digital media are written and produced. These teachers encourage active comprehension. They ask students in this grade range to ask questions and make predictions. In this process, students become more goal directed. They listen or read to satisfy their own purposes rather than the teacher's.

A critical feature of teaching students to actively comprehend in this grade range is helping them relate their prior knowledge to the content of what they are hearing or reading. Text connections are thought of in three ways: (1) text-to-self, often called "making a connection"; (2) text-to-text; and (3) text-to-world (Keene & Zimmermann, 2007). A text-to-world connection is inferential in that it goes beyond the story or nonfiction piece. A first grader's text-to-world connection for *The Giving Tree* (Silverstein, 1964) might be, "The story makes me think of how much trees give us and what we don't give back to them. I think we need to take care of trees."

In some classrooms, when discussions occur, the teacher or a few vocal students can quickly dominate. This is especially true in K–2 classrooms. To keep a discussion moving forward, some teachers may rapidly ask too many questions. Often, young children are reticent about participating when discussions are monopolized either by the teacher or by a few peers.

We advocate skillful use of the turn-and-talk strategy (page 122), particularly in kindergarten through grade 2 classrooms. This way, every student expresses their thoughts to a classmate, and then many ideas are shared with the whole group. Each student has an opportunity to share their ideas. You may use these best practices to support K–2 students as they build on comprehension skills in a natural progression toward perspective comprehension, which includes systems thinking. In grades 3–5 and beyond, the three cycles of comprehension are more explicitly taught during Green Literacy practice.

The following vignette comes from one lesson within a thematic unit with the overarching thematic question, "How does extreme weather connect our communities?" In the vignette, second-grade teacher Janet shares *Hide and Seek Fog* by Alvin Tresselt (1965) with her class. This picture book concerns an extreme weather event, an environmental issue that more people experience as the climate warms. Note that in K–2 classrooms, it's important to spark students' interest in the topic before diving into a book. For young students, a brief and engaging prereading activity helps them connect to the content and feel excited about the story. With older students, we often spend more time on conceptual prereading activities to involve them in an environmental issue before they read about it. This gives them a chance to think about the big ideas related to the environmental issue at hand before they start reading.

To begin, Janet reads Hide and Seek Fog several times. With her second-grade class, she discusses what happened in the book to make sure students comprehend the story. Janet then breaks the class into small groups. Now each student has the opportunity to think critically and contribute to the small-group discussion.

Each group is assigned one of the following groups of characters or implied characters from the book: the lobstermen, the children on the beach, their vacationer parents or caregivers, or the weather reporters on television who discuss the extensive fog. Group members talk among themselves about the worst fog in twenty years and how it affects their assigned characters. Janet has her students focus on the question of what each character would be thinking and saying about how the fog affects them.

During the group discussions, Janet walks around the room and listens.

"We can't swim. We can't build sandcastles," says Mindy from the children-on-the-beach group.

"No lobster for us," says Fernando from the lobstermen group.

"I can't report on the weather except I have to keep saying there is fog, fog, fog," says Tyquan from the weather-reporter group.

Satisfied that each group has collaboratively developed what the fictional characters would be thinking and talking about, Janet calls the students to return back to a whole-class setting.

On the board, Janet writes, "How to Be Prepared for a Future Fog." She says, "Now we are going to pretend that there is a village picnic. I'm going to be the mayor and call all of the groups together and ask each group to tell me what they think needs to be done to prepare our town for the next fog. Remember to be 'in character' and say what the character you are would say."

As the student groups present, Janet notes their suggestions on the board.

- "We got so bored. We need lots of games if there is another long fog." (children)

- "We were so mad! We couldn't find any nets. We couldn't see inside the shed because the fog was so thick!" (Lobstermen)

- "Everybody watched me all the time. They wanted to know when the fog would go away. I kept saying, 'Fog, fog, fog!' It was embarrassing. I am going to make a list of jokes I can tell that might help." (weather reporters)

After the presentations, the class makes a list of extreme weather events in addition to the one they read about in Hide and Seek Fog. Then Janet asks, "Do you think people in other extreme weather events have discussions like ours? Why?"

"Yes," says Fernando. "Mayors need to know what people think. Everybody can help to figure out how to help for big storms."

Marla asks, "I wonder, what would my mom do in a tornado?"

"Interesting," Janet says and begins to hand out paper. "Here is what I want you to do tonight to add to our class discussion tomorrow. Ask your parent, your grandparent, or the adult in your household to talk about any extreme weather event that they experienced or know about. Ask them what they think people should do to prepare for extreme weather."

"Wow," says Mindy. "Then we will have more people's ideas on how to prepare for bad weather."

Although the class continued beyond this point, we end this vignette here with the second-grade students going home to interview their parents or other adults about extreme weather events and if and how one should prepare for such events. This kind of interviewing on the environmental issue at hand extends the conversation, as can be seen in the Luke and colleagues (1996) study cited in chapter 1 (page 9). This interviewing process opens up the conversation to more points of view and often to a perspective shift.

We have found that a shift in perspective often leads to a desire for student-initiated action. Janet and her students, for instance, could consider local weather events such as tornadoes, and their shift in perspective may lead to students seeking safe places for all pets to go during a tornado and carrying out the safety plans with their parents or caregivers.

Janet and her students offer an example of how Green Literacy practices play out in K–2 classrooms, especially in student dialogue. In a K–2 classroom, Green Literacy often revolves around curiosity and observation, with students exploring environmental topics through storytelling and simple discussions. The dialogue focuses on making connections to their everyday experiences and expressing wonder about the natural world. In contrast, students in grades 3–5 and beyond engage in more complex discussions that require thinking critically and making connections to broader environmental issues. Their dialogue often includes predictions, evidence-based arguments, and reflections that explore multiple perspectives, preparing them to take meaningful action. This progression shows how Green Literacy adapts to developmental stages, encouraging all students to think critically about their role in caring for the planet.

As you move on to chapter 3, keep in mind the various ways to engage your students in critical thinking.

CONCLUSION

This chapter explored how to design a thematic unit as the focus of Green Literacy in practice. We outlined the elements of designing a Green Literacy thematic unit, including developing a thematic question, fostering your thinking through commentary, curating Green Reads and Views (books and digital media), selecting Green Literacy strategies, and developing Green Literacy ideals, using the template to brainstorm and organize through these steps.

Now, consider how this chapter has impacted your learning as a teacher. We offer a dedicated space for you to do so in the following "Teacher's Corner" reproducible tool (also available at **go.SolutionTree.com/literacy**). Whether you're working on your own, with a teaching partner, or within a schoolwide learning network, after exploring chapter 2, we encourage you to reflect on what you've learned.

Teacher's Corner

Here are some questions to support your reflection.

- Consider why you have *The Green Literacy Handbook*. What are your goals in reading it? How will being part of Green Literacy help (or hinder) you?

- How can teacher freedom in curriculum design enhance students' personal engagement with and response to environmental issues?

Here are prompts for journaling.

- Recall a teaching experience constrained by a set guide that limited addressing a pressing environmental issue. How would a more personalized approach have made a difference?

- Write about a time when the need for structured content had to be weighed against fostering students' personal connection to environmental issues. Discuss the decision and its effects.

Here are discussion guidelines.

- How do you judge when to move away from provided resources to incorporate your own, especially to make urgent environmental topics more personally relevant for students?

- How do you strike the right balance between setting rigorous educational goals and nurturing students' personal exploration of environmental issues?

PART 2

TEACHING OF
GREEN LITERACY

CHAPTER 3

Creation of the Green Literacy Model

People are the solution to the challenges facing our fabulous biodiversity on Earth. Young people are more supportive of caring for our natural world than any previous generation.

—JAMES DANOFF-BURG

The his chapter provides context for Green Literacy by showing how our professional development efforts, particularly a yearlong one in an urban setting, shaped the Green Literacy process and practice. We describe some of our engagements with teachers and include descriptions of how they developed and taught a thematic unit around the question, "How do you become an environmental leader?"

THE GREEN LITERACY MODEL DEVELOPS DURING PROFESSIONAL DEVELOPMENT

We led many professional development efforts as we developed Green Literacy in theory and practice. Over the years, we've guided a variety of Green Literacy programs, including a yearlong, grant-funded Green Literacy professional development initiative. This long experience, as well as shorter professional development sessions, helped us create what we now call the Green Literacy model. We share the context for the model to illustrate how working through complex environmental

Chapter Snapshot— What You'll Explore

In this chapter, we share with you how to:

- Determine the context for Green Literacy professional development efforts

- Follow the steps used to develop a Green Literacy thematic unit

- Use the Green Literacy Thematic Unit Planning Template

- Understand the process used in deciding a thematic unit question

- Create commentaries and use them to launch discussions during professional development sessions

- Choose Green Reads and Views for the thematic unit

- Select teaching strategies to pair with their chosen Green Reads and Views

- Implement the thematic unit

- Create Green Literacy ideals

issues builds relationships between teachers and their school communities. Specifically, when teachers participate in Green Literacy professional development, their school contexts play a key role in how they implement Green Literacy in their classrooms.

In the context of our yearlong professional development experience, we engaged in biweekly sessions with grades 2–5 teachers who were teaching together in the same school and volunteered to partake in the professional development. The school was urban and multicultural, with many students supported by English as a second language (ESL) teachers.

At the beginning of the professional development, some teachers worked alone while other teachers often worked in pairs to develop lessons they taught in their classrooms. During professional development sessions, the teachers shared their teaching experiences; we reflected together. For example, we collaborated with the teachers on two single-book Green Literacy lessons using *Common Ground* by Molly Bang (1997) and *The Boy Who Harnessed the Wind* by William Kamkwamba (Kamkwamba & Mealer, 2009). We supply an example commentary for the first book at **go.SolutionTree.com/literacy** and a vignette on the second book on page 23.

In describing the development of the model, we focus on two teachers (composites of various teachers we worked with), whom we'll call Maribel and Sarah. We share their responses to a precursor to the Green Literacy Thematic Unit Planning Template (chapter 2, page 34) and other responses so that you get a sense of how one might think through the Green Literacy process based on their experience.

Maribel and Sarah, Grade 5
Teachers at an Urban Public School

Maribel: *I am a seasoned educator with over fifteen years of experience. I bring expertise in classroom management, differentiated instruction, and relationship building with diverse learners. I am excited to mentor and share insights while remaining open to fresh ideas.*

Sarah: *I am newly hired with less than five years of experience. I am eager to participate in Green Literacy professional development. I seek guidance from Maribel on navigating the school's community and classroom dynamics.*

Together, we co-plan lessons. We volunteered for the Green Literacy professional development because we want to build environmental awareness in our classroom and want more classroom library books about environmental topics.

PROFESSIONAL DEVELOPMENT FOR GREEN LITERACY IS COLLABORATIVE AND FLUID

Green Literacy addresses diversity and is designed to be tailored to unique contexts, interests, and learning needs. This flexibility was evident from the beginning of our work developing Green Literacy, and was and is a core part of Green Literacy professional development. As we worked with teachers in the yearlong professional development experience, we focused on details—one book or media source at a time, for instance—and collaboratively moved to a cohesive vision, rather than attempting to apply a ready-made vision to all participants from the outset. This mode, while still in formation at the time of our professional development, exemplifies the importance with which Green Literacy holds all voices.

To provide pedagogical background knowledge and vocabulary, we often focused on the three cycles of comprehension and reading and writing strategies as well as drama strategies as we engaged with each Green Literacy read or view. Near the end of the professional development, as a culminating effort, we developed with the teachers what we now call the Green Literacy model, which includes the following steps, of which you are already aware: (1) develop your thematic question, (2) foster your thinking through commentary, (3) cultivate a list of Green Reads and Views, (4) select Green Literacy strategies, and (5) develop Green Literacy ideals. Our yearlong collaboration, and other shorter professional development work, provided profound engagement. We estimate a teacher independently teaching a similar thematic unit could complete the teaching process in two to four weeks. Shorter durations can also suffice to honor the Green Literacy values of holding all voices as important and allowing participating individuals time to evolve their own ideas and truly hear others' ideas, particularly as we've streamlined the Green Literacy process in this book. In terms of preparation, we believe that prep time may vary depending on the teacher's process. For example, we have seen teachers be inspired and create a unit in a day, while others may take a week. In general, we believe the prep process is three to four days.

In the following sections, we share a streamlined reconstruction of our work in each step, including examples of how students responded to lessons. This gives you a sense of how we developed the Green Literacy process and its inherent values, and it promotes thinking about what your own work may look like as you create Green Literacy learning experiences that speak to your students' interests and needs, urgent environmental issues, and the time constraints in your school and teaching schedule.

Note: Maribel and Sarah, our example teachers, used a precursor to what is now the Green Literacy Thematic Unit Planning Template. Throughout this chapter, we reconstruct their responses and, at times, generalize how teachers in our professional development responded to the different steps.

Step 1: Teachers Develop the Thematic Question

In what is now step 1 of the Green Literacy process, Maribel and Sarah engaged with us, as did the other participating teachers, in a brainstorming discussion dedicated to what thematic question we would use to organize the thematic unit.

After this session, Maribel and Sarah responded to the questions the group developed during brainstorming and completed the process of selecting a thematic unit question. As you can see from Maribel and Sarah's thought process, both Maribel and Sarah zeroed in on the question, "How do you become an environmental leader?"

Maribel and Sarah's brainstorm follows.

- What issue that could lead to a big idea about the environment are you most passionate about exploring with your students?

    - Maribel: *I'm passionate about helping my students explore what makes someone an environmental leader. We've studied leadership in other units before, and now I'd like to take that foundation and connect it to the environment. It's such a meaningful way to show them how leadership can create real change.*

    - Sarah: *As someone new to teaching, I really care about helping my students figure out what it means to be an environmental hero. I think it's so important for them to see that anyone, no matter where they come from, can make a difference for the planet. But honestly, I feel like we're always telling the same stories about the same people, and it's kind of boring. I want my students to hear different, more diverse stories—especially ones that reflect the world we live in now, not the same old stuff from years ago. I want my students to learn that heroes aren't famous people— they're individuals who take action for the planet, no matter how big or small.*

- What current events or real-world examples resonate with you and can help bring environmental issues to life for your students?

    - Maribel: *I'm really worried that with all the problems with the climate and weather, my students might feel overwhelmed. I want to keep things hopeful. When I was a new teacher, I focused so much on teaching the facts, but over time, I've realized how important it is to also inspire hope. I think showing them real-world examples of people actively solving environmental issues could really make a difference. I want them to see that change is possible and that they can be part of making a difference too.*

    - Sarah: *I think one of the biggest environmental issues we face is not realizing how powerful we can be when we work together. As someone from a generation that's super connected online, I feel like we have so much potential to come together and make a difference, but sometimes, we don't know how. I want my students to see that their voices matter and that, when we combine our efforts, we can really create change. I'm still figuring out the best way to teach this, but I'm excited to learn alongside them.*

While brainstorming can definitely produce thought-rich results, you may ask at this point, "How do I prioritize when there are many good ideas or when I have more than one environmental issue I'd like to explore with my students?" Our answer would be this: Think about which one will create the most meaningful conversations and learning, and consider what your students already know about environmental issues and how your school community might respond to the topic. Think, too, about the ways your administration can support you as you teach this lesson. How can you shape your question so it encourages collaboration and reduces any challenges? What is your willingness to engage with the environmental issue?

Here is an example of how Maribel and Sarah engaged in this process of prioritization.

- Maribel: *I've been teaching long enough to see that my students often know the basics about environmental issues, but they don't always see how their actions connect to bigger solutions, and they don't often think critically about them. I want to help them make those connections and show them they can make a real difference. I know the administration would back us. I see teaching environmental issues as learning facts and inspiring students to be leaders who take action for the planet.*

- Sarah: *Honestly, I feel like my students probably know some basics about environmental issues, like recycling or climate change, but I don't think they've had the chance to connect what they know to their own lives or community. The great thing is I have Maribel on my team, so we can work together to make this really engaging for the students. Our admin is super supportive and would totally help us out, whether it's with resources, planning, or getting the whole school involved in something like a project or event. I didn't go to college to study environmental issues, so I know I'm a little nervous about figuring out what I need to know as a teacher before I share it with my students.*

As you engage in a prioritization process like Maribel and Sarah's, write your thematic question. Here are some sentence stems that might be useful.

- How can/do . . . ?
- What might . . . ?

In the following, Maribel and Sarah decide on their thematic question.

- Maribel: *I suggested we focus on the question, "How can we become environmental leaders in our school and community?" because I know how important it is for students to see themselves as capable of making a difference. With my years of experience, I can help guide the lesson to show them how small, consistent actions can lead to big change. It's a question that not only encourages collaboration but also gives students a sense of purpose.*

- Sarah: *I love the idea of asking, "How can we become environmental leaders in our school and community?" It feels super fresh and exciting, and I know it's something that will totally click with our students. I want to bring in fun, hands-on ways to dive into this, like cool projects or interactive activities that show leadership in action. For me, this question makes the topic feel real and inspiring for today's students—it's something they can actually see themselves doing.*

As you can tell from the way Maribel and Sarah thought and dialogued, they came together on the same thematic question, clarifying it by including the phrase "in our school and community" at the end. Cohesion in selecting and finalizing the thematic question in this professional development experience came from the teachers' desire to use the same books and media in their Green Literacy work.

When you engage in this process using the thematic unit planning template, you may want to brainstorm with a colleague or on your own about how to complete the first section around environmental leadership (or whatever your chosen theme is). Consider how your answers may be different from Maribel and Sarah's.

Step 2: Teachers Foster Thinking Through Commentary

While the teachers in our yearlong Green Literacy professional development experience agreed that young people have the potential to be influential leaders in environmental activism, they saw their students as often needing to be empowered to take on these roles. They agreed that one way to empower their students was to involve them in critical thinking. They expressed that in order to facilitate critical thinking in their students, teachers would first have to reevaluate their own beliefs and ideas surrounding the question, "How do you become an environmental leader?"

During the professional development experience, we wrote the commentary for the thematic question the teachers developed. To do this, we researched the theme and continued talking with the teachers, gathering ideas for empowering students through critical thinking. The research and gathered ideas then framed our commentary, which we designed to support and foster the teachers' thinking as they continued their work.

During our professional development sessions, we shared the commentary with teachers on a printed handout. When we presented our commentary to the teachers, our aim was to give them a concrete resource to reference as they planned and implemented their thematic units. We specifically created this commentary to provide a foundation for discussing how to incorporate narratives into lessons on environmental leadership. This commentary aligned with existing research on the use of narratives and role models in environmental education. For instance, in *Childhood and Nature: Design Principles for Educators*, David Sobel (2008) discusses how personal stories can inspire environmental action by connecting children to relatable experiences, fostering a sense of agency, and encouraging empathy toward the natural world.

We provided commentary on two topics.

1. Complexity of environmental issues and young people

2. The Green Literacy approach to personal narrative

We used the two commentary topics as points of departure for our professional development conversations after the teachers had read and reflected on them. We created the following commentary on the first topic—complexity of environmental issues and young people—due to the many questions that arose during discussions with teachers. The commentary for the second topic is available as a reproducible at **go.SolutionTree.com /literacy**.

> We see environmental issues are complex, multilayered, and needing multiple perspectives in order to attain sustainable solutions. Many environmental challenges draw young people into hard dilemmas of determining solutions that may require sacrifices.

Many young people involved in environmental issues participate because they believe their actions can help address the degradation of the natural world. They often ask, "If I help and nothing changes, why should I care? If I work hard and create a viable solution, yet people in power ignore or belittle me, why should I try?" How do adults, people in power over young people, answer these questions? What message can society instill in young people so that they can discover answers, push back, and demand that the adult world pay attention to them? In many ways, the question, "Why should I try?" speaks to the reality that young people are not always invited into conversations. "Why should I try?" reflects the reality that young people are often left out of important conversations because adults sometimes overlook their ideas or don't create space for their voices. When this happens, we miss out on their unique perspectives and the chance to help them feel empowered to take action and be part of meaningful solutions.

Through storytelling and teaching, tellers explain that humans must work together to sustain individual motivation for a project. Consider the advent of the skyscraper, the development of the internet, or the foundation of robotic surgery. These accomplishments cannot be attributed to one individual. Sure, the seed idea may belong to an individual, yet collectively, many people contributed to each of these achievements, and in turn, growth and movement evolved. We believe that young people may follow a leader and need to work as a group as environmental stewards. We believe effective change happens when we work collaboratively—while you might not see immediate results, your efforts continue and inspire others. For example, a group of students organizing a beach cleanup may not see lasting change that day. They may acknowledge their teamwork raises awareness and motivates others to care for the environment. Young people thrive as environmental stewards when they work together, turning small actions into lasting impact.

Environmental leaders, such as the ones we'll highlight in this thematic unit, began by acting locally. They started where they lived and discovered a problem in their local world. This problem ignited in them the willingness to speak up, and in doing so, they became leaders. They received a wider audience and thus influenced people in their local community and beyond, and in this way, their efforts gained collective momentum.

Why do you think environmental solutions often begin at the local level? Additionally, why do you think environmental leaders tend to look beyond traditional approaches to problems and instead focus on creating solutions that strengthen community relationships while promoting earth stewardship?

While many commentaries in this handbook center on books and our analysis of them, we also offer commentary on ways to engage with an environmental issue without links to books. Both approaches are beneficial. We see our commentary as a springboard for dialogue during the sessions.

We offered Maribel and Sarah the following questions, which are now part of the Green Literacy planning template. Here is how they responded.

- Whose voices or stories do you need to hear to understand this issue, and why are they important to you?

  - Maribel: *After years of teaching, I've realized that truly understanding environmental leadership requires listening to a variety of voices and stories. I want to hear from people who've been working on the ground for decades— activists, community leaders, and farmers or Indigenous groups—because their lived experiences show the real challenges and triumphs of environmental work. These stories are important to me because they add depth and authenticity to what I share with my students. I want my students to see the diversity of leadership and understand that everyone's voice matters in solving these issues.*

  - Sarah: *I am a newer teacher. I know I have so much to learn, and I think it's so important to listen to voices that don't always get the spotlight. I want to hear from diverse leaders—Indigenous activists, young changemakers, and communities directly affected by climate issues—because their stories are raw, real, and inspiring. Representation matters, and I want my students to see that leadership doesn't look one way. These voices can show them that anyone, no matter where they're from or what they've been through, can step up and make a difference.*

- What unfair systems or problems do you want your students to think about when learning about this issue, and how can you help them ask questions and find ways to make things better?

  - Maribel: *I know how unfair systems keep some people on top while leaving others behind, and it drives me crazy. I don't focus on environmental issues, mainly because I am not sure how. My own son, who's disabled, has struggled with systems that aren't built for everyone, and that's shaped how I teach. I want my students to ask, "Who's being left out, and why?" and to know they can challenge unfairness. If we're not teaching them that, what's the point?*

  - Sarah: *As a younger African American teacher, it's important to me that my students see leaders of all races, classes, and genders making a difference. Growing up, I didn't see enough role models who looked like me, and I want my students to know leadership can come from anyone. I'll ask them questions like, "Who benefits from this system, and who doesn't?" to help them think critically and see how they can be part of the solution.*

While creating commentaries is something you will come to do on your own as you design units, we provide commentaries in this chapter that we used during our professional development experience. Additionally, we encouraged the teachers to do research independently, and many of the participants did so.

If you decide to teach this unit on environmental leadership, you can use the planning template's Foster Your Thinking Through Commentary section to brainstorm and then compare your commentary to how Maribel and Sarah responded. Your answer will depend on your teaching context.

Step 3: Teachers Curate Green Reads and Views

We supported the teachers in the professional development experience as they selected the following texts and digital media, which we now refer to in Green Literacy as Green Reads and Views. During the professional development sessions, we gave brief "book talks" or "view talks"—that is, quick oral reviews of books or films we thought would work in this thematic unit and align with exploration of the thematic question. Some of the teachers brought in books they thought would work with the theme and shared their own book talks.

From a longer list we developed, the teachers chose these books and digital media for the unit.

- *Seeds of Change* by Jen Cullerton Johnson (2010)
- *A River Ran Wild: An Environmental History* by Lynne Cherry (1992)
- *Seedfolks* by Paul Fleischman (1997)
- *Jane's Journey*, a short film by Lorenz Knauer (2011)
- An excerpt from *No One Is Too Small to Make a Difference* by Greta Thunberg (2021)

Since the teachers appreciated and learned from reading, reflecting on, and dialoguing about the topic commentaries we wrote, we also wrote a commentary based on each book or view the group chose to include in the thematic teaching unit. We followed a similar process with the commentaries on specific books and views as we did with the overall commentaries. The teachers found the background we provided in each read or view commentary supportive as they worked with their students on how to teach the specific Green Reads and Views in this thematic unit.

Here, as with the previous steps in the process, you can use the planning template to frame your selection of Green Reads and Views for your teaching about environmental leadership. A way to do this is to brainstorm a list of possible Green Reads and Views in the template space, first looking over the list the teachers used and then adding to it through your own knowledge of books and media as well as through internet research. Notice the template asks you to write down key insights for each selection, which will push you to think about all possible Green Reads and Views to use in the unit. After you have created this longer list, you need to prioritize which books and media would work in your specific teaching situation.

Step 4: Teachers Select and Use Green Literacy Strategies in the Thematic Unit

We supported the teachers in the professional development experience as they carefully chose strategies to facilitate their students' thinking, dialoguing, and learning about environmental leadership toward taking a critical stance and ultimately creating sustainable action to help preserve our natural world.

To choose strategies, we collaborated on how the specific books and digital media the teachers chose could pair with strategies we drew from best practices in literacy education. For example, we decided to pair the Free Response strategy (inviting students to respond in an open-ended way to teacher-chosen places as the teacher reads the book aloud) with *A River Ran Wild*. As we read aloud, we paused at places in the text and asked the teachers to write what they were thinking. Then we asked them to share their thoughts. We dialogued about the environmental ideas that arose from reading *A River Ran Wild* as well as their experience using Free Response to get a sense of teaching and learning with this strategy. Recall the three cycles of comprehension (chapter 1, page 9). Since the three cycles of comprehension are essential to Green Literacy learning, we had the teachers think out loud about how different strategies might support their students as they moved through simple comprehension, criteria comprehension, and perspective comprehension. We settled on these strategies as useful for each type of comprehension.

- **Strategies toward simple comprehension:** As the teachers focused on the following strategies aimed at developing simple comprehension, we used these organizing questions: "What does the author say about becoming an environmental leader?" and "How do you become an environmental leader?" As you will recall, simple comprehension occurs when students retell or summarize the story, nonfiction text, or digital media, including making inferences about what the author wrote. The teachers became familiar with this terminology in the previous professional development sessions.

  - *Free Response*—When using the Free Response strategy, the teacher invites students to answer open-ended questions about environmental topics, which promote critical thinking and personal expression. Students write their thoughts in short form at specific stopping points in the text that the teacher chooses, connecting their background knowledge of the topic to the reading. The classroom dialogue leads students to be able to articulate and comment on what the author says about becoming an environmental leader.

  - *Dear Agony Letter*—The Dear Agony Letter strategy involves having students choose a character in the text that has a problem and writing from the character's point of view. This reading and writing strategy aids students in understanding what happens in the text as well as encourages them to see different perspectives.

- *Develop a Timeline*—Students create timelines of important environmental events. This helps them see how events connect and have an impact over time. They visualize and gain a better understanding of environmental progress.

- **Strategies toward criteria comprehension:** During the professional development, teachers selected these strategies to encourage critical thinking and facilitate meaningful classroom discussions toward criteria comprehension. As you may recall, criteria comprehension occurs when students support their thinking about the story, nonfiction text, or digital media with criteria either prompted by the teacher or established from their own thinking. We used the guiding question, "How can you support your ideas of how to become an environmental leader by drawing from the text?"

  - *Dear Character Letter*—The Dear Character Letter strategy has students write letters to a character from a story or a real-life environmental leader. This exercise helps them explore the person's motivations, decisions, and actions related to environmental issues.

  - *Think-Pair-Share*—Students are asked to first think on their own about a prompt related to the text; then, they discuss their ideas with a partner, and finally, they share their thoughts with the larger group. This collaborative approach encourages all students' participation and enhances their understanding through peer interaction.

- **Strategies toward perspective comprehension:** We guided the teachers as they chose the strategies toward perspective comprehension. Recall that perspective comprehension includes systems thinking and occurs when students engage in the story, nonfiction text, or digital media so it becomes less an end than a doorway through which they explore the social world and their relationship to it. This incorporates explicit and implicit perspectives, characters debating different sides of issues, and the valuing and development of assumptions and beliefs that make sense to young people. The teachers considered the following questions: "Can you, as an environmental leader, see perspectives other than your own?" and "Can you consider systems thinking?" The following strategies help students see different viewpoints and think about how systems work in environmental issues. During professional development, we guided the teachers as they chose these strategies that would lead classroom discussions, encourage empathy and big-picture thinking, and build critical and comprehensive understanding.

  - *Compare Behaviors*—With this strategy, students examine the attitudes and behaviors of different groups of people, exploring how the different groups view and respond to environmental issues. This helps them understand diverse perspectives and the reasons behind various actions.

  - *Engagement*—The Engagement strategy (Long & Gove, 2004) has two parts: (1) finding the voices and (2) engaging through creating a drama. Students explore different perspectives on environmental issues by considering what different stakeholders in texts would say to each other. Then they use the voices they have considered to create an impromptu drama. Through this experience, students often begin to realize the social complexity of environmental issues.

- *Examining Preachiness of Language*—Students in small groups rate two different books using the following rating scale of 1–5; they provide reasons for their ratings and support their ideas with evidence from the text. For this strategy, we suggest using *No One Is Too Small to Make a Difference* and another book of the students' choice.

  ▸ 1 = Informative, interesting, and not preachy at all

  ▸ 2 = A little preachy, but I don't really notice it

  ▸ 3 = Somewhat preachy; only bothers me a bit

  ▸ 4 = Fairly preachy, and it feels rude

  ▸ 5 = Really gets on my nerves, preaching or lecturing to me; seems rude to me

  Follow this with a whole-class discussion where you support students when they have differing opinions about the appropriate "preachiness" of language, considering who they are talking to and in what context.

- *Compare and Contrast Texts*—This strategy helps students explore how different texts handle similar ideas; they look at what the authors are trying to say, how their messages are alike, and how they're different. It's a great way to encourage critical thinking and help students see topics from multiple perspectives.

After selecting strategies, the grades 2–5 teachers in the professional development sessions collectively chose to begin with *Seeds of Change*, followed by *A River Ran Wild*, *Seedfolks*, and the short film *Jane's Journey*, and ending with the excerpts from *No One Is Too Small to Make a Difference*. Because all the teachers used the same books in their teaching, they were able to debrief with one another and us as they engaged their students in the thematic unit. We believe it is best to collaborate with other teachers in teaching Green Literacy thematic units. However, many teachers begin teaching units alone and later bring in fellow teachers. We believe it is possible to work as a solo teacher, though we think that is more challenging. We offer some advice in the epilogue (page 183) on how to collaborate with other teachers, as well as how to consider this Green Literacy work in your own school context. In our professional development experience, we created commentaries for each book and the excerpt to help with good thinking, group discussions, and the strategies.

A reading selection and a paired strategy that you may be particularly interested in reviewing are excerpts from *No One Is Too Small to Make a Difference* by Greta Thunberg and Examining Preachiness of Language. Since Thunberg has been accused of being "pushy" in her rhetoric, teachers can explore the implications of this reaction to Thunberg's words and see what students themselves think.

The following commentary includes these excerpts, largely allowing Thunberg (2021) to speak for herself. In the full paired strategy discussion (available in the reproducible "Chapter 3 Commentaries With Paired Teaching Strategies" at **go.SolutionTree.com /literacy**), we describe how teachers support their students to consider whether forceful language is useful.

Following is the first excerpt from "Unpopular," a speech given at the United Nations Climate Change Conference in Katowice, Poland, in December 2018:

> You are not mature enough to tell it like it is. Even that burden you leave to your children. But I don't care about being popular, I care about climate justice and the living planet. We are about to sacrifice our civilization for . . . a very small number of people to continue to make enormous amounts of money. We are about to sacrifice the biosphere so that rich people in countries like mine can live in luxury. But it is the sufferings of the many which pay for the luxuries of the few. . . . Until you start focusing on what needs to be done rather than what is politically possible, there's no hope. We cannot solve a crisis without treating it as a crisis.
>
> And if solutions within this system are so impossible to find then maybe we should change the system itself?
>
> We have not come here to beg world leaders to care. You have ignored us in the past and you will ignore us again. You've run out of excuses and we're running out of time. We've come here to let you know that change is coming whether you like it or not.
>
> The real power belongs to the people. (Thunberg, 2021, pp. 13–14)

Following is the second excerpt from "Our House Is on Fire," a speech given at the World Economic Forum in Davos, Switzerland, on January 25, 2019:

> We are facing a disaster. . . . And now is not the time for speaking politely or focusing on what we can or cannot say. Now is the time to speak clearly. . . . Adults keep saying: "We owe it to the young people to give them hope." . . . I don't want you to be hopeful. I want you to panic. I want you to feel the fear I feel every day. And then I want you to . . . act as you would in a crisis. I want you to act as if our house is on fire. Because it is. (Thunberg, 2021, pp. 19, 22)

The third excerpt, "I Am Too Young to Do This," given in Stockholm, Sweden, on February 2, 2019, follows:

Some people mock me for my diagnosis. But Asperger is not a disease, it's a gift. People also say that since I have Asperger I couldn't possibly have put myself in this position. But that is exactly why I did this.

And I agree with you, I am too young to do this.

We children shouldn't have to do this. But since almost no one is doing anything, and our very future is at risk, we feel like we have to continue. . . .

I thank everyone for your kind support! It brings me hope! (Thunberg, 2021, pp. 28, 31)

The fourth and last selection excerpts a speech from the European Economic and Social Committee's Civil Society for rEUnaissance citizens' convention in Brussels, Belgium, on February 21, 2019, called "You're Acting Like Spoiled, Irresponsible Children":

We need a whole new way of thinking. The political system that you have created is all about competition. . . . We need to cooperate and work together and to share the resources of the planet in a fair way. . . . Let me remind you that our political leaders have wasted decades through denial and inaction. And since our time is running out we have decided to take action . . . to clean up your mess and we will not stop until we are done. (Thunberg, 2021, pp. 34, 38)

> **Pause and Consider:**
> What do you think of Thunberg's demands for prioritizing the health of our planet over consumerism? What do you think of her language choices, which some consider "pushy"? How do her words impact you personally?

The commentaries for *A River Ran Wild*, *Seedfolks*, and *Jane's Journey*, along with discussion on strategy pairings, are available in the reproducible "Chapter 3 Commentaries With Paired Teaching Strategies" at **go.SolutionTree.com/literacy**.

Additionally, we offer an example of the commentary we created for *Seeds of Change* (which we consider the commentary of a personal narrative), followed by some details about how we paired discussion with strategies for that book.

The picture book *Seeds of Change* by Jen Cullerton Johnson (2010) exemplifies a personal narrative of both a person and an environmental movement. One storyline centers on the leader and catalyst of the movement. The other parallel storyline focuses on the movement and the people who supported and shared the leader's vision. Both perspectives blend together to make the whole story.

Seeds of Change tells the life story of environmentalist Wangari Maathai, who was the first African woman to win a Nobel Peace Prize. She blazed a trail across Kenya, using her knowledge and compassion to promote the rights of women in her country and to help save the land by planting trees.

In many ways, Maathai's life story mirrors the Green Belt Movement, an organization she founded that involves women in Kenya traveling to towns and villages planting seeds and trees—the Green Belts. At each stepping stone in the process of developing the movement, people embraced Maathai's activism. Her vision became a mutual mission with others in the Green Belt Movement. The women dug in the dirt. They carried seeds. They planted trees. Women influenced other women to join the movement.

When Maathai (2004b) accepted the Nobel Prize, she said:

> Although this prize comes to me, it acknowledges the work of countless individuals and groups across the globe. They work quietly and often without recognition to protect the environment, promote democracy, defend human rights and ensure equality between women and men. By so doing, they plant seeds of peace.

The Green Belt Movement's message to young girls and women was simple: Work together and results will come. We can take that message one step further and interpret it as evidence that when we work together, our results have a domino effect, inviting others to participate with us.

How can you evaluate Wangari Maathai's life and the lives of those within the Green Belt Movement? Does she represent a universal truth that touches all our lives? If so, what is that truth? What can you and your students learn from how she worked with other women around troubling issues, like deforestation and poverty?

In the professional development sessions, we discussed the preceding questions at the end of the commentary for *Seeds of Change*. The teachers talked about how women who lived in extreme poverty and hardship caused by deforestation were able to get out of poverty *and* address deforestation in Kenya by collaborating with one another and with Wangari Maathai. Next, we move to how the teachers paired *Seeds of Change* with teaching strategies.

Already familiar with the three cycles of comprehension from earlier sessions, the teachers used the cycles as they planned how they would work with their students on *Seeds of Change*. During simple comprehension, the teachers aimed to create with students a shared understanding of what took place in the story and in the lives of Maathai and the people who shared her vision. To do this, the teachers used the Free Response strategy as they read the book aloud with their students. This strategy gave students time to write comments about the story, plot, or characters, which revealed their perceptions of the story. There are no wrong answers in Free Response as long as the responses relate to the text in some way. In preparing for this strategy, the teachers read the book to themselves and decided on four or five places to stop; when the teachers read the story aloud, the students wrote their comments at each stopping place and then shared them with the class.

As students moved from simple comprehension to criteria comprehension, they made strides in understanding and application. The teachers moved their students into criteria thinking by having them make personal connections to the book. With *Seeds of Change*, they used think-pair-share (Lyman, 1981). Such a strategy is useful for encouraging even the shyest student to become involved.

- **Think:** Start with a question or prompt that gets students thinking about the story, and provide a short amount of time for students to reflect on the question or prompt.
- **Pair:** Have students pair up and share their responses. The goal is for the pairs to compare their information and come up with the most complete response to the question or prompt.
- **Share:** Ask each student pair to share their response with the class.

Teachers asked why students' connections were pertinent, and students explained during their think-pair-share responses as part of their criteria comprehension thinking. For example, after reading about the protagonist Wangari Maathai, one student said his connection was that he saw a bulldozer take down a grove of trees for a condominium development in his neighborhood. The student elaborated on how this connected to Maathai's life by saying in both situations, trees were taken down.

As you move through step 4 when developing your own thematic unit, you might again use the Green Literacy Thematic Unit Planning Template as you pair teaching strategies with each of the books and media use in your teaching unit. As before, you can consider the strategies the professional development teachers used and teaching strategies you and your students often employ together.

Next, we offer an example to illustrate how Katie, a K–2 teacher in our professional development sessions, works with her second graders with the thematic unit question "How do you become an environmental leader?" The following vignette shows how she engages second graders in coming up with wonderings, questions, and thoughts during a read-aloud of *The Mangrove Tree: Planting Trees to Feed Families* by Susan L. Roth and Cindy Trumbore (2011).

After Katie reads the book's title, she shows her students the cover. "What observations can you make about the cover?"

Jasmine says, "Maybe they have seeds to plant."

Katie says, "Yes, maybe so," and then poses, "What about their clothes?"

"Most of them are dressed like the people in the rainforest," says Terrell.

"The man in the blue suit looks like our clothes," Victor says, and makes a connection between the man's clothes and where his father works.

As Katie begins reading the book, she wonders aloud, "How could a tree make families not hungry anymore?"

Students respond with different ideas, including "growing food" and "animals living in the trees." To these and other answers, Katie says, "Great ideas."

In a similar fashion, Katie guides her students with questions about the text as she reads. Periodically, students make observations about the collages in the book. Other students offer wonderings such as, "What do they use the tree trunk for?" Another student concludes, "Houses and boats." Students build a connection with another book about the rainforest in which animals make their homes in trees as they do in the mangrove trees.

Supportive of all observations, Katie encourages connections and wonderings her students make. On two occasions, she asks, "What is your evidence? Why do you think so?"

After the discussion, students take out their wonder journals to write any questions that went through their minds as they listened to the story. Katie says, "Also, write about changes that happened in the village of Hargigo because of the planting of the mangrove trees. Tomorrow, we will get out our tablets and see if we find answers to some of our wonderings. Plus, we will share changes that occurred to Hargigo because of the mangrove trees."

One student says, "I don't have any wonderings."

Katie says, "No wonderings? Here, look at the book to help you." The student gets her journal, looks at the book, and begins writing.

This example illustrates how primary teachers can engage in Green Literacy teaching. Next, we describe how teachers worked with students in creating their Green Literacy ideals.

Step 5: Teachers Lead Students to Reflect on Learning by Creating Green Literacy Ideals

As you may recall, Green Literacy ideals are a set of agreed-on, shared values about the environment and our interactions with it that a class creates after much dialogue and reflection together throughout the Green Literacy thematic unit. These shared values are developed through collaboration and consensus at the unit's end. The values emerge when students engage in meaningful dialogue, reflect on experiences, and consider how to work together to address environmental issues. Further, creating Green Literacy ideals encourages young people to investigate and balance multiple perspectives. We saw during the professional development that this nuanced process of creation discouraged easy, oversimplified answers to complex issues for both teachers and students. It led to the creation of substantive, thoughtful ideals that considered multiple points of view.

Here are some Green Literacy ideals that the professional development pairs developed with their classes and shared and that the classes agreed to display in their rooms.

- Environmental leaders are committed to their project and the community; the leaders work hard and inspire others to help.

- Environmental leaders need to take time and have patience because environmental issues are complex and need to be looked at through multiple perspectives.

These ideals make clear that the teachers led their students to come to some generalizations about people who become environmental leaders; all classmates agreed these ideals were important. In the professional development sessions, we, and the teachers, expressed hope that this developing understanding would initiate some small or large actions on the part of the students that would lead to a more sustainable Earth.

As we wrapped up our professional development experience, having explored the personal narratives of environmental leaders like Jane Goodall, Wangari Maathai, and Greta Thunberg, many powerful truths emerged. One in particular was these leaders' journeys began with understanding themselves. Whether they were quiet observers, bold activists, or patient nurturers of ideas, they honored their unique strengths and found ways to make an impact that resonated with who they were. Moreover, these leaders all demonstrated the ability to hold two seemingly opposing ideas or modes at the same time—hope and urgency, an objective perspective and an emotional one, and action and patience. Wangari Maathai knew that planting a single tree could spark global change and that empowering women and communities required relentless advocacy. Jane Goodall has combined groundbreaking research with an unshakable optimism about humanity's ability to protect wildlife. Greta Thunberg wields the hard facts of climate science with a fearless, emotional call to leaders to act now. Rachel Carson united meticulous scientific inquiry with poetic storytelling that awakened the world to environmental harm. Their ability to balance these dualities allowed them to inspire action while staying grounded in the realities of the challenges they faced.

Maribel and Sarah's Reflection on the Green Literacy Ideals and Professional Development Experience

Maribel: *Whew. That was a process! Helping our students write their class Green Literacy ideals was rewarding, but I wasn't expecting them to get stuck.*

Sarah: *Right? I thought they'd jump right in, but some really struggled. When we asked them to define what mattered most to them, a few got overwhelmed and didn't know where to start.*

Maribel: *I'm so glad we suggested going back to the authors' messages in the books we read. When students saw how different writers approached environmental activism—from Wangari Maathai planting trees to Lynne Cherry writing about the life of a river—they realized there's more than one way to make an impact.*

Sarah: *Yes! And when we gave them space to reflect, they really surprised me. One group came up with "We listen to the Earth, and we listen to each other," and another student suggested, "Caring for nature means caring for our community."*

Maribel: *I loved that. If we had given them a list of Green Literacy ideals to choose from, I don't think the process would have been as meaningful. The empty space on the page really mattered—it let them create, not just copy what we think they should believe.*

Sarah: *Exactly! And when they started seeing multiple perspectives—like how some environmental leaders focus on restoration while others work on policy such as cleaning up a river, or speaking up to powerful leaders who could change policy—they realized environmental leadership isn't one-size-fits-all. That made it easier for them to define their own approach.*

Maribel: *Now that they have their class Green Literacy ideals, I feel like they have a real foundation for moving forward. I can already see them applying these Green Literacy ideals to future projects.*

Sarah: *Same. And honestly? This experience made me feel more confident too. I used to hesitate about guiding students in environmental leadership, but now I see that giving them a framework like Green Literacy—along with room to explore—is key.*

Like Maribel and Sarah, as you plan to lead a discussion on creating Green Literacy ideals, you may start by refreshing your thinking about how to lead a Green Literacy ideal creation discussion. You may go to chapter 1's Tips for Teachers to Create Green Literacy Ideals (page 16) for this refresher. You may also begin by reflecting on your own strengths, values, and unique perspective to model self-awareness and curiosity that inspire your students. Your willingness to explore the question of your thematic unit becomes a guide for your students, encouraging them to do the same. Through your example, they learn to hold multiple perspectives at once as the teachers who considered Amy Krouse Rosenthal's (2009) picture book *Duck! Rabbit!* did (see the preface, page xv), and as the environmental leaders we mentioned earlier also did. While the Green Literacy Thematic Unit Planning Template serves as a planning tool, it can also be used for reflection. We intentionally left the ideals section of the template open because Green Literacy ideals emerge from your class discussions and engagement with Green Reads. Comparing and contrasting different authors' messages helps students explore multiple perspectives on environmental issues. As you approach the end of your unit, we encourage you to guide students in synthesizing these messages to develop their own Green Literacy ideals.

When you, as the teacher, embrace duality—hope and urgency, respect for objective facts and storytelling driven by emotional significance, action and patience—you help your students develop the critical thinking and empathy needed to engage with complex environmental issues. When you shift your own perspective, you teach your students to see a future as they might imagine it to be—inclusive, vibrant, and sustainable. In doing so, you empower them to take their own steps inward and outward, becoming environmental leaders in their own right.

CONCLUSION

After exploring how a group of teachers led by us engaged their students in the thematic question, "How do you become an environmental leader?" we encourage you to reflect on what you've learned from reading and hopefully engaging your students in all or some of the books and media shared in this chapter. You can think of this chapter as your compass, guiding you through teaching Green Literacy thematic units. It can help you understand what Green Literacy looks like in action and may serve as your starting point. You can refer back to this chapter whenever you need clarity or support as you determine your thematic units, either those we support you in teaching in chapters 5–7 or those you develop around your own thematic questions using the Green Literacy model. You may want to use other profiles of environmental leaders and negative environmental impacts you are aware of, such as loss of habitat for forest creatures because of widespread human developments. Since environmental issues are complex and multilayered, multiple perspectives are needed to attain possible solutions.

Now, consider how this chapter has impacted your learning as a teacher. We offer a dedicated space for you to do so in the following "Teacher's Corner" reproducible tool (also available at **go.SolutionTree.com/literacy**). Whether you're working on your own, with a teaching partner, or within a schoolwide learning network, after exploring chapter 3, we encourage you to reflect on what you've learned.

Teacher's Corner

Here are some questions to support your reflection.

- Reflect on how your understanding of environmental issues has deepened through this thematic unit. How do you see yourself contributing to positive environmental change in your community?

- Think about the environmental leaders you've learned about during this unit. What qualities or actions do you admire them for, and how might you develop those same qualities in your own life?

Here are prompts for journaling.

- In what ways do you think young people can make a real impact on environmental issues? What steps can you take right now to start becoming an environmental teacher leader?

- How can you use technology and social media to inspire others and advocate for environmental change? What strategies might you use to ensure your efforts are both impactful and sustainable?

Here are discussion guidelines.

- Who is a teacher in your school who exhibits a deep connection to the environment within their classroom, and how do they promote environmental awareness?

- What events or schoolwide assemblies or celebrations does your school use to promote environmental awareness in your unique school context?

CHAPTER 4

Thematic Unit Design and Customization With Twelve Insights Into Green Literacy Teaching

Instead of worrying about what you cannot control, shift your energy to what you can create.

—ROY T. BENNETT

In this chapter, we offer guidance for using and customizing the ready-made Green Literacy units found in part 3 of this handbook. We share with you our reflections on how Green Literacy teaching is inherently collaborative and continually transformative. We also share twelve insights into Green Literacy teaching. We've seen these insights help students and their teachers succeed. We know these tips are not stagnant, nor is your progress. They'll grow and shift as you adapt them to fit your unique classroom. We encourage you to experiment, explore, and make these insights your own, trusting that each step will lead to deeper trust, curiosity, and understanding for you and your students. Think of this chapter as a bridge to creating and teaching your own units and as a collection of tools and inspiration to reinforce your journey.

DESIGN, CUSTOMIZE, OR USE GREEN LITERACY THEMATIC UNITS

Through the yearlong Green Literacy professional development experience and collaboration, we discovered that we, too, were transforming alongside the

Chapter Snapshot—What You'll Explore

In this chapter, we share with you how to:

- Design, customize, or use ready-made Green Literacy units

- Be empowered through autonomous implementation

- Foster thinking through commentary

- Discuss and guide students to Green Literacy ideals

- Include immersive strategies

- Consider the twelve insights into Green Literacy teaching

teachers and students engaging with Green Literacy. Each session became an opportunity to reflect on the material we shared and the dynamic ways teachers adapted it for their classrooms. We listened to teachers' stories, observed their challenges, celebrated their successes, and realized that these experiences were reshaping how we thought about Green Literacy.

The insights we gathered became invaluable; they shaped the ideas and strategies we present later in this book and sparked new directions for future projects and resources. It became clear that Green Literacy is a living, breathing way of teaching that evolves through the collective wisdom of those who engage with it. Our reflections reinforced that transformation happens when a community of learners and educators discover shared values together.

The importance of appreciating Green Literacy teaching as inherently collaborative and continually transformative is why we shared experiences of developing the model in chapter 3, and it will guide you going forward into part 3, "Support to Design Your Own Green Literacy Thematic Units." By understanding our thinking and the challenges and decisions that shaped this model, you can better adapt it to your own teaching context. As Margaret J. Wheatley (2002) reminds us, "There is no power [for change] greater than a community discovering what it cares about" (p. 145). This collective journey of reflection and feedback continues to inspire us, reminding us that the strength of Green Literacy— and ourselves—lies in its ability to grow through the shared passion and commitment of those who bring it to life.

Next, you will explore how four connected focus areas will support your planning of Green Literacy thematic units in part 3. Each focus area—teacher autonomy, commentary, student discussion, and immersive strategies—helps make Green Literacy a collaborative, transformative, and evolving process.

Empower Teachers Through Autonomy in Implementation

A key decision we made during both yearlong and shorter professional development was to allow teachers the autonomy to implement Green Literacy units in their classrooms without direct interference or prescriptive guidance. After teachers selected their Green Reads and strategies, which we may have suggested, they designed and executed their lessons independently. Our approach was intentional—we stepped back to create space for teachers to observe, reflect, and adapt based on their students' responses and their own insights. We chose not to burden teachers with additional paperwork or standardized worksheets. Instead, we encouraged them to use their own systems of note taking and reflection, trusting in their professional expertise and familiarity with their classrooms. This flexibility meant teachers documented their experiences in ways that felt natural and meaningful to them, whether through journals, digital notes, or even informal observations.

By embracing this loose, open-ended style, we aim to foster a sense of ownership and creativity in how teachers integrate Green Literacy into their teaching. As you explore the chapters in part 3, you'll find opportunities to make their ready-made units your own— adapting lessons to fit your teaching style, adjusting activities to support your students, and incorporating resources that reflect your school community. Your experience, school setting, and available support will shape how you bring these units to life. Part 3 offers flexibility, letting you implement Green Literacy in a way that feels both structured and adaptable to your unique classroom.

Foster Thinking Through Commentary

From the beginning, we always provided teachers with foundational information and seeded ideas related to the big-picture concepts behind thematic unit questions. These starting points sparked initial engagement and ensured teachers had a strong foundation for deeper exploration.

What we learned from our professional development sessions was how powerful the discussions and feedback among teachers were during the process of designing their Green Literacy thematic questions. These dialogues not only clarified the thematic questions themselves but also served as a natural springboard for developing rich and reflective commentary. Teachers found that engaging in our commentary—analyzing existing ideas or, if they chose, generating their own from ours—deepened their thinking and connected their thematic questions to meaningful classroom discussions.

To build on this insight, we incorporated opportunities for teachers to foster their thinking through commentary into the Green Literacy resources. The questions within the commentaries are meant to spark active engagement. In chapters 5–7, although the units have suggestions and choices for you, the Green Literacy Thematic Unit Planning Template includes a dedicated section for teachers to design their own commentary, if they are interested in doing so.

Support Teachers With Discussions and Guide Students to Green Literacy Ideals

Through our professional development sessions, we discovered that teachers needed additional support in facilitating meaningful discussions with their students. Many teachers shared that navigating student dialogue on complex environmental themes required more guidance and tools. In response, we developed resources to enhance these discussions, such as the Turn-and-Talk Conversation Cards, which provide prompts and strategies to generate engaging, student-centered conversations. You can integrate this strategy—and others from the handbook—into the ready-made units, adapt them to fit your own units, or use them as a foundation for designing new Green Literacy units. Whether you're leading peer-to-peer discussions, small-group conversations, or whole-class reflections, these tools will help you foster meaningful dialogue that deepens student engagement and critical thinking.

One of the most significant insights from our professional development sessions was that teachers face a challenge with the final step of the Green Literacy process: creating Green Literacy ideals. This step requires students to reach a consensus on shared values, which can be a complex process. To support teachers in guiding students through this transformative phase, we incorporated reflection questions into the Green Literacy Thematic Unit Planning Template. The questions help teachers ponder their teaching practices and their students' responses throughout the unit, enabling them to plan more effectively for this critical step. This added layer of support ensures that the process of creating Green Literacy ideals is achievable and enriching and that it empowers both teachers and students to collaborate meaningfully. In part 3, you'll find ways to inspire meaningful student dialogue, encourage collaborative thinking, and connect learning to real-world environmental challenges. These interactions help students express diverse perspectives and work toward shared and agreed-on values.

Each chapter in part 3 provides opportunities to deepen these conversations. In chapter 5, students can explore how their environment influences identity, culture, and community. In chapter 6, they can reflect on the impacts of climate events and consider collective action. In chapter 7, they can examine interconnected systems and how small changes lead to broader transformation.

Include Immersive Strategies

An *immersive strategy* is a deeply engaging and interactive activity that allows students to fully connect with a subject or environment through multiple senses, emotions, and perspectives. In the context of Green Literacy, immersive experiences are designed to foster a tangible and meaningful connection to environmental concepts, whether through hands-on activities, sensory exploration, or collaborative projects. These experiences give students opportunities to actively engage with their surroundings, reflect on their relationships with the natural world, and internalize the lessons in a way that feels personal and impactful. Immersive experiences can take place outdoors in nature, within the classroom through simulations or sensory activities, or even virtually, so all students can participate regardless of their access to natural spaces. These strategies were designed to meet students where they are, whether they have direct access to nature or they are learning in urban or classroom environments.

Based on teacher input from our professional development sessions, we recognized the transformative power of shared immersive experiences within Green Literacy teaching. Teachers emphasized the need for activities that engage all students to foster a collective understanding of and emotional connection to environmental topics. Their feedback highlighted how such experiences build community among students and deepen their ability to engage critically and empathetically with the material.

In response, we integrated immersive strategies into chapters 5–7. In chapter 5, we include Wonder Walk and Imagination Station. These strategies encourage students to use their senses, observe their surroundings, and use creativity to deepen their connection to the environment. In chapter 6, we introduce Human Knot and Web of Life, strategies that emphasize interconnectedness and collaboration, mirroring ecological systems. Finally, in chapter 7, we incorporate the Thumb-Wrestling Game, a playful yet insightful activity designed to illustrate concepts like competition, cooperation, and problem solving. You can employ these strategies as they are, adapt them to fit your classroom needs, or use them as inspiration to create your own content in part 3. Each chapter provides flexible guidance, so you can customize Green Reads and Views and strategies to best support your students and teaching goals.

Weaving immersive experiences throughout the teaching ensures that every student, regardless of their background, can connect with Green Literacy. These activities engage students, spark curiosity, and inspire collective action, laying the groundwork for lifelong environmental stewardship.

CONSIDER THE TWELVE INSIGHTS INTO GREEN LITERACY TEACHING

As you transition from the concepts explored in the previous sections to the insights ahead, consider how these ideas will guide your approach to the unit chapters in part 3. The themes of collaboration, adaptability, and student engagement shape meaningful Green Literacy experiences.

The following twelve insights provide practical guidance on how to apply Green Literacy in your teaching. They will help you reflect on your role as an educator, support student inquiry, and create dynamic, student-centered learning experiences. As you engage with chapters 5–7, you can implement these insights as they are, customize them to fit your students' needs, or design your own Green Literacy units with confidence and creativity.

Insight 1: Make Trust the Foundation of Learning

In your Green Literacy thematic units, trust can serve as the cornerstone of a thriving learning community. By creating a supportive and inclusive environment, you might encourage your students to feel safe expressing their ideas and exploring new sustainability concepts without fear of judgment. Actively building this trust can empower your students to take risks, engage with the subject matter, and embark on a meaningful learning journey.

To establish trust, you could start by actively listening to your students and valuing their diverse perspectives on environmental issues. For instance, when a student shares an idea, you might respond with something like, "That's an interesting thought. Can you tell me more about how you see this working?" Starting units with listening circles might help create a safe space for sharing. In our experience, these circles work well to foster respect and curiosity, as each student has an opportunity to share their thoughts while peers ask questions or offer encouragement. That said, it might help to set clear ground rules for listening and respect, as we've noticed that without this structure, some students hesitate to share.

You might consider integrating immersive or team-building exercises into your units. Activities like Web of Life (page 148), where students connect parts of an ecosystem with string, could illustrate interdependence and prompt thoughtful discussions. We found that adding a reflection session after this activity works well, allowing students to share insights such as, "I didn't realize how much pollinators like bees and butterflies affect our food system." Similarly, paired discussions could help students feel connected to each other. For example, when one student shares how their family grows vegetables at home, another might ask for tips on starting their own garden, sparking a deeper dialogue.

Encouraging students to reflect on their learning might enhance participation. Strategies like think-pair-share (page 72), in which students consider a question individually, consider it with a partner, and then share thoughts with the whole class, could keep students engaged, especially when used in conjunction with tools like project journals. In one instance, a student used their journal to sketch a recycling system for the cafeteria, which inspired their classmates to expand on the idea. Offering sentence stems such as, "One thing I noticed was _____" or "I wonder if we could _____," might give quiet students the confidence to share their thoughts.

Finally, modeling vulnerability could help build trust over time. You might share moments when you learned from a mistake or had to adjust a plan. For example, during a pollinator garden project, we underestimated how much time students needed to research local plants. Admitting this and brainstorming a revised timeline together solved the issue, as well as demonstrated that learning is an ongoing process for everyone. Through weaving these trust-building practices into your Green Literacy thematic units, you might create a nurturing space where students feel confident to grow their knowledge, experiment with ideas, and contribute to a sustainable future.

Insight 2: Consider School Context and Thematic Questions

In the thematic unit planning template, in the Develop Your Thematic Question section, we suggest you gauge your willingness and your administration's openness to engage with the environmental issues for which you may develop thematic questions. As you work through *The Green Literacy Handbook* and the template, you may identify ideas you're excited to try or consider some of the suggestions we've offered. After reflecting on your school's context and your administration's willingness to engage with environmental issues, you may realize that challenges lie ahead. If you find that your administration is hesitant or not fully supportive, don't be discouraged. Rather than feeling disheartened, we've found that approaching the situation with professionalism, collaboration, and respect for their priorities makes a significant difference.

In particular, we've noticed that if we modify a thematic question to inspire creativity while respecting different perspectives, it creates more opportunities for collaboration and support. By framing the question in a way that invites curiosity and constructive dialogue, we can engage others without alienating them. This approach allows us to advocate for environmental awareness in a way that aligns with our school's values and priorities, fostering a positive environment for change. For instance, consider the thematic question, "How are long-term fossil-fuel consequences of climate change impacting our way of life and the planet?" In places that have implemented policies that limit or influence how the topic is addressed in classrooms, educators may be discouraged from using terms like *climate change*, so this question might conflict with administrative guidelines. An alternative question might be, "How do human choices impact our local environment and resources?" This version still encourages students to think critically about environmental issues while working within administrative policies.

To cultivate environmental awareness in schools, you and other teachers should explore the policies and guidelines in your area, as well as understand the priorities of your administration and community. We encourage you to see this as a journey rather than a quick fix. Respect the constraints your administration may face, and approach change with professionalism and patience. When you focus on incremental progress, you're laying a strong foundation for fostering environmental awareness, which can grow and flourish *over time*.

Insight 3: Differentiate Instruction

We have two related insights connected to differentiating instruction: (1) the *Matthew effect*, the issue of varied reading ability in a classroom, and (2) ways to support K–2 learners with differentiated instruction as they begin their journey of critical agency.

The Matthew Effect and Strategies to Counteract It

We realize that every classroom features young people whose readability levels vary widely and that the gaps widen as students move to higher grade levels. Some educators call this the *Matthew effect*—that is, students who avidly read often outdistance those who do not develop a reading habit in their daily lives. Thus, the phenomenon is one in which "the rich get richer, and the poor get poorer" in terms of reading ability and academic success (Pfost, Hattie, Dörfler, & Artelt, 2014; Stanovich, 1986). Green Literacy teachers need to consider this in planning and conducting instruction.

Children who start reading early and become successful readers continue improving and enjoying reading, allowing them to benefit from a positive feedback loop where their skills are consistently reinforced and expanded. Conversely, children who struggle with reading early tend to read less, thereby missing chances to improve their reading skills and acquire new knowledge. This cycle results in a growing disparity between proficient and struggling readers, emphasizing the importance of early and effective reading interventions.

We have emphasized that Green Literacy teaching engages teachers and their students in the ideas in the text, which leads to critical thinking. However, some students, especially those who struggle with decoding, may find it hard to access the ideas in written form. To support these students, teachers can use auditory strategies, like reading aloud, having students read in pairs, or using audio versions of texts. Listening allows students to fully engage with the content and participate meaningfully in discussions if reading on their own is challenging.

Visual resources, such as Green Views—short videos, infographics, and photographs— offer another powerful way to make environmental concepts accessible. For example, while reading aloud a book like *Hurricane* by David Wiesner (2008) or *Flood* by Alvaro F. Villa (2013), you could enhance the story with a short video showing how extreme weather forms and impacts communities. Similarly, a book like *The Water Princess* by Susan Verde (2016) can spark discussions about how water systems connect people, nature, and communities. Adding an infographic about the global water cycle can further help students see these connections in action.

When paired with engaging Green Reads, these visual and auditory strategies ensure that all students, regardless of reading ability, can grasp and explore the interconnected systems behind environmental challenges like extreme weather, pollution, or deforestation. This inclusive approach empowers every student to fully participate in the journey of Green Literacy.

Following are additional specific strategies to counteract the Matthew effect.

- **Differentiated instruction:** Tailor teaching methods and materials to accommodate students' diverse learning needs and abilities, providing additional support to those who require it (Dosch & Zidon, 2014; Tomlinson, 2001).

- **Personalized learning:** Offer individualized learning paths that consider each student's strengths, interests, and areas for growth and allow all students to progress at their own pace (Tomlinson, 2017).

- **Collaborative learning:** Encourage peer-to-peer collaboration and cooperative learning activities where students can support and learn from one another, fostering a sense of community and shared success (Tullis & Goldstone, 2020).

- **Culturally responsive teaching:** Acknowledge students' diverse backgrounds, cultures, and experiences and integrate them into the curriculum to create a more inclusive and engaging learning environment for all (Shareefa, Moosa, Zin, Abdullah, & Jawawi, 2019).

- **Scaffolded support:** Provide gradual and structured support for complex tasks, breaking down learning objectives into manageable steps to help all students achieve success (Pozas & Schneider, 2019).

- **Feedback and reflection:** Offer constructive feedback and opportunities for students to reflect on their learning progress; encourage them to set goals and take ownership of their academic journey (Tomlinson, 2015).

With these strategies, you can create an inclusive classroom where all your students can thrive. By tailoring your instruction, fostering collaboration, and providing scaffolded support, you'll ensure every student feels supported and engaged.

Support for Grades K–2 and 3–5 Learners With Differentiated Instruction

In the primary grades, particularly kindergarten through second grade, educators in the Green Literacy program adapt their instructional strategies to align with the developmental stages of young learners. For K–2 students, the focus is on making environmental concepts tangible, relatable, and connected to their everyday experiences. Activities like storytelling, hands-on projects, and visual aids simplify complex ideas and help young learners build intuitive relationships with the environment (Tomlinson, 2001). For instance, reading a picture book like *Over and Under the Pond* by Kate Messner (2017) or *The Curious Garden* by Peter Brown (2009) can spark discussions about habitats, ecosystems, and the importance of caring for the environment. A hands-on activity like creating a class mural of a local ecosystem or planting a small garden can reinforce these ideas in a creative, collaborative way.

These foundational experiences foster curiosity, empathy, and environmentally responsible behavior that can grow as students progress to higher grades (Dosch & Zidon, 2014).

The foundational experiences so important for K–2 students lay the groundwork for the deeper, more abstract thinking students encounter in grades 3–5. In a K–2 classroom, students might role-play sunny- versus rainy-day activities or explore "what happens next" scenarios through storytelling. As these students move into grades 3–5, those activities evolve into more structured explorations of cause-and-effect relationships and systems thinking (Pozas & Schneider, 2019). For example, a K–2 student who has acted out the effects of weather might later, in third grade, use a weather wheel to analyze how seasonal changes impact plants, animals, and people. By fourth grade, they might build on that knowledge by discussing how climate change disrupts those patterns and what actions can mitigate those effects (Tullis & Goldstone, 2020).

Similarly, simple observation activities in K–2 lead to more structured data analysis in grades 3–5. A K–2 class might explore their schoolyard to look for signs of plants and animals, drawing or journaling their observations. This observational habit forms the foundation for a third-grade project where students map the biodiversity of their schoolyard and discuss the roles that different organisms play in the ecosystem. By fifth grade, the students may use this knowledge to create a systems diagram, connecting how human actions like planting a pollinator garden can positively impact the environment (Tomlinson, 2017).

Using differentiated strategies such as storytelling, sensory engagement, and visual learning in K–2 creates a pathway for students to build skills progressively. These methods help students develop empathy and curiosity early on, which seamlessly transition into critical thinking and problem solving as they mature. By connecting environmental themes to their daily lives and gradually introducing complexity, you'll empower your students to explore, question, and act for a more sustainable future, no matter their age or developmental stage. Following are some tried-and-true strategies for starting dialogues with K–2 students with questions geared toward Green Literacy.

- **Emotion check-ins:** Ask students how different weather conditions or places in nature make them feel—for example, "How does it feel when you play outside on a sunny day versus a rainy day?"

- **Story starters:** After reading a story that includes elements of nature, ask questions like, "What do you think would happen if the forest in our story lost all its trees?"

- **Themed show-and-tell:** For a theme like "My Favorite Animal," students can talk about an animal they love and discuss simple things people can do to protect that animal's habitat.

- **Role-playing scenarios:** Set up scenarios in which the participants have to make decisions that impact the environment, like choosing to walk or drive, and discuss the outcomes.

- **Question cubes:** Include questions such as, "What can we do to keep our air and water clean?" or "Why is recycling important?"

- **Interactive journals:** Encourage students to draw or write about an experience in nature, such as a visit to a park, and discuss what they observed during the experience, such as litter or wildlife.

- **Classroom meetings:** Bring in a "mystery object" related to nature, such as a pine cone or a shell, and let students ask questions or share what they know about it.

- **Puppet dialogues:** Use puppets to act out stories about environmental issues, such as water conservation. One puppet might teach the other how to save water at home.

Differentiating instruction makes Green Literacy accessible for all learners; it helps K–2 students build foundational knowledge through storytelling, hands-on activities, and visual aids. These strategies prepare them for more complex thinking in grades 3–5 while fostering curiosity, empathy, and a lifelong connection to environmental stewardship.

Insight 4: Consult Subject-Matter Experts as You Explore Commentary

In chapters 2 and 3 (pages 31 and 57), we offered ways to create commentary through tried-and-true methods of gathering information, such as researching databases, using Google, consulting books and videos, and more. Now, we return to this topic and encourage you to consider seeking out professional subject-matter experts.

We recommend this approach because connecting with subject-matter experts from Wangari Maathai's Green Belt Movement and Jane Goodall's Roots & Shoots program in Tanzania enhanced our understanding of their impactful work. These interactions deepened our appreciation for the nuances of their movements. You can achieve similar results by building relationships with experts in thematic environmental topics.

Here are a couple of ways you might find subject-matter experts.

- **Locally:**

  - Consider reaching out to nearby universities or colleges to connect with professors, researchers, or students who specialize in environmental studies.

  - Explore partnerships with local environmental organizations or nonprofits. They often host workshops and community events, which offer opportunities to meet potential speakers or collaborators.

  - Look within your community for environmental activists, park rangers, or leaders of conservation projects who might bring valuable insights to your classroom.

- **Globally:**

  - Try using online platforms like LinkedIn to find professionals in specific environmental fields, and don't hesitate to send these professionals a polite message outlining your goals.

- Attend webinars or virtual conferences on environmental topics to network with global experts who are passionate about sharing their knowledge.
- Reach out to international organizations like UNESCO, Greenpeace, or the World Wildlife Fund. Many of these organizations have educational outreach programs and can connect you with experienced representatives.

Engaging with experts helps you broaden your understanding of complex environmental issues, uncover fresh perspectives, and develop a richer context for the topics you teach. We believe that bringing in subject-matter experts, whether local or global, can inspire your students and add authenticity to their learning.

Insight 5: Encourage Student Participation in Environmental Discussions

Many teachers find it challenging to start and maintain good discussions among their students, especially when the topics touch on urgent environmental issues. Engaging students in meaningful classroom dialogue often requires more than presenting a topic of interest; it involves creating a space where students feel comfortable sharing their perspectives and genuinely listening to one another.

In chapters 5–7, we explore Turn-and-Talk Conversation Cards, which can initiate meaningful discussions about big-picture ideas connected to the thematic question. We suggest using tried-and-true strategies like think-pair-share to ease students into discussions. This way, students can first gather their thoughts individually before sharing with a partner and eventually contributing to a group discussion. For instance, after reading *The Lorax* by Dr. Seuss, you could ask students to think about the question, "What message do you think the Lorax was trying to share with the Once-ler?" Giving students time to reflect individually and with a peer can help quiet students feel confident enough to share their thoughts with the larger group.

Another strategy that can work particularly well is scaffolding discussions with sentence starters or guiding questions. Providing tools like, "I think this because _____" or "One thing I learned from this story is _____," helps ensure that all students have a way to participate if they're less familiar with the topic. This scaffolding creates a foundation of confidence and inclusivity so students can connect the lessons from books to real-world environmental issues.

In our experience, a combination of structure, encouragement, and flexibility makes the biggest difference in fostering meaningful classroom discussions. For example, during a discussion inspired by *The Great Kapok Tree* (Cherry, 1990), we noticed that students struggled to respond when we asked a broad question like, "What do you think about deforestation?" However, when we broke the topic into smaller, specific questions like, "How do the animals in the story feel about the tree being cut down?" and "What would you say to the man with the ax if you were one of the animals?," the conversation became much more focused and productive.

What didn't work as well were unstructured discussions where students were left to navigate complex themes on their own. For instance, when we asked students to "talk about the environment," the conversation became scattered, and many students didn't participate. Students are much more engaged and thoughtful in their responses if a discussion is tied to a specific moment in a story or a character's actions.

Five Adaptable, Simple Prompts to Use for Meaningful Student Discussions About Environmental Issues

1. Have you ever wondered how our actions can help or hurt the Earth?

2. Let's think about what happens when we do or don't take care of our planet.

3. What are some things we can do to protect nature and all its creatures, including humans?

4. Imagine what the world would look like if everyone did their part to keep it clean.

5. How do you think the Earth, animals, plants, or other people feel when we pollute the air and water?

Be sure to recognize and celebrate what your students bring to the table—this helps build trust and creates a real sense of community in your class. It's about inspiring them, giving them the chance to think, and encouraging them to learn from each other rather than talking to them.

As teachers, we've all encountered moments when students hesitate to participate in discussions, particularly when the topics are complex or tied to urgent environmental issues. Following are some observed barriers and suggestions based on what we've noticed when implementing Green Literacy. You may have noticed similar patterns in other ways while working with your own students. By recognizing these barriers and using strategies that connect classroom conversations to larger environmental challenges, you can create a space where students feel empowered to contribute their perspectives and engage meaningfully. The following ideas (using, in this case, water conservation as an example topic) are meant to prompt reflection and adaptation, so feel free to modify them to fit your students' unique needs and your teaching style.

- **Fear of being judged:** Students may worry about how their peers or the teacher will perceive their contributions. For instance, a student might hesitate to share their ideas about protecting water resources, fearing they'll be judged as idealistic or uninformed.

    - *What you can try*—Start with anonymous idea-gathering activities to create a safe space. For example, ask students to write their thoughts on sticky notes or use a digital platform like Padlet to answer a question such as, "What are some ways people can protect rivers and lakes?" Use their responses as a starting point for class discussion, ensuring no one feels singled out. This approach encourages students to focus on the environmental issue rather than worry about judgment.

- **Lack of confidence:** Some students may have ideas about water conservation or pollution but feel unsure about articulating them, especially when discussing complex topics like clean water access or wastewater treatment.

  - *What you can try*—Provide scaffolded sentence starters to help students organize their thoughts. For example, prompts like, "One way we could help keep our water clean is _____" or "I wonder how we can make sure everyone has access to safe water by _____," give students a clear structure for participation. By connecting these prompts to real-world water challenges, students can contribute with confidence, knowing their ideas are relevant.

- **Shyness or introversion:** Naturally reserved students may find it intimidating to participate in discussions about big environmental topics like water rights or pollution, preferring to observe rather than contribute.

  - *What you can try*—Small-group or partner activities, like think-pair-share, can ease these students into participation. For example, after reading *We Are Water Protectors* (Lindstrom, 2020), you might ask students to reflect individually on the question, "Why do you think protecting water is so important to the people in the story?" Then, have them discuss their answers with a partner before sharing with the larger group. This gradual process helps shy students feel more comfortable sharing their thoughts about significant environmental issues.

- **Language barriers:** English learners or students with limited vocabulary may struggle to express themselves effectively, especially when discussing terms like *conservation*, *pollution*, or *sustainability*.

  - *What you can try*—Introduce visual aids and preteach key vocabulary to make discussions more accessible. For example, display images of polluted rivers, clean water systems, or community efforts to protect water resources. Pair these visuals with words like *watershed*, *contamination*, and *restoration*. Also, pairing these students with supportive peers during discussions can help them feel more confident contributing to conversations about protecting these vital resources.

- **Fear of making mistakes:** Students might avoid participating in discussions about water policy or pollution prevention if they're unsure about their facts or worried about making errors in front of others.

  - *What you can try*—Create a classroom culture where mistakes are celebrated as part of the learning process. Reinforce this by saying things like, "We're all here to learn from one another," and model how to build on incorrect answers. For example, if a student says, "I think using less water is the only way to save rivers," you might respond with, "That's a great starting point!

Let's think about other ways communities can help, like cleaning up litter or planting trees along riverbanks." This approach encourages students to take risks and think critically about water-related solutions.

- **Lack of engagement:** Some students might feel disconnected from large-scale water issues, like water shortages or ocean pollution, making it hard for them to engage.

  - *What you can try*—Make the topic personal and relatable. For example, ask students questions like, "What's one thing you love about a nearby lake, river, or beach?" Then connect their answers to larger environmental systems. If a student mentions loving a local creek, you could explain how pollution upstream can affect the health of that creek and the wildlife that depends on it. This helps students see the connections between their own experiences and global water challenges.

- **Peer pressure:** Students may feel pressured to conform to their peers' opinions or behaviors, leading them to withhold their thoughts about water issues or climate justice.

  - *What you can try*—Normalize diverse perspectives by using activities like agree–disagree lineups or four corners discussions. For example, present a statement like, "People should have the right to unlimited water, even during a drought," and have students move to the corner of the room that represents their opinion—agree, disagree, strongly agree, or strongly disagree. This visual activity shows students that it's OK to have different perspectives while fostering a respectful environment for discussing complex water-related topics.

By addressing barriers to student participation and grounding your strategies in larger environmental issues, you can help students connect their classroom discussions to real-world challenges. Whether you use anonymous idea sharing, sentence starters, or relatable connections, these tools can transform hesitant participation into lively, thoughtful conversation about the environment. Together, we can create a space where every student feels empowered to contribute their voice to the urgent issues facing our planet today.

Insight 6: Set Boundaries and Expectations for Whole-Class Conversations

Setting boundaries and expectations may come naturally to many teachers. Whether on the playground or in the classroom, they are constantly guiding behavior and communication to create safe and productive learning environments. When it comes to fostering effective and meaningful discussions about environmental issues, like climate change or climate anxiety, setting boundaries and expectations can make all the difference. Following, we suggest some key strategies that you might adapt in your Green Literacy classroom. We've included examples of how these can connect directly to environmental topics and issues, as well as where you can find related activities and ideas in the chapters of this book.

- **Active listening:** Encouraging students to give their full attention to the speaker, take interest, and avoid interruptions can set the stage for open and respectful dialogue.

  - *What you might try and explore further*—Ask students to practice active listening by reflecting back what they hear. For example, when discussing global warming, a student could say, "So, you're saying that rising temperatures are affecting sea levels. Is that right?" This simple technique helps students stay focused while promoting deeper understanding. In chapter 5 (page 107), we explore how listening to diverse cultural perspectives about landscapes—such as Indigenous views on land use—can deepen students' environmental awareness. You might find inspiration there to guide your students in listening to one another with care and curiosity.

- **Respectful and constructive communication:** When students use polite and respectful language, avoid personal attacks, and offer constructive feedback, discussions become safe spaces for exploring sensitive topics. This is especially important when addressing issues like climate anxiety or other emotionally charged environmental concerns.

  - *What you might try and explore further*—Consider using sentence starters to model respectful communication. For example, students could begin with, "I see your point, and I wonder if we could consider _____" or "I appreciate what you said, and I'd like to add _____." These stems guide students toward constructive responses while reducing the likelihood of conflict. In chapter 6 (page 133), we offer examples of how empathetic communication fosters collaboration when communities respond to natural disasters. You might use this insight to show students how respectful communication leads to productive teamwork during challenging conversations.

- **Inclusivity in participation:** Making sure all voices are heard and shared airtime is respected can prevent discussions from being dominated by a few individuals. This approach is especially important when students are sharing their ideas about issues like conservation or deforestation, where diverse perspectives can enrich the conversation.

  - *What you might try and explore further*—Try structuring discussions with group roles, like facilitator, note taker, and timekeeper, to encourage equitable participation. Use a round-robin format where every student has a chance to share their thoughts. For instance, during a conversation about conservation strategies, you might prompt each student with, "What's one way you think we can protect forests for future generations?" In chapter 3 (page 57), we discuss how the Green Literacy teaching model emphasizes equitable group participation to ensure all students feel valued and included in the learning process. You might find helpful strategies there to implement in your classroom.

- **Engagement through clarification and staying on topic:** Encouraging students to ask clarifying questions and stay focused on the discussion topic can lead to more productive and meaningful conversations. This skill is especially valuable when discussing technical or multilayered topics like renewable energy solutions.

  - *What you might try and explore further*—Teach students to ask clarifying questions, such as, "Can you explain more about how wind power works?" or "What do you mean when you say solar panels are more efficient?" Providing students with question stems like these can help them engage with the material while staying on track.

By setting clear boundaries and expectations and tying them to environmental issues, you can help your students participate in meaningful discussions about the world around them. The strategies of active listening, respectful communication, inclusive participation, and focused engagement can help create a classroom environment where students feel confident and inspired to share their ideas.

Insight 7: Consider Choice Boards for Authentic Learning

Choice boards are flexible tools that provide students with a menu of activities to choose from, allowing for differentiation, creativity, and autonomy in their learning. You can adapt them based on your students, your classroom, and the time you have available. Each square on the board represents a unique task or project, and students have the freedom to select the activity that best matches their interests, strengths, or preferred learning style. This structure fosters engagement and ensures that students feel empowered in their educational journey.

In the context of Green Literacy, choice boards embed environmental themes and perspectives into every option on the board. This ensures that each activity supports academic growth and autonomy as well as nurtures environmental awareness and action. Students are encouraged to think critically, empathize with the natural world, and envision solutions to real-world challenges—all while doing creative, student-driven work.

To give you an idea of how choice boards may be used in Green Literacy teaching, here are some examples for if you are using a single text. Any choice board activity can be modified to connect to one or more texts. The modification comes in when curating your Green Reads and Views list, making sure the authors' messages connect to the thematic question.

- After reading *All the Water in the World* by George Ella Lyon (2011), students discuss the importance of conserving water. The choice board might include:

  - Writing a letter to their community about water conservation tips

  - Creating a comic strip about the journey of a raindrop from cloud to ground

  - Designing a poster that illustrates actionable ways to save water at home

  - Performing a short skit showing the consequences of wasting water and how small changes can make a big difference

- Using *The Thing About Bees: A Love Letter* by Shabazz Larkin (2019), students explore the role of pollinators in ecosystems. The choice board could include:
  - Writing a poem about a day in the life of a bee
  - Constructing a bee hotel out of recyclable materials and writing instructions to share with others
  - Researching and presenting on a local pollinator species, explaining its role in the ecosystem
  - Designing a game that teaches others about pollinators and their importance

These example options allow students to integrate science, art, and advocacy to showcase their unique talents while deepening their understanding of pollinator conservation. Incorporating an environmental perspective into choice boards deepens students' respect for the interconnectedness of their lives, their communities, and the planet. Choice boards let students approach environmental issues through multiple entry points, and they foster creativity, critical thinking, and a sense of agency. Through these activities, students actively engage with topics that matter to their surroundings and their future, making the abstract tangible and the global personal. They are empowered to act, reflect, and create in ways that inspire change.

If you are interested in incorporating choice boards into your teaching, we provide an appendix filled with boards designed to align with the units in chapters 5–7 (appendix B, page 197). These are meant to inspire you, but you'll know best what works for your students and their interests. We recognize that using choice boards does take some preparation on your part—such as creating rubrics or determining how to assess student work, depending on your school culture. We've done the groundwork by offering engaging learning activity ideas. You can customize and expand these to suit your teaching style and learning goals, including rubrics and student assignments. Those choice boards can be used for a single book, like the examples we present, or for several books.

Insight 8: Assess Students for Understanding

Frequently in our Green Literacy professional development process, we encourage teachers to use an action research framework to refine their teaching practices. This framework involves actively reflecting on how assessments inform and improve instruction to ensure that lessons remain responsive to students' needs. In particular, we ask teachers to consider three types of assessments they can use daily to gauge student understanding and engagement. These assessments identify where students are in their learning journey. They provide actionable insights to guide instructional decisions, especially when working with interdisciplinary topics like environmental literacy.

1. **Observe your students:** Observation provides valuable insights into how students engage with activities and ideas. For example, during a role-playing activity inspired by *Saving American Beach* by Heidi Tyline King (2021), you might have students act out the story of MaVynee Betsch advocating for the preservation of a historically

significant beach. Observe whether students take initiative in their roles, contribute dialogue about environmental justice, or ask questions about the importance of protecting natural spaces. These observations can help you identify students who are connecting with the content and those who may need additional support to engage fully.

2. **Analyze their written work:** Students' drawings and written reflections can reveal how they process and connect with the material. After reading *The Ocean Gardener* by Clara Anganuzzi (2024), for example, you could ask students to create an illustrated plan for protecting coral reefs. Their work might include ideas like setting up marine reserves, educating their community about ocean conservation, or reducing pollution. Analyzing these responses allows you to assess how well students understand the relationship between marine life and human actions, and it provides insight into their ability to think critically about real-world solutions.

3. **Ask what they think:** Engaging students in dialogue about their learning helps you understand their perspectives and areas of growth. After a lesson inspired by *Compost Stew* by Mary McKenna Siddals (2014), ask students reflective questions like, "What can we add to a compost bin to make healthy soil?" or "How does composting help reduce waste in landfills?" These conversations, whether they occur through informal discussions or quick written responses, reveal what students have learned and how they are beginning to see the practical applications of Green Literacy concepts in their own lives (Gove & Kennedy-Calloway, 1992).

Observing, analyzing, and asking for feedback ensure that your instruction meets students where they are while fostering critical thinking, creativity, and environmental stewardship. These tools strengthen students' understanding. They help them see their role in creating a sustainable future.

Insight 9: Reflect as a Tool for Change

Reflection is a powerful tool for fostering change, especially in Green Literacy classrooms, where students are navigating the complexities of environmental issues. Together, teachers can cultivate a reflective mindset that encourages learners to form personal connections with ecological topics, transforming abstract ideas into actionable responsibilities.

In part 3, we recommend fostering a reflective mindset through engaging activities that connect students to ecological topics in meaningful ways. Each of these activities can easily be added to units in chapters 5–7. While we don't embed them directly into those chapters, we offer them here with examples from books that are part of our Green Reads and Views collection. Some of these tools for reflection may already be familiar to you and your students. These are strategies young people can easily participate in, but we've added an environmental lens to deepen their impact and relevance.

- **Environmental learning journals:** Maintaining journals focused on environmental studies can help students reflect on what they've learned, document observations, and connect global issues to their local ecosystems.

- *What you might try*—Invite students to start "eco-journals" where they can write or draw their reflections. For example, after reading *Don't Let Them Disappear* by Chelsea Clinton (2019), students could reflect on the story's message about endangered animals. They might document their thoughts about a species they love, such as sea turtles or elephants, and write about what people can do to protect that species.

- **Eco–exit tickets:** At the end of a Green Literacy lesson, students can share brief reflections on what they've learned, ask questions, or suggest ways to apply the lesson to real-world challenges.

  - *What you might try*—Use prompts like, "What's one thing you learned today that surprised you?" or "What's one way you could help protect the environment after today's lesson?" For example, after reading *Compost Stew* by Mary McKenna Siddals (2014), students could reflect on how composting reduces waste and improves soil health.

- **Sustainability think-pair-share:** This strategy has students reflect individually, discuss with a partner, and share their ideas with the class to foster a collaborative understanding of environmental issues.

  - *What you might try*—After reading *Kate, Who Tamed the Wind* by Liz Garton Scanlon (2018), ask students to reflect on the question, "How can planting trees help solve environmental problems?" Students can first think quietly, then share their ideas with a partner before discussing those thoughts as a group.

Insight 10: Gain Consensus on Environmental Issues

Reaching consensus in your classroom is an opportunity to teach young people the value of collaboration and respect for differing opinions. We feel strongly about this because we've seen how seeking consensus mirrors the real-world challenges of addressing environmental issues. These issues often touch on personal values, like balancing the need for financial stability with the responsibility to protect the planet. For us, consensus is about empowering students to listen, reflect thoughtfully, and grow as compassionate, collaborative problem solvers.

Of course, finding consensus isn't always easy, and it's normal for students to struggle with this process. Imagine a discussion about fracking, where one student might worry about its environmental impact while another shares how their family relies on the industry for income. Or consider a conversation about electronic waste, where a student's enthusiasm for reducing tech-related pollution could clash with their knowledge that a family member works in the computer industry. These tensions are natural, and as new ideas and personal circumstances emerge, students may find their initial opinions shifting.

Helping our students reach consensus reminds us that compromise and flexibility are essential when addressing environmental challenges—skills that are as important in the classroom as they are in the wider world. When students work through these discussions, they practice patience, learn to listen to diverse perspectives, and begin to appreciate the complexity of real-world problems. For teachers, facilitating this process helps build a sense of community and creates a classroom culture where all voices are valued.

When working toward consensus in Green Literacy discussions, it can help to start with shared goals that everyone can agree on. For example, if your students are debating renewable energy options, you might guide them to focus on the common goal of reducing fossil-fuel use, even if their preferences for solar or wind power differ. Perspective taking is another powerful tool; in role-playing activities, students step into different shoes and see how various priorities shape decisions. For example, during a discussion on wildlife conservation inspired by *Last: The Story of a White Rhino* by Nicola Davies (2020), students might take on roles as park rangers, farmers, or conservationists. This activity helps students empathize with the complexities of real-world challenges and think critically about protecting endangered species. If discussions become heated or stuck, pausing for individual reflection can give everyone time to process their thoughts.

Simple prompts like, "What's one thing you learned from a classmate's perspective?" can cause students to reengage with a more open mind. Finally, remember to celebrate progress, not perfection. Reaching full agreement isn't always the goal—consensus is as much about the process as the outcome. Take time to reflect with your students on what they learned during the discussion and how their thinking evolved. By focusing on these strategies, we can create spaces where everyone feels heard and valued, fostering the collaborative mindset needed to tackle complex environmental issues.

For us, consensus building isn't about resolving classroom debates—it's about giving students the tools they'll need to address the environmental challenges of their time. We believe that when students learn to work through disagreements thoughtfully, they're building a foundation of empathy, respect, and resilience. These are the qualities that will empower them to make a difference in their communities and beyond.

So, as you guide your students through these discussions, remember that every step—even a messy, imperfect one—is an opportunity for growth. Together, we can model the kind of collaborative thinking the world needs to tackle its most pressing environmental challenges.

We offer these three steps you might try to foster consensus. We've included reflections on what worked best for us in similar activities.

1. **Start with a group discussion:** Begin by gathering your students and introducing the topic. You might encourage everyone to share their thoughts and feelings while emphasizing the importance of listening to one another. Open-ended questions like "How do you feel about this issue?" or "What concerns or ideas do you have?" can help spark conversation and ensure every voice is heard. This initial discussion builds a sense of community and sets the stage for collaborative decision making (Fisher & Frey, 2014).

    • *What worked for us*—When discussing the environmental impact of fast fashion, we started with the question "What happens to clothes we don't wear anymore?" This allowed students to share personal experiences; for example, one student talked about donating clothes to a local charity, while another expressed concern about waste in landfills. Starting with personal stories made the discussion more relatable and helped students connect emotionally to the topic.

- *Where we might improve*—Sometimes, more vocal students dominated the initial discussion. Next time, we'd use a talking stick or assign turns to ensure quieter students have a chance to share.

2. **Use role playing to understand different perspectives:** Role playing can be a powerful way to help students empathize with others and consider different viewpoints. You might have students take on roles like a factory worker, an environmental activist, a consumer, and a clothing company CEO during a discussion on fast fashion. This kind of activity engages students actively while promoting empathy (Jensen, 2001).

- *What worked for us*—During a role-playing activity inspired by *Don't Let Them Disappear* by Chelsea Clinton (2019), students took on roles such as conservationists, community members, and government officials debating how to protect endangered species. One student, acting as a government leader, said, "We want to protect animals, but we need to make sure people have jobs." Another student, playing a conservationist, responded, "What if we create jobs that focus on protecting the animals instead?" This exchange showed how role playing helps students see different perspectives and work toward creative solutions.

- *Where we might improve*—Not all students were initially comfortable with role playing. In the future, we'd offer sentence stems or prompts like, "As a factory worker, I would feel _____," to help them ease into the activity.

3. **Reflect and recap:** After the group has reached consensus, take time to reflect on the process together. You might ask questions like, "What worked well during our discussion?" or "What could we do differently next time to make sure everyone feels heard?" Reflection solidifies what students have learned and encourages continuous improvement in their collaborative skills (Costa & Kallick, 2008).

- *What worked for us*—After a class decided to advocate for a no-waste lunch initiative inspired by *Compost Stew* by Mary McKenna Siddals (2014), we asked them to reflect on the process. One student said, "I liked how we all shared ideas before making a decision." Another added, "Next time, we should ask everyone to vote anonymously so it feels fair." This reflection let students celebrate their success. It gave them ownership of how to improve future discussions.

- *Where we might improve*—Some students found it hard to pinpoint areas for improvement. Next time, we'd provide specific prompts like, "Was there a moment when you felt stuck? What helped you move forward?" to guide their reflections.

Reaching consensus isn't always easy, but it's a process worth exploring with your students. By starting with an open discussion, incorporating role playing, and reflecting on the process, you can help your students build the skills they need to navigate complex environmental challenges collaboratively. These steps create a classroom culture where every voice matters, fostering both empathy and critical thinking.

Insight 11: Acknowledge Challenges When Teaching Systems Thinking

Many understand (and agree) that systems thinking involves shifting perspectives from viewing issues in isolation to understanding their interconnectedness within larger systems. This perspective shift is crucial for comprehending complex environmental challenges and devising practical solutions. Yet, even though many may understand and agree with systems thinking and its result of shifting perspectives, acting on understanding is a different story.

From our experience both as learners of systems thinking and as teachers of it through Green Literacy, we acknowledge that several common factors may hold teachers back from teaching systems thinking (effectively or at all). Here's a concise list of experiences many of us share in making a change and our responses as we work toward systems thinking.

- **Stepping out of your comfort zone:** As teachers, we often rely on traditional teaching practices because they feel familiar and safe. But introducing new approaches like systems thinking means stepping out of your comfort zone and trying something new in your classroom. It's not always easy, but taking small risks like this can lead to meaningful growth—for both you and your students.

- **Overcoming resistance to change:** Change can feel daunting, especially when others—like fellow teachers, administrators, or even parents—might be hesitant to embrace new methods. You may encounter resistance when introducing systems thinking in your classroom, but together, we can show the value of fresh, innovative approaches that empower your students to think critically and creatively.

- **Addressing gaps in training:** Trying something new without the right support can be frustrating. If you haven't received much training in systems thinking, it's normal to feel unsure about how to get started or how to facilitate discussions about complex topics in your classroom. That's why professional development and accessible resources are so important—they ready you to guide your students through these exciting ideas.

- **Navigating curriculum limitations:** Sometimes, rigid curriculum guidelines can make it hard to bring deeper, interdisciplinary learning into your classroom. If your school's standards prioritize covering content over fostering critical thinking and connections, it may feel like there's little room for systems thinking. But with some creativity, you can incorporate it into your lessons and help your students see how everything connects in the real world.

Trying new ways of thinking and doing can also be difficult for students. We've learned that overcoming resistance, hesitation, or refusal requires a thoughtful, flexible approach. With young students, it's important to make systems thinking accessible and engaging while addressing any uncertainties you may feel about teaching this concept. Here are some ideas for addressing the difficulties of taking on the shift to systems thinking.

- **Resistance to new approaches:** Resistance often arises when new approaches feel overwhelming or disconnected from the realities of daily learning. To ease this, start by fostering an inclusive classroom environment where students feel comfortable exploring big ideas. For example, you might ask students to think about how their school lunch connects to the broader system of food production, transportation, and waste. By helping them see these connections in their everyday lives, you make systems thinking relatable and relevant (Sterling, 2001).

- **Hesitation due to uncertainty:** Hesitation may stem from not knowing where to begin. For third to fifth graders, visual tools like systems maps or simple cause-and-effect charts can provide a clear entry point. A lesson on the water cycle, for instance, could show how rain supports plants, which in turn provide oxygen and food. Using stories or picture books as a springboard is another effective approach. A Green Read, such as *Seeds of Change* (Johnson, 2010), can inspire discussions about how one person's actions, like planting trees, can positively impact the environment and their community (Capra & Luisi, 2014).

- **Refusal to try systems thinking:** If you're facing outright refusal to try systems thinking, it can help to reframe the concept by sharing success stories. For young students, these stories can include real-world examples, like how schools have created butterfly gardens to support pollinators or implemented recycling programs to reduce waste. Incorporating hands-on activities, such as creating a classroom compost bin or designing posters to encourage energy conservation, gives students a chance to see their ideas in action. Demonstrating the practical benefits of systems thinking through such projects can reduce hesitation and build engagement (Meadows, 2008).

- **Lack of engagement in real-world applications:** One of the most powerful ways to engage students in systems thinking is through real-world applications that make a difference. A class project to reduce single-use plastics in the cafeteria, for instance, shows students how their actions can create change within a larger system. By tying these projects to their lives and communities, you empower students to think critically and act responsibly (Sterling, 2001).

Adopting systems thinking means shifting perspectives and sometimes trying new approaches that you might be skeptical of or that do not fit into your comfort zone for your students and your classroom. Systems thinking provides an opportunity for your students to see the world in a new way. In chapter 7 (page 159), we offer specific examples of how systems-thinking strategies may be implemented in grades 3–5 classrooms, with consideration for grades K–2, including tools and ideas to guide you.

Insight 12: Help Students Get Beyond Surface-Level Answers

When we explore Green Literacy and systems thinking with young people—and adults—it becomes clear that their first responses often feel too simple. Surface-level answers may stem from thinking that focuses on familiar solutions, lacking the depth needed to tackle environmental challenges. We can guide students to move beyond these initial ideas and uncover the dynamic relationships that shape our world. We suggest using stories, practical activities, and reflective discussions, which have worked best for us, to inspire young minds to think critically and engage deeply with complex environmental issues.

In our experience, the following general approaches push young people to go beyond their most common surface-level answers.

- **Moving beyond quick-fix solutions:** One of the most common responses we hear from students is the belief that environmental problems can be solved with one action or quick fix. It's tempting to think that planting one tree or recycling one bottle will solve the issues, but we know these challenges are part of much larger systems. To help students grasp this complexity, we suggest starting with stories that illustrate interconnectedness. *Palm Trees at the North Pole: The Hot Truth About Climate Change* by Marc ter Horst (2021) is a favorite of ours because it explains how climate change influences a variety of global systems and why solutions require more than isolated actions. You could also guide students to map the ripple effects of a single action. For example, some students traced the journey of a piece of litter, exploring its impact on marine life, waste systems, and human communities. This activity opened their eyes to how quick fixes often have unintended consequences, such as replacing one harmful material with another.

- **Bringing environmental issues closer to home:** Another frequent misconception among students is that environmental problems affect distant places or animals—not humans. To help bridge this gap, we suggest using stories like *Antarctica: The Melting Continent* by Karen Romano Young (2022), which vividly illustrates how climate change is reshaping one of the most fragile ecosystems on Earth, and connects these changes to human activity. What worked best for us was pairing this book with a local investigation, such as exploring how pollution affects water quality in nearby rivers or how extreme weather events disrupt local communities. Discussions tied to real-world examples make abstract concepts tangible for students. Researching their own communities fosters a deeper understanding of how global problems impact their lives.

- **Demonstrating the power of individual actions:** Perhaps the most disheartening response is that individual actions don't make a difference. This belief can leave students feeling powerless in the face of large-scale problems. We've found that stories like *A Wild Promise* by Allen Crawford (2023) are incredibly effective for showing how personal efforts can ripple outward. This beautifully illustrated book celebrates the resilience of nature and the impact of collective human effort. What worked best for us was encouraging students to take small, meaningful actions and then reflect on the results. For instance, one class participated in a monthlong challenge to reduce single-use plastics and measured their impact. Seeing the results made them feel empowered and showed that their actions mattered.

- **Understanding the emotional impact of environmental issues:** Last, we've noticed that environmental challenges often evoke strong emotional responses from students. Books like *The Lonely Polar Bear* by Khoa Le (2018) can help students process these emotions by fostering empathy and understanding. We suggest using this story as a springboard for discussions about how people can positively respond to environmental degradation rather than feel overwhelmed by it. What worked best for us was guiding students to channel their emotions into action. It showed them how they can create change.

CONCLUSION

In moving through this chapter, you've discovered the layers of understanding within Green Literacy teaching. This chapter has provided you with twelve key insights into Green Literacy teaching, all of which offer valuable perspectives on how to cultivate environmental awareness and responsibility among young learners. These insights highlight the importance of integrating nature into education, fostering a deep connection to the natural world, and empowering students to become environmental stewards. As you move forward, consider how you can weave these ideas into your teaching practices, guiding your students to understand and actively protect the environment.

While reading this chapter, you may have gained insight into some ways to create a smooth and successful thematic unit. We offered you insights from our own teaching and examples from teachers who participated in Green Literacy professional development. Now it's time to reflect on your own teaching journey and draw from unique experiences to shape your approach to Green Literacy in part 3.

Consider how this chapter has impacted your learning as a teacher. We offer a dedicated space for you to do so in the following "Teacher's Corner" reproducible tool (also available at **go.SolutionTree.com/literacy**). Whether you're working on your own, with a teaching partner, or within a schoolwide learning network, after exploring chapter 4, we encourage you to reflect on what you've learned.

Teacher's Corner

Here are some questions to support your reflection.

- What potential challenges do you anticipate when implementing Green Literacy thematic units, and how might you address them?

- How does reflection work in your classroom? How might the reflection strategies offered (for example, journals, eco-exit tickets) help you bring in reflection as a tool for change? How do you think they will support your teaching and student engagement?

Here are prompts for journaling.

- How might planning to implement a Green Literacy thematic unit—either one we offer or one of your own—influence the way you collaborate with other teachers?

- Which of the twelve insights is something you already do in your daily practice, and how might you improve it for talking about Green Literacy?

Here are discussion guidelines.

- How might you begin to work with other teachers to implement Green Literacy?

- How might you create a time management plan for working with Green Literacy?

PART 3

SUPPORT TO DESIGN YOUR OWN GREEN LITERACY THEMATIC UNITS

In part 3, "Support to Design Your Own Green Literacy Thematic Units," we guide teachers through thematic units, offering both ready-made unit content and ideas for customization while also moving along a continuum of three units that starts with personal connection and expands to broader communal and global perspectives. Drawing on our experiences in Green Literacy professional development (as recounted in chapter 3, page 57), we have organized chapters 5–7 around the phases or actions of engage, empower, and shift, reflecting the natural process of profoundly comprehending an idea.

Chapter 5, "How Landscapes Shape Us," is the starting point, focusing on personal connections. This chapter helps students explore how the landscapes around them shape their identities and how these connections—or the lack of them—affect their relationships with nature and their communities.

Chapter 6, "How Extreme Weather Events Connect Our Communities," transitions from personal to communal themes, examining the impacts of extreme weather events, the plight of weather refugees, and the effects of climate anxiety on young people.

Finally, chapter 7, "How Systems Thinking Changes Our World," brings students to the heart of Green Literacy and explores how systems thinking can transform their understanding of interconnectedness and the power structures that sustain or disrupt ecological balance.

The ready-made units in these chapters show how you might explore these big-picture environmental questions with your students. For each of the chapters, we've included a completed Green Literacy planning template from the lens of a composite teacher, along with commentary, a curated Green Reads and Views list, suggested Green Literacy strategies, and space to develop Green Literacy ideals.

We like to call this approach *design your own unit* because you're welcome to use our example as it is, tweak it to better fit your needs, or use it as inspiration to create something entirely new. Think of chapters 5–7 as plans we suggest to spark ideas and help you envision how you might build a unit of your own. That being noted, you are not merely observing suggested classroom units; you should actively adapt and implement these ideas for your unique classroom context.

The Green Literacy Handbook supports you every step of the way. If you need help, here's a quick guide for your reference.

- Consult chapter 1 on Green Literacy theory for ways to move into a critical stance.

- Confer with chapter 2 for information about Green Literacy practice.

- Refer to chapter 3 as our model of the Green Literacy thematic unit.

- Return to chapter 4 for guidance on moving toward designing your own Green Literacy thematic unit and for insights into Green Literacy teaching.

CHAPTER 5

> *The land knows you, even when you are lost.*
>
> —ROBIN WALL KIMMERER

How Landscapes Shape Us

This chapter ventures into the personal, inviting you to help your students discover their individual connections to the landscapes around them. Homing in on the power of attention and observation, you and your students may explore how to acknowledge and empower a sense of place within landscapes, and find those connections to landscapes in the selected Green Reads and Views. The chapter provokes this by guiding readers through a ready-made sample thematic unit about how landscapes shape us, following the three phases of Green Literacy teaching: (1) engage, (2) empower, and (3) shift. We offer a completed Green Literacy Thematic Unit Planning Template through the lens of a composite teacher to support and inspire you. In this chapter, you can follow along and customize the blank template, considering your teaching context.

PHASE 1: ENGAGE

In this section, you will:

- Develop your thematic question
- Foster your thinking through commentary

Chapter Snapshot— What You'll Explore

In this chapter, we share with you how to:

- Discover various ideas about landscapes and how landscapes connect with and shape who students are and their perspectives

- Organize a unit

- Pick Green Reads and Views and Green Literacy strategies, including K–2 consideration

- Navigate critical thinking, reading, speaking, and writing to create Green Literacy ideals

The *engage* phase focuses on your growth as a teacher; it invites you to explore environmental issues, develop thematic questions, and immerse yourself in meaningful commentary. Specifically, in this chapter, the engage phase invites you to explore the many ways landscapes influence our lives and shape our realities. It examines how these insights can foster deeper connections—or create disconnections—with the spaces and places where we coexist with the natural world.

In this section, we provide you with a thematic question and thoughtful commentary to support your journey and ensure you have the tools needed to navigate these complex topics. This section prioritizes your learning, helping you build confidence with environmental issues, gain a solid foundation, and prepare to bring these key ideas into your classroom.

On the planning template, you will note that addressing questions about your willingness to engage and how your school community might react is part of this process. Only you can answer these questions. As you move through this section, keep in mind how you learn, how your students may react, and the level of commitment your school community has. All of this will influence how you engage with big-picture environmental issues surrounding the thematic question of this unit on how landscapes shape us.

We will next guide you through the individual steps that compose the larger engage phase: developing a thematic question and fostering commentary for a topic.

Develop Your Thematic Question

Landscapes shape who we are and how we understand the world. Mountains, rivers, forests, and deserts influence the ways we live, the stories we tell, and the communities we build. The geography around us determines our physical environment and shapes our cultural practices and even our perceptions of the world. These connections demonstrate how landscapes are intertwined with our identities economically, socially, and emotionally.

We offer this thematic unit as the first of the three ready-made units because discovering personal connections to local landscapes creates a meaningful entry point for deeper exploration of connections to the natural world. We chose the thematic question, "How do landscapes shape us?" as it invites you to reflect on how landscapes shape both our inner and outer worlds and to guide your students in doing the same. This thematic question encourages you to explore how landscapes influence your and your students' daily lives and broader sense of place in the world.

While we provide a sample thematic question for this unit, you can choose to create your own thematic question if ours does not fit your needs. Consider the following variations.

- How do different landscapes shape the ways people live and work?
- What can we learn from how people and animals adapt to changing landscapes?
- How can we help protect the landscapes around us?

By reviewing the completed section for developing your thematic question on the sample Green Literacy planning template (figure 5.1), you'll see how we crafted our question

Name: Daniel (five years of teaching experience)

Grade level: Third grade

School context: Rural

PHASE 1: ENGAGE

Develop Your Thematic Question

Here are some guiding questions to consider as you develop your thematic question. Reflect on these prompts to clarify your focus.

1. Brainstorm

- What issue that could lead to a big idea about the environment are you most passionate about exploring with your students?

    My students are rural kids. They love technology and embrace it just like anyone else. I want them to think beyond the screens and explore how they're connected to the land—not just because they live on it, but because it's part of who they are. I want them to reflect on a special place in nature that means something to them and start observing the environment around them in new and thoughtful ways. It's about helping them see their relationship with nature as deeper and more personal, beyond the routines of everyday life.

- What current events or real-world examples resonate with you and can help bring environmental issues to life for your students?

    One thing that really stands out to me is how the land around us is changing. Places that used to feel wild and untouched now seem more worn down; there are fewer trees, more empty fields, and less space for the things we used to take for granted, like the creek where we'd fish or the woods we'd explore.

2. Prioritize

You might have more than one environmental issue you'd like to explore with your students. Now, think about which one will create the most meaningful conversations and learning.

    There's the mindset in the community. Don't get me wrong, people here care about the land—they depend on it—but there's resistance to change. Talking about pollution or conservation sometimes feels like I'm stepping on toes because no one wants to admit how certain practices might be part of the problem. I may have to figure out ways to engage without rubbing parents the wrong way. As for my willingness to engage with the topic, I'm all in. Teaching about environmental issues is personal for me—I want my students to feel proud of their community and motivated to protect it.

Figure 5.1: Completed "develop your thematic question" segment of the Green Literacy Thematic Unit Planning Template.

Continued ▶

> Through this brainstorming and prioritization process, write your thematic question. Some stems that might be useful are:
>
> - How can/do . . . ?
> - What might . . . ?
>
> Write your thematic question here.
>
> *How do landscapes shape us? A question like this is a big-picture idea and can bring my students and our school community together.*
>
> *See page 38 in the book for more information on creating thematic questions.*

based on the lens of third-grade teacher Daniel. He is from a rural school in a farming community.

Daniel collaborates with an administration rooted in an agricultural setting, where there is a shared focus on fostering environmental understanding. In this case, Daniel's collaboration with the administration and his ability to build on students' personal connections to landscapes made the big-picture question successful for his class and school.

Now that you have explored and chosen a thematic question, we support your thinking by providing commentaries designed as starting points for deeper reflection and planning.

Foster Your Thinking Through Commentary

The commentaries we provide in this chapter are designed to serve as springboards, or seed ideas, to ignite your curiosity and spark complex thinking. These commentaries are intentionally crafted to give you a solid starting point as you explore the chapter's environmental issues. At the same time, commentary is meant to be active—it encourages you to begin thinking critically about how to connect ideas to your classroom.

Following, you'll find ideas based on the thematic question, "How do landscapes shape us?" We offer commentary through these focus areas to help you consider the complexities of our relationships with various types of landscapes that influence us.

- **Landscapes and belonging:** Explore Richard Louv's (2008) idea of the third frontier and the importance of personal connections to nature.

- **Landscapes and distraction:** Address how technology "fracks" our attention. Through awareness, we can help ourselves refocus from distractions.

- **Landscapes and acknowledgment:** Use mindfulness to develop relationships with the landscapes around us.

- **Landscapes and emergence:** Understand anthropogenic ecotones and how human activities impact natural environments.

As you read the commentary in the following focused sections, you'll find Pause and Consider questions threaded throughout. These questions will engage you and spark your curiosity so that as you progress through this chapter and the steps in developing a Green

Literacy thematic unit, you will feel confident in considering these environmental issues for your students.

Landscapes and Belonging

Did you have regular and meaningful interactions with nature as a child? Many of us had a special place where we could escape, reflect, and be ourselves. Yours might have been the woods behind your house, a quiet corner of a park, the shore of Lake Michigan, or a nearby creek, like Bear Creek. Nature felt accessible. There were green spaces, few barriers, and a general freedom to explore. You may have grown up throwing stones into rivers, building forts among trees, and catching fireflies in the backyard until it was too dark to see. These experiences weren't planned or scheduled; they were part of everyday life. Walking down trails, biking along paths, or spending lazy afternoons having family picnics in the park might have shaped your connection to the land.

Direct engagement with nature is more than simply fun; it helps one mature. Creating such memories in nature leads one's identity to develop around the local landscape. These moments, full of wonder and curiosity, shaped who we, the authors, are and our appreciation for the natural world.

In his groundbreaking book, *Last Child in the Woods: Saving Our Children From Nature-Deficit Disorder*, Richard Louv (2008) invites us to consider young people's relationship with nature and how adults, teachers, and parents influence that relationship. Young people today have a different reality and relationship with nature than their parents and grandparents did. Louv claims young people today are living in what he calls the *third frontier*. He states that in the third frontier, the reality of nature for young people looks like this:

> a severance of the public and private mind from our food's origins; a disappearing line between machines, humans, and other animals; . . . the invasion of our cities by wild animals (even as urban/suburban designers replace wildness with synthetic nature); and the rise of a new kind of suburban form. (Louv, 2008, p. 19)

Pause and Consider: How might your memories in nature have shaped your identity and connection to your local landscape?

As adults, we must acknowledge that the young people in our classrooms have experiences of nature that are not similar or close to what ours were. Our young people have different opportunities to engage in nature than we did, and we had different engagement opportunities than our grandparents and great-grandparents. For one generation, what was once "wild" becomes "tame," whereas another's learned "wild" becomes "extinct." While our planet cannot return to what it once was before climate change, there is room for acceptance of what is, such as what the landscapes are now and what this environment is like.

Being in the *now* with our connections forces us to act and be responsible for our actions in the present moment. That is not to say we need to forget past eco-disasters or allow nostalgia to wane for childhood memories of planting trees, which are valuable and meaningful and add to our awareness. Rather, we must signal to young people that we accept the landscape we live in with them, not force our memories onto them. We must respect our young people's experiences with nature and avoid trying to create ones that are no longer available. Considering their backgrounds and the state of our young people's lives will help

Pause and Consider:
How does the landscape around you shape your sense of self, influence your beliefs, or affect the choices you make? In what ways does your environment contribute to your sense of belonging and connection to the world?

them, and in this way, we will facilitate more profound personal connections with each other and landscapes.

Knowing this, we ask, "What is a landscape? How is it defined, and by whom? Can we identify with more than one at the same time rather than none at all? Is our understanding of landscape fluid or stifled? Does it matter if we perceive our landscapes as fragmented rather than whole? And how do our definitions shape who we are and how we interact with, protect, or play in the landscapes around us?"

While many agree that *landscape* refers to the physical environment, including natural features like mountains and rivers and manufactured elements like buildings and infrastructure, it may be much more. That juxtaposition is rich for mining a better understanding of ourselves, others, and the natural world. The interplay between landscape and identity explores how the physical environment shapes our perception of self and the world, thereby influencing our choices, beliefs, and sense of belonging.

Landscapes, as personal canvases, evoke a myriad of emotions, extending beyond picturesque scenes to encompass the rich tapestry of human experience (Tuan, 1977). They serve as repositories of memories, where laughter and joy echo through school playgrounds, while shadows of past play and moments of shared learning linger during family field trips to nature observatories. These spaces are intertwined with the lives of young people, shaping their understanding of the world and their place within it (Louv, 2005). The landscape may also hold the nuances of a young person's fears, serving as a space that may spark anxiety or evoke a sense of disconnect.

In some instances, landscapes bear the weight of generational hurts, silent witnesses to the struggles and traumas that have unfolded across time (hooks, 2009). The land itself often tells stories of historical injustices and environmental changes, both of which can leave lasting impacts on the communities that inhabit it. Each contour and feature becomes a storyteller, weaving tales of both resilience and vulnerability within the expanse of personal and shared histories for young people to discover and articulate (Gruenewald, 2003).

Pause and Consider:
In what ways have you considered exploring and reflecting on your local environment to uncover deeper connections to it?

Land Acknowledgment Statements

In many North American classrooms, students and their teachers acknowledge that they are standing on Native lands by evoking a land acknowledgment statement. They begin school meetings, club events, or classes with a land acknowledgment statement that recognizes and respects the Indigenous peoples who have traditionally stewarded the land where they live. We the authors, Jen and Mary, write from the lands of the Council of Three Fires (Potawatomi, Ojibwe, and Odawa; Chicago) and Seminole (Gainesville), respectively. We express gratitude and appreciation to those whose territory we reside on as a way of honoring the Indigenous people living and working on the land from time immemorial.

Understanding the land's history, geography, and significance, regardless of whether it is now urban and no longer resembles what it once was, instills a sense of belonging and attachment, sometimes reverence. Native poet CMarie Fuhrman (2021) declares, "Acknowledgment means too late for an apology," and without change and equality, "Land Acknowledgment is not but another broken treaty."

> **Pause and Consider:** How might you and your students develop a sense of belonging, attachment, and reverence by acknowledging how the land's history, geography, and significance have changed over time?

If you and your students wish to participate in acknowledging the Indigenous peoples who have historically cared for the land, consider crafting a land acknowledgment statement and incorporating it into your classroom and larger school community. Land acknowledgments do not exist in a past-tense or historical context; colonialism is an ongoing process, and we need to build mindfulness of our present participation. When you and your students begin creating a land acknowledgment statement, reflect on your connection to the land, dive into researching the Indigenous history of your area, and choose language that recognizes both past and present injustices while honoring Indigenous resilience (Native Governance Center, 2019).

As you think about the planning and teaching of this unit, consider how your experiences with nature growing up differ from those of your students. For example, consider the number of wild animals like deer, raccoons, or squirrels you saw in your neighborhood. Was this, or another example, different for you as a young person than for your students? Also, you may be interested in knowing about the Native tribes who formerly lived where your school is located. Reflect on how comfortable you feel working with your students in acknowledging these Native American or First Nations peoples.

Landscapes and Distraction

Many K–5 teachers are bringing learning to life by organizing trips to farms, nature centers, and animal habitats. These explorations give students the chance to see plants and animals up close, explore how ecosystems work, and connect what they learn in class to the world around them. For example, a farm visit might include seeing how plants grow, learning about sustainable farming, or meeting farm animals. A trip to a nature center could include a guided hike to spot local wildlife, while an animal habitat visit might spark curiosity about how animals live and adapt. These hands-on experiences inspire students to ask questions, care for the environment, and develop a lifelong love for nature.

Despite these endeavors, smart devices often divert students' attention, hindering their connection with the natural environment. As youth reflect on their relationship with the landscape, the question emerges: How can they learn to be present in nature without succumbing to digital distractions?

Teachers face a dilemma—should devices be eliminated for the moment or incorporated in a way that fosters presence? Some may believe that balancing technology and nature engagement is a critical challenge that school communities must address.

Technologies can be incredibly helpful when observing nature, especially for young people. For example, using apps to identify specific plants and animals, taking photos to document findings, or using a GPS to explore new trails can enhance the learning experience and make nature more engaging. However, there is a significant difference between productively using technology and simply scrolling through social media. We recognize this difference and promote using technology as a tool for learning and discovery in nature rather than as a distraction.

As educators, we are concerned that high technology use increases the challenge for critical thinking about the environment. We have seen it in ourselves and recognized it with our friends, students, and family members. Most individuals use technology without thinking. Psychologist Gloria Mark (2023), author of *Attention Span: A Groundbreaking Way to Restore Balance, Happiness and Productivity*, has been tracking people's attention over the years using unobtrusive and sophisticated computer logging techniques. Mark has found evidence that attention spans have shrunk in recent years, at least as measured by how long people spend on task on computers. How much have attention spans shrunk? In 2004, she and her researchers found the average attention span on any screen to be two and a half minutes. Throughout the years, it has become shorter. By 2012, she and her researchers found it to be seventy-five seconds.

In this crisis of fragmented attention caused by significant time spent on devices, members of the Friends of Attention (a coalition of artists, scholars, and activists) and the connected entity the Strother School of Radical Attention (which offers seminars and experiential workshops to cultivate radical attention) advocate for attention education, recognizing the negative impact of technology-induced attention deficits. By fostering collective experiences and self-awareness through innovative exercises, the Strother School's curriculum aims to reclaim shared learning spaces. In practical terms, this means taking time to go to a park or another outside place without a technological device, observing what is around, and then reflecting and sharing with others about what is observed in this time and space. This kind of attention activism seeks to build a coalition of individuals committed to valuing and preserving true attention for longer than forty-seven seconds, which is essential for thinking that can lead to informed citizenship and a vibrant democracy. This focus on building true attention directly connects to how people engage with landscapes and the natural world. When they slow down and truly pay attention, they can form richer, more meaningful connections with the environments around them.

Attention is a tool for fostering empathy and meaningful relationships. It becomes a gateway to deepening connections with landscapes. Intentionally focusing on the environment cultivates greater awareness of its rhythms, beauty, and needs, fostering a deeper sense of care and responsibility for the natural world.

As you navigate the planning and teaching of this unit, we see a dilemma for you, which we, too, experience. This idea of how people's attention is being fracked, affecting both the focus needed for learning and their ability to think critically, is challenging for us as teachers and nature lovers. For each experience we have with young people, we consider whether they would benefit from leaving their technology behind or it is an occasion to use technology such as the iNaturalist app, which aids learning about natural processes. In your context, consider whether you feel comfortable requesting that your students leave their phones behind when they go into nature with the purpose of noticing how they respond.

Pause and Consider: How can technology enrich your relationship with nature?

Landscapes and Acknowledgment

The art of observation emerges as a powerful antidote to distraction. We teachers play a pivotal role in honing this skill among our students. Helping young people pause to observe the landscape around them enhances their connection to the present moment (Hickey, 2010; Husgafvel, 2016). In time, they become open to nature as it is presently unfolding before them. Observation is more than a skill; it is a gateway to heightened awareness and mindfulness. Teaching young people to intentionally observe their landscapes allows them to regain control over their attention and make deliberate choices about where to direct their focus. This focus on the present moment becomes a sanctuary from overwhelming technological stimuli. In this way, deliberate observation becomes a transformative tool for students to navigate the digital age, anchor themselves in the present, and savor the world's richness rather than be lost.

Green Literacy recognizes the significance of mindfulness as a practice, yet we contend that the term *mindfulness* has become commonplace, often diluted in meaning, and sometimes political and divisive. Our approach encourages you and your students to craft your distinct definitions of mindfulness, ensuring a personal resonance that transcends ubiquitous usage of the term. When young people own their language, they are emboldened by it.

Frequently, we have seen teachers change the word *mindfulness* to *awareness*, *paying attention*, or *using your imagination*. Whatever words you and your students deem appropriate will be what they connect to, and hopefully, your students will be able to be still and observe the world around them. For *The Green Literacy Handbook*, mindfulness is about stillness and observation, devoid of any religious affiliation. This neutral approach respects diverse beliefs and allows for a genuine and meaningful exploration of these practices.

Jon Kabat-Zinn (1994), a pioneer in mindfulness practices and the developer of the Mindfulness-Based Stress Reduction (MBSR) program, emphasizes that mindfulness in education can enhance student well-being, resilience, and performance. These practices have become a cornerstone of many educational settings, providing tools to foster emotional and cognitive growth.

Key benefits of mindfulness for students include the following.

- **Improved focus and attention:** Regular mindfulness practice has been shown to improve students' ability to concentrate on tasks, which can lead to better academic performance (Zenner, Herrnleben-Kurz, & Walach, 2014).

- **Stress reduction:** Mindfulness techniques help students manage stress and anxiety, promoting overall well-being and mental health (Meiklejohn et al., 2012).

- **Emotional regulation:** By learning mindfulness, students develop the skills to identify and regulate their emotions, which leads to improved self-control and stronger interpersonal relationships (American Psychological Association, 2019).

- **Enhanced resilience:** Mindfulness fosters resilience, equipping students to handle challenges and setbacks with greater confidence and adaptability (Greenberg & Harris, 2012).

- **Increased self-awareness:** Through mindfulness practices, students gain deeper insight into their thoughts and emotions, fostering personal growth and self-understanding (Kabat-Zinn, 1994).

- **Better decision making:** Mindfulness enables students to approach situations with clarity and calmness, which improves their ability to make thoughtful decisions (Zenner et al., 2014).

As Kabat-Zinn (1994) highlights, mindfulness gives students tools for navigating life's challenges while fostering a deeper connection to themselves and the world around them.

As you plan, take a minute to assess your comfort with mindfulness both on a personal level and with implementing it in your classroom. What's your experience with it? How can mindfulness be more than skill building? How can it be a transformative experience that ignites students' imaginations and builds their relationships with nature?

Landscapes and Emergence

Many people live in *anthropogenic ecotones*, transitional border areas made by humans that separate different types of natural environments or habitats. Anthropogenic ecotones show how human activities can impact, intersect with, and change natural environments, affecting plants, animals, and overall biodiversity. Consider the following student examples, which may resemble experiences of young people in your classroom.

- In Boston, Massachusetts, where fifth-grade student Norma goes to school, a large park borders several busy streets. The edge between the manicured park lawns and the concrete sidewalks is an example of an anthropogenic ecotone. This area, Norma learns, supports a variety of urban-adapted wildlife, such as squirrels, pigeons, and sometimes foxes.

- Near Jacob's school in La Porte, Indiana, there are fields where crops are grown right next to a small wetland area. The edge where the farmland meets the wetland is an anthropogenic ecotone. Here, Jacob finds both agricultural pests and wetland creatures like frogs and dragonflies, demonstrating the interaction between the two environments.

- Regina's school in Spokane, Washington, has a small forest at the back. Regina learns that the transitional area between her neighborhood gardens and the natural forest is an anthropogenic ecotone. This edge hosts a mix of garden plants and wild forest species, creating a unique habitat for insects and birds.

The preceding examples show how anthropogenic ecotones introduce various natural elements and influence the character of the spaces we inhabit. These intersections enrich our experiences by evoking emotions and connections that arise from the dynamic interplay of different ecological realms—like where Central Park's trees meet Manhattan or where a Vermont garden borders a wild meadow. They stir memories of childhood play, peaceful walks, or the blend of nature and community life. Anthropogenic ecotones, the meeting grounds of diverse ecosystems, are portals through which our personal landscapes emerge. Marked by an interplay of different natural elements, these transitional zones bring forth a tapestry of biodiversity that enriches our perceptions of the land we inhabit. Table 5.1 features some examples of anthropogenic ecotones.

Pause and Consider: How could integrating mindfulness into your classroom help you and your students enhance academic success while fostering personal growth and a more positive, balanced learning environment?

Pause and Consider: How might you and your students explore the ways environmental connections shape experiences and provide a sense of continuity across varied realms?

Table 5.1: Human Impact on Natural Boundaries—Anthropogenic Ecotones

Urban Green Spaces	Parks, gardens, and green urban areas serve as ecotones where human infrastructure meets natural elements. These spaces balance urban developments and natural ecosystems.
Rural–Suburban Transitional Zones	Areas where rural landscapes transition into suburban developments represent ecotones. These zones may feature a mix of agricultural land, natural habitats, and residential areas.
Agricultural Landscapes	The interface between cultivated fields and natural habitats creates an ecotone. Agricultural areas often coexist with remnants of native vegetation, forming transitional zones.
Urban Wetlands	Wetlands within urban settings, such as constructed ponds or urban marshes, serve as ecotones between human developments and natural wetland ecosystems.
Brownfield Sites	Areas with abandoned or repurposed industrial facilities become ecotones as nature reclaims the human-altered landscape. These sites often undergo ecological succession.
Riverfront Developments	The interface between urban areas and riverfronts forms an ecotone. It can include constructed riverwalks, parks, or green buffers along the water's edge.
Transitional Zones Around Infrastructure	Areas around roads, highways, and other infrastructural developments can serve as ecotones, adapting to both human activities and natural processes.
Nature Reserves Near Urban Centers	Protected natural areas near urban centers act as ecotones, offering buffers between pristine ecosystems and human settlements.
Eco-Friendly Developments	Sustainable or eco-friendly developments that integrate natural features and green design principles create anthropogenic ecotones that prioritize environmental coexistence.

By understanding the ways human activity shapes and disrupts natural boundaries, you can better equip students to explore their role in fostering balance within these ecotones. More than likely, if you share this list with them, your students will be able to name ecotones in your local environment. Many of the Green Reads noted in this chapter highlight anthropogenic ecotones.

While you are considering how to bring the idea of anthropogenic ecotones into your classroom, think about where you teach and what landscape is around you. If you live on the edge or border of an urban, suburban, or rural area, might this inform your discussion with your students? In essence, anthropogenic ecotones prompt you to consider how people can coexist with nature without dominating or annihilating it. As you begin to plan and teach your unit, consider where ecotones are in the vicinity of your school. For example, do any parks abut urban development? Or does farmland lie next to housing?

The four commentaries that we provide for the thematic question, "How do landscapes shape us?" aim to deepen your understanding of how personal and communal interactions with landscapes shape identity, attention, and connection to the environment. The unifying thread among these themes is intentionality in how we inhabit and interact with the world around us. Land acknowledgment invites us to respect the past and those who have nurtured the Earth before us. Meditation helps us cultivate presence, connecting us to the land here and now. Anthropogenic ecotones challenge us to consider the future; they inspire us to make thoughtful decisions that balance human activity with ecological integrity.

As you immerse yourself in the commentaries, consider how teacher Daniel approached them. Figure 5.2 includes Daniel's insights on this chapter's commentaries in the corresponding segment of the template.

As you move on to the empower phase of the Green Literacy process, take ideas from the commentaries as you review our Green Reads and Views selections for this unit and consider how you might customize with your own selections.

PHASE 2: EMPOWER

In this section, you will:

- Cultivate a list of Green Reads and Views

- Select Green Literacy strategies

The empower phase builds on the foundation created in engage, where you reflected on environmental issues related to the thematic question. Now, the focus shifts from consideration of environmental issues to the choices you will make to empower your students and enhance their environmental awareness.

In this section, we point to thematically relevant Green Reads and Views and pair them with strategies that align with the unit's theme, modeling the importance of carefully pairing specific texts and media with powerful teaching strategies. These selections serve as examples of how thoughtfully chosen texts and strategies work together. Our decisions are reflected in the corresponding part of the planning template. You're welcome to follow our example or adapt it to suit your students' needs and your teaching style.

As you move through empower, consider:

- How Green Reads and Views can foster environmental awareness by exposing students to diverse perspectives

- How strategies can inspire creativity, collaboration, and critical thinking

- How planning can balance structure with flexibility to meet your students where they are

This phase empowers you to create your own thematic unit tailored to your students' needs. While we recommend designing a unit that spans two to four weeks, you have the flexibility to make it as long or short as necessary to meet your goals.

Foster Your Thinking Through Commentary

First, review the following questions and respond to a few or all of them. Use a list or brainstorm freely to capture your ideas.

- Whose voices or stories do you need to hear to understand this issue, and why are they important to you?

  I'd like to find out more about the Native Americans' presence and how they took care of the land around our town. I think my students might be interested in writing land acknowledgment statements.

- What unfair systems or problems do you want your students to think about when learning about this issue, and how can you help them ask questions and find ways to make things better?

  I want them to consider why some places have better access to clean water, healthy soil, or support for sustainable farming practices than others do.

- Whose experiences or ideas are sometimes left out when this issue is talked about, and how can you share those voices in your classroom to help everyone learn more?

  Many families here have roots in farming, and the land once supported small, independent farms where people worked closely with nature. However, over time, many of these farms were lost to large companies that took over the land for industrial-scale farming or development.

From your responses, begin to find springboards that will help you develop commentary that deepens your thematic exploration.

Springboards to Support Commentary

- Springboard 1: *writing a land acknowledgment statement*
  - Title or source: *Local library*
  - Key insights: *I learned about the history of Native American people in our areas and their respect for landscapes, food they grew, and customs with stories about the land.*
- Springboard 2: *Getting my students to observe nature*
  - Title or source: *Meditation ideas (Brown University and Jon Kabat-Zinn)*
- Key insights: *Meditation may help my students observe their natural surroundings better.*
- Springboard 3: *Learning about the history of the farming areas*
  - Title or source: *Local library*
  - Key insights: *I found out information about farming in our area.*

See page 40 in the book for more information on developing springboards for commentary.

Figure 5.2: Completed "foster your thinking through commentary" segment of the Green Literacy Thematic Unit Planning Template.

Cultivate a List of Green Reads and Views

The book and digital media suggestions we provide for this thematic unit encourage young people to consider various types of landscapes and those landscapes' impact on their lives. This chapter's suggested Green Reads and Views may become touchstones as you and your students gain confidence and draw on your personal experiences with your local landscapes. If there are books or digital media you want to use that we do not reference, consider revisiting chapter 2 (page 31), which provides insightful questions to guide your Green Reads and Views selections.

You can find a full list of resources for this chapter at **go.SolutionTree.com/literacy**. The selections highlighted in this chapter appear in the leaf features throughout the chapter. As you go through the choices for Green Reads and Views within this section, try visualizing how they would play out in your own teaching space and what adjustments you'd make to ensure they resonate with your students.

While you are deciding on the Green Reads and Views, consider Daniel's choices (figure 5.3) and how they relate to his brainstorming and choices in the previously completed sections of the Green Literacy planning template.

Home, and Other Big, Fat Lies
by Jill Wolfson
(2006)

Select Green Literacy Strategies

The strategies outlined in this section support critical thinking and empower students to make meaningful connections among their lives, the texts they read, and the larger world. At the same time, we encourage you to incorporate any of your own tried-and-true methods that have proven effective. As the teacher, you are in the process of curating strategies to align with your thematic unit, ensuring they resonate with your students' needs and your classroom's goals. Here, you are not merely observing a suggested classroom unit; you are encouraged to actively adapt and implement these ideas in the unique context of your classroom. As you move through this section, ask yourself, "How could this look in my classroom? What changes would make this approach most effective for my students?"

We present the following strategies for you to explore, many of which are paired with a Green Read to illustrate their applications.

- **Turn-and-Talk Conversation Cards:** These cards frame a prereading and postreading discussion strategy.

- **Immersive strategies:** Immersive strategies fully engage students by sparking curiosity and creativity through hands-on experiences.
  - *Wonder Walk*—Students engage in mindful exploration of their surroundings.
  - *Imagination Station*—Students have a creative space to reflect and innovate based on observations.

- **Strategies toward the three cycles of comprehension:** These strategies focus on an author's ideas about how landscapes shape us and how young people can support their ideas through personal connection, text-to-text connection, and text-to-world connection.

PHASE 2: EMPOWER

Cultivate a List of Green Reads and Views

Consider the three cycles of comprehension as you choose your strategies: simple comprehension (retell and summarize), criteria comprehension (support thinking), and perspective comprehension (investigate explicit and implicit perspectives and move to systems thinking).

Select texts and digital media that flow from your thematic question and your commentary research. If you need help finding texts or digital media, consult **go.SolutionTree.com/literacy**, our companion website (www.greenliteracy.org), or your school or local librarian.

What types of texts or stories (fiction, nonfiction, poetry, or multimedia) can you use to help your students connect emotionally and critically to this environmental issue? What is the author's message?

Green Reads
Title: <u>Home, and Other Big, Fat Lies</u> by Jill Wolfson (2006)
Author's message: Sense of place and belonging
Title: <u>Remember</u> by Joy Harjo (2023)
Author's message: Wonder and importance of the natural environment with Native American perspective
Title: <u>Butterflies on Carmen Street</u> by Monica Brown (2007)
Author's message: Connections between geographic areas through natural phenomena
Title: <u>A Park Connects Us</u> by Sarah Nelson (2022)
Author's message: Wonder of nature, importance of communal natural spaces
Title: <u>Letting Swift River Go</u> by Jane Yolen (1992)
Author's message: Outdoor adventure, environmental stewardship

Figure 5.3: Completed "cultivate a list of Green Reads and Views" segment of the Green Literacy Thematic Unit Planning Template.

- *Literature Circle*—Students are organized into small groups to discuss books in depth, with each group member having a specific role.

- *Tableau*—Students create frozen scenes or tableaux to represent key moments or concepts from a text.

- *Sketch-to-Stretch*—Students create quick sketches that represent their interpretations of key ideas, themes, or emotions from the story.

- *Compare and Contrast Authors' Messages*—Students compare and contrast themes within texts chosen for the teaching unit.

Jayden's Impossible Garden
by Mélina Mangal
(2021)

As you choose your Green Literacy strategies, remember that chapter 3 (page 57) offers a model thematic unit created during a Green Literacy professional development experience. Chapter 4 (page 79) offers tips for developing a unit. Please refer to either chapter if needed as you use this ready-made unit, customize it, or develop your own new unit.

Next, we provide descriptions and examples for each strategy to model how you can implement them in your context.

Turn-and-Talk Conversation Cards

We recommend starting with the Turn-and-Talk Conversation Cards for this unit. These cards are a great way to spark excitement among your students. You can revisit them throughout the unit to review your students' thinking and use them to reflect after the unit is complete.

We provide Turn-and-Talk Conversation Cards for chapters 5–7 (see figure 5.4), but we also encourage you to tailor them to your classroom. Creating your own questions will build a valuable resource for future discussions. You can undertake these questions with your whole group, have students discuss them with an elbow partner in a turn-and-talk, or use them as journal prompts. To guide your students into perspective comprehension, you could revisit the cards after they have read and discussed the reading selections; students could discuss how the characters in the books or media you're focusing on might answer these questions.

Wonder Walk

During a Wonder Walk, students observe and explore their surroundings and jot down findings or observations. This immersive experience aims to stimulate students' curiosity about the environment, mirroring experiences in the book *Wonder Walkers* (Archer, 2021). The sense of place students feel can transform how they understand their world, helping them reimagine their relationship with natural and cultural communities (Judson, 2010, 2015). This strategy works for multiple grade levels and is a helpful early strategy for kicking off this unit.

To do the Wonder Walk strategy, we suggest you read *Wonder Walkers* to your class and encourage students to share their responses to it. Following the reading and sharing of responses, take your students on a class Wonder Walk within the school neighborhood or grounds, adapting the activity to suit your school setting. After the Wonder Walk, you can facilitate a debrief session where you ask students to share their individual observations; encourage them to articulate what they noticed during the walk and to draw connections to the concepts presented in the book. This reflective discussion allows your students to express their thoughts and enhances their ability to make connections between theoretical knowledge and practical experiences.

A Wonder Walk can be done several times in the school year. Some teachers incorporate one every season. You may prefer to do the walk at the start and end of the school year. Imagine this strategy coming alive in your classroom—what would the students be doing, saying, and feeling?

Wonder Walkers by Micha Archer (2021)

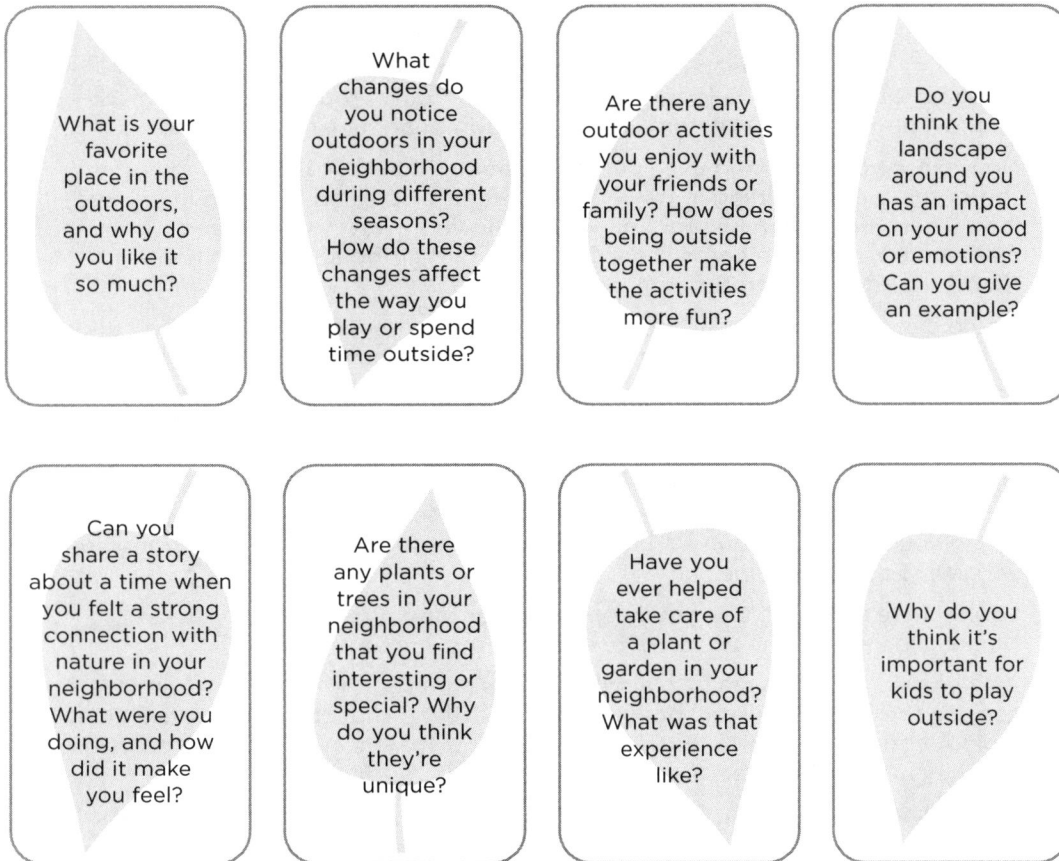

Figure 5.4: Turn-and-Talk Conversation Cards.

*Visit **go.SolutionTree.com/literacy** for a free reproducible version of this figure.*

Imagination Station

This activity is grounded in guided meditation, a process known for inspiring creativity. While meditation serves many purposes, such as reducing stress and achieving balance, in the context of Green Literacy, we focus on its capacity to enhance the imagination of young learners as they engage in the natural world around them (Kabat-Zinn, 2003).

To begin the Imagination Station activity, you can instruct students to take their seats and put their heads down if they are comfortable doing so. Encourage them to relax, and you can suggest closing their eyes if they feel safe. You will then read from the provided script (figure 5.5, page 124) to prompt them to visualize their local landscape and the landscapes depicted in the books and digital media covered in this chapter. While we offer a complete script, we emphasize the flexibility for teachers to modify it as needed. You can tailor the experience for your students, ensuring the best possible outcomes and honoring your local landscapes. Once you finish reading the script, prompt your students to write about what they envisioned in the Imagination Station activity.

Remember
**by Joy Harjo
(2023)**

Let's start with a big, deep breath. Breathe in through your nose like you're filling up a big, bright balloon. Now, slowly let it out through your mouth. Can you feel it—that gentle rhythm, like a soft drumbeat, moving all around us?

Now, close your eyes and use your imagination. Picture yourself standing on top of the tallest building in town. The sky feels close, and the air is crisp. But look! There's a garden just for you—bright flowers swaying, tall green plants reaching up, and little herbs waving hello from their pots. It's like a happy, friendly garden waiting for you!

Listen closely—do you hear the birds singing? Their songs mix with the sounds of the city below. A soft breeze moves through the leaves, making its own little melody. Can you feel the sunshine? It's warm and golden, wrapping around you like a hug. Even the shadows on the buildings are part of the magic, dancing and changing as the day goes on.

Now, let's go on a little adventure. Imagine stepping into a big, beautiful park. The trees stand tall like gentle protectors, and their leaves rustle in the wind. When you walk, the ground crunches under your feet. What kinds of trees do you see? Each one is special!

Look—there's a pond! Can you hear the water tapping against the rocks? Ducks glide across the surface like dancers, moving so smoothly.

As we walk, we find a small, playful hill. Let's climb to the top! From here, we can see the whole city—tall buildings, busy streets, and a big, endless sky. And look! A curious squirrel, a fluttering butterfly, or maybe even a sleepy cat joins us. They make this adventure even more special.

Now, take a deep breath. Can you tell what season it is? Maybe it's warm and sunny, or maybe there's a cool breeze telling us that autumn is near. Each season has its own magic, don't you think?

Before we open our eyes, take one last look around. Is there something special you noticed? Something you want to explore more? Let's say thank you to this wonderful place—for its beauty, for its peace, and for the joy it brings.

Now, let's pick up our pencils and write about our adventure! What did you see? What did you feel?

Figure 5.5: Imagination Station script for teachers.

Literature Circle

Literature circles are small groups of students who have discussions about a specific book or text. The original Literature Circle strategy, developed by Harvey Daniels (1994), organized small student groups to discuss books in depth. These discussions promote critical thinking, collaboration, and a nuanced understanding of the text.

There are several vital components to literature circles. First, students choose a book to read together, often based on a common theme or genre. Once the book is chosen, each student takes on one of the roles within the group, such as the following. These roles help guide discussions and keep everyone engaged. In this case, for this unit, we link the roles to the book *Home, and Other Big, Fat Lies* (Wolfson, 2006).

No Bad News
by Kenneth Cole
(2001)

- **Discussion director:** This group member develops open-ended questions about the text to spark discussion. For this book, the student may act as a kind of investigator.

For example, what would the investigator ask about Termite and Striker for staying up in an old-growth tree to save it from being logged?

- **Summarizer:** This group member prepares a brief summary of the assigned reading. For this book, the summarizer may take on the role of reporter, communicating via text, providing the essential details in as few words as possible. For example, the text reporter could write a piece about why many foster children are in this logging town in Northern California.

- **Connector:** This group member makes connections between the text and other texts, their own life, or the world. In this case, this discussion may start with considering the lives of the characters beyond the story—for example, advising how this community in Northern California may want to proceed by considering the perspectives at the end of *Home, and Other Big, Fat Lies*. Connections could then grow from there.

- **Word wizard:** This group member identifies interesting, challenging, or important vocabulary in the reading. For example, the group member may find the following words to talk to their group about in chapter 1 of *Home, and Other Big, Fat Lies*: *overgrown kids*, *oogabloga*, *moogablogo* (Alaskan words for "wet snow" and "flaked snow"), *deciduous trees*, and *night owl*.

- **Illustrator:** This group member draws a visual representation of a scene, character, or concept from the reading. In this case, the student might illustrate scenes of how Termite, who has spent her life in foster homes in the city, becomes interested in spending time in the forest.

- **Passage picker:** This group member selects significant or memorable passages for the group to discuss. They guide others toward significant passages that indicate important changes for characters. For example, they might consider how Termite, Striker, and Josh grow more mature toward the story's end and pick a passage that illuminates how.

Groups meet regularly to discuss assigned parts of the text, exchanging ideas and exploring different perspectives. One task of the discussion director is to make sure all the group members have turns and "airtime." After discussions, students reflect on their learning and their process and may do projects or further research. While the teacher offers guidance and support to the groups, the focus is on student-led exploration and analysis. Literature circles help students take ownership of their learning, develop critical thinking skills, and enjoy reading and discussing books. The teacher may also choose to have each small group share their learning with the whole class in some specific way.

Tableau

Authors Carole Miller and Juliana Saxton (2004) describe the Tableau strategy as an instructional technique where students create frozen scenes, or tableaux, to represent key moments or concepts from a text, a historical event, or any subject matter being studied. Each tableau consists of students posing as characters or elements from the text or event, arranged in a still image that captures a specific scene or idea. Tableau is a drama strategy, and drama strategies are excellent ways for young people to learn multiple perspectives.

This strategy encourages engagement and comprehension by having students interpret and visualize the material. It supports kinesthetic learning, as students physically embody the content; this often fosters a profound understanding of complex concepts. It promotes collaborative learning, as students work together to create and analyze the tableaux. After creating the tableaux, students present their scenes to the class, explaining the significance of their choices and how they relate to the text or topic at hand. This presentation encourages communication skills and critical thinking as students articulate their interpretations to their peers.

When paired with *Home, and Other Big, Fat Lies*, this strategy helps students connect with environmental issues by giving them the chance to physically and emotionally step into the perspectives of people impacted by logging and climate change. Through this process, students can explore the challenges of balancing people's need to earn money with the importance of protecting nature. By embodying these perspectives, they can develop empathy and critical thinking skills while gaining a deeper understanding of the story's themes.

As the rest of the class observes each tableau, they will describe what they see—such as the emotions, conflicts, or actions portrayed in the still frames. To extend the activity, students can answer reflective questions like, "Who should we (the participants in the tableau) speak to about resolving this conflict?" This discussion will naturally lead to a closer look at two big ideas in *Home, and Other Big, Fat Lies*.

1. The value of logging to make a living
2. The importance of preserving old-growth trees as the "lungs" of the Earth, especially during climate change

Connecting the Tableau strategy to the environmental and social themes in *Home, and Other Big, Fat Lies* will help your students see the complexity of real-world issues and empower them to think critically about solutions. How might your students surprise you with their reactions to this approach, and how could you prepare to embrace their creativity?

Sketch-to-Stretch

Sketch-to-Stretch is a reading strategy that helps students visualize and deepen their understanding of a text (Short & Harste, 1996). After reading, students create quick sketches that represent their interpretations of key ideas, themes, or emotions from the story. These sketches are not meant to be works of art; rather, they are a creative way to think critically and symbolically about the content. Following sketching, your students explain their drawings, either in writing or through discussion, to reflect on and connect with the text on a deeper level.

After reading *A Park Connects Us* (Nelson, 2022), your students can use Sketch-to-Stretch to think about how the park brings the characters and community together. For example, one student might draw a simple sketch of people holding hands around a tree in the park to represent unity and friendship. Another student might draw a scene of children playing on the swings, symbolizing joy and connection. After sketching, the students can share their drawings with the class and explain why they chose to represent the story in certain ways; this will spark a thoughtful discussion about the book's themes of community and togetherness.

Compare and Contrast Authors' Messages

Compare and Contrast Authors' Messages was a key strategy used by the teachers in the Green Literacy professional development sessions that helped participants pull together (chapter 3, page 57). Comparing and contrasting involves examining similarities and differences in how authors present ideas, themes, or perspectives in their works. This strategy helps students see how different authors approach the same topic; in this way, students uncover unique messages and perspectives. It is a powerful way to encourage critical thinking, deepen understanding, and develop the ability to consider multiple viewpoints.

Butterflies on Carmen Street
by Monica Brown (2007)

Encourage your students to compare and contrast the messages and themes in the texts they have explored in class. As you support them in recognizing the central themes across the books, guide them to probe deeper by examining how the texts intersect, differ, and influence their understanding of how landscapes shape us—both broadly and personally. For example, grouping *Wild Wings* (Lewis, 2011), *A Park Connects Us* (Nelson, 2022), and *Home, and Other Big, Fat Lies* (Wolfson, 2006) allows students to explore common themes of environmental stewardship while observing how the books each highlight different approaches to taking action. *Wild Wings* emphasizes the global connection of protecting wildlife, *A Park Connects Us* focuses on community-based efforts to preserve nature, and *Home, and Other Big, Fat Lies* explores individual choices and the conflicts between economic needs and conservation.

You can challenge students to analyze how different authors approach similar ideas from distinct perspectives, how cultural contexts shape the portrayal of themes, and how characters navigate comparable challenges. For instance, your students can compare Joy Harjo's (2023) *Remember*, which emphasizes the wonder and importance of the natural environment and the interconnectedness of living things, with Denise Fleming's (1996) *Where Once There Was a Wood*, which explores the impact of commercial development on animal habitats. These comparisons let your students see how authors can highlight different aspects of environmental themes while still connecting to broader ideas about the relationship between people and nature.

You may refer to chapter 3, where we provided practical examples of how teachers used such methods during professional development sessions.

Grades K–2 Consideration

For those teachers focused on K–2, we offer the following strategy that can, of course, be adapted for higher grades.

The Directed Reading Thinking Activity (or Directed Listening Thinking Activity) "builds critical awareness of the reader's role and responsibility in interacting with stories by involving readers in predicting, verifying, judging, and extending thinking about the text" (Vacca et al., 2011, p. 363). Before reading, you identify story parts and decide on logical stopping points. You may want to record the students' responses at each of the following steps using large chart paper. For example, we use the wordless book *One Winter Up North* (Owens, 2022) for this activity.

1. As a first step, present the book's title, *One Winter Up North*, and display the cover, featuring a snowy scene. The cover depicts a warmly dressed girl holding snowshoes with a sled nearby. Engage the class by asking, "What do you think the story will be about? Why do you think so?" After generating initial ideas, proceed to read aloud, covering the setting, the introduction of characters, and the beginning event. Use the second picture, which showcases many trees and a father, a mother, and a young girl on skis or snowshoes pulling packs on sleds, with a sign indicating "BWCA Wilderness: Superior National Forest."

2. Transition to step 2 (prediction round 1) by asking, "What do you think will happen next? Why do you think so?" Encourage students to share predictions, such as the family will find a spot, set up camp with a tent, and possibly spend the night.

3. Move to step 3 (prediction round 2) with the same question: "What do you think will happen next? Why do you think so?" Read aloud and discuss attempts made to address challenges and achieve goals. For example, suggest a possible prediction like, "A young girl will get lost."

4. Continue this prediction pattern throughout the narrative, exploring subsequent events, attempts, and resolutions in the story. Highlight that predictions may initially be off the mark but can become more accurate as the story unfolds, fueled by background knowledge and experiences.

A follow-up activity is for the class to write a story with the same format as *One Winter Up North* describing a family camping trip in a different environment. For example, what would occur on a family camping trip in southern Florida near a park in the Everglades? Also, have the class consider how the experiences of the characters in the two stories—that is, *One Winter Up North* and the story written by your K–2 class—would be similar and different.

Notice how Daniel decided on strategies to best help his students engage (figure 5.6).

You've put a lot of time and effort into planning and teaching your thematic unit, and you've likely seen areas of growth and spots where there's room to improve. Before wrapping up this section, you might revisit chapters 3 and 4 if you need additional guidance.

PHASE 3: SHIFT

In this section, you will:

*   Develop Green Literacy ideals

This section, the shift phase of Green Literacy, invites you and your students to dive deeper into environmental themes by working together to create Green Literacy ideals. Through thoughtful discussions, students can share their ideas, find areas of agreement, and build a vision rooted in consensus. Unlike parts of this unit where you encourage individual

A Park Connects Us by Sarah Nelson (2022)

Select Green Literacy Strategies

What reading, writing, and drama strategies will encourage your students to express their thoughts, analyze the issue, and explore solutions?	How can you support all your students—no matter their reading level or background—to engage deeply with the issue and build their understanding?
Reading, Writing, and Drama Strategies:	Immersive Strategies:
Free-Write	Wonder Walk
Tableau	Imagination Station
Compare and Contrast Authors' Messages	

See page 45 in the book for more information on selecting Green Literacy strategies.

See page 16 in the book for more information on the three cycles of comprehension.

Figure 5.6: Completed "select Green Literacy strategies" segment of the Green Literacy Thematic Unit Planning Template.

thinking, this step is about what you and your students agree on together. While we offer a few suggestions to guide you, this is also your opportunity to create something authentic and uniquely reflective of your classroom's shared goals and collective voice.

Develop Green Literacy Ideals

At this point, encourage your students to look back at their experiences and insights to see how landscapes shape their own lives and communities. This reflection isn't about reviewing what they've learned—it's about shifting their perspectives to collectively recognize the subtle ways landscapes influence them. Reflecting together and developing Green Literacy ideals will help them connect the dots between their observations and broader environmental impacts, leading to a more nuanced and meaningful appreciation of the landscapes around them.

Green Literacy ideals generated by your class will be influenced by the books and media you choose, the themes you discuss, and whether you involve your students in the suggested immersive activities—in this case, Wonder Walk and Imagination Station.

If you decide to engage your students with the books *Remember* and *Where Once There Was a Wood*, the Green Literacy ideals your class thinks of may be similar to the following: "Animals, like all living things, must be respected and allowed to have places to live." If you engage your students with *Home, and Other Big, Fat Lies*, a corresponding ideal may be this: "Sometimes making a living can bring challenges around taking care of nature."

Letting Swift River Go
by Jane Yolen
(1992)

As we have noted, developing Green Literacy ideals is an intentional and impactful action step, one that is hard-earned and meaningful. Without this critical step, and without commitment to further or future action, the work risks losing its longevity. It is through the depth of critical thinking, the consensus-building process, and the shared ownership of Green Literacy ideals that students can ensure their learning endures and continues to inspire. As you go through that deep reflective work with your students, ask them as a final reflection, "How can working together on Green Literacy ideals help make a lasting difference?" and "What can you do to help Green Literacy ideals stay strong and meaningful?"

Creating Green Literacy ideals is a process, and in that process, we suggest you consider how Daniel approached it. Figure 5.7 features his answers for this step of the planning template.

Consider referring to chapter 2 for more guidance on creating Green Literacy ideals and to chapter 3 for how teachers and their students created them. Please refer to chapter 4 for more insights.

CONCLUSION

This chapter explored how different landscapes influence our identity and sense of belonging and how personal relationships are fostered with the places that shape us. It encouraged reflection on land acknowledgment statements and inspired meaningful discussions about the natural world and our connections with it.

As you progressed through the chapter, you found practical supports in Green Reads and Views and strategies to help students explore environmental themes. These tools guided you in either using our ready-made thematic unit, designing your own unit around the same themes, or doing a combination of both. They connect students to the landscapes around them, encouraging both critical thinking and emotional engagement.

You may have found that as your students' perspectives shifted, your own understanding of your landscape deepened or shifted as well. This journey was a chance to honor those changes and new perspectives.

Now, consider how this chapter has impacted your learning as a teacher. We offer a dedicated space for you to do so in the following "Teacher's Corner" reproducible tool (also available at **go.SolutionTree.com/literacy**). Whether you're working on your own, with a teaching partner, or within a schoolwide learning network, after exploring chapter 5, we encourage you to reflect on what you've learned.

PHASE 3: SHIFT

Develop Green Literacy Ideals

As you work with your students to create their Green Literacy ideals, remember this is something that happens naturally during your teaching. You can plan all the other steps ahead of time, but for this last part, you'll need to pause and observe how your students respond.

Reflection 1

As you plan how to guide your students in creating their Green Literacy ideals, take a moment to think about the lessons you've already taught. How did your students respond during these activities? What really stood out to you? Write down some notes or free-write about what you noticed happening in your classroom.

> Students were intrigued by how the land in our area has changed over time. They asked thoughtful questions about what the landscape might have looked like when their grandparents were young and how those changes affected families and their work.
>
> Discussions about families losing their farms to large companies prompted students to reflect on what it means to lose something tied to your identity. They showed a lot of empathy during these conversations.

Reflection 2

In your free-writing, think about what stood out to you during class discussions about the books. What were some interesting things your students said about using the reading and writing strategies?

> What stood out most was how students responded when learning about how Native Americans lived sustainably, in harmony with the landscape. They were fascinated by the idea of using resources like rivers for transportation and forests for food without harming the land for future generations.
>
> We also discussed how many Native American tribes were displaced from their ancestral lands as settlers arrived and reshaped the area for farming and urban development. Students expressed empathy, with several asking questions about what happened to those communities and where they are today.

See page 47 in the book for more information on how to facilitate the Green Literacy ideals discussion.

Figure 5.7: Completed "develop Green Literacy ideals" segment of the Green Literacy Thematic Unit Planning Template.

Teacher's Corner

Here are some questions to support your reflection.

- How can nurturing a personal appreciation for nature enhance your ability as a teacher to instill similar values in your students?

- How can sharing personal experiences with nature create a more inclusive and engaging learning environment in your classroom?

Here are prompts for journaling.

- Describe a lesson or activity you have implemented in your classroom that aimed to cultivate a sense of environmental appreciation among students. What challenges did you face, and what positive outcomes did you observe?

- What Green Literacy ideals did your class come up with? What observations did you make about your students? How did their thinking shift? Did your own thinking shift? How different (or similar) would your Green Literacy ideals be to your students' ideals?

Here are discussion guidelines.

- Why is sharing your experiences and understanding of nature essential for teaching? How did you share them before Green Literacy, and how can modeling this process help students build environmental awareness and reach consensus?

- How can educators play a pivotal role in shaping a school culture that prioritizes appreciation of nature and consequently contributes to broad conservation efforts?

CHAPTER 6

How Extreme Weather Events Connect Our Communities

> If we are to have a chance of minimizing further irreparable damage, we now have to choose: either we safeguard living conditions for all future generations, or we let a few very fortunate people maintain their constant, destructive search to maximize immediate profits.
>
> **—GRETA THUNBERG**

In this chapter, we provide ideas on how extreme weather events connect our communities, examine the challenges faced by weather refugees, and ponder how climate anxiety affects young people. You'll learn about resilience and the power of collaborative courage when dealing with extreme weather. Here, you are not simply presented with a ready-made unit to use as is; instead, you are encouraged to tailor and implement these concepts to suit the unique needs and dynamics of your classroom. We guide you through the individual steps that compose the larger Green Literacy actions of engage, empower, and shift. As in chapter 5, we offer a completed Green Literacy Thematic Unit Planning Template through the lens of a composite teacher to support and inspire you. You can follow along and customize the blank template, considering your teaching context.

PHASE 1: ENGAGE

In this section, you will:

- Develop your thematic question
- Foster your thinking through commentary

Chapter Snapshot—What You'll Explore

In this chapter, we share with you how to:

- Discover ways that extreme weather connects our communities and impacts our connections with the world and our places within it

- Organize a unit

- Pick Green Reads and Views and Green Literacy strategies, including K–2 consideration

- Navigate critical thinking, reading, speaking, and writing to create Green Literacy ideals

In the engage phase in this chapter, we examine the impacts of extreme weather events and provide thematic questions and commentary to help you navigate this complex issue in your classroom. This section is designed to support your exploration of environmental challenges in how extreme weather impacts our communities, offering a foundation for meaningful discussions and unit development.

In our completed example sections of the planning template, we have provided a composite example as a guide, framed from the perspective of a fourth-grade teacher in an urban setting, whom we call Helen. You can directly use this unit, modify it, or create your own approach, as outlined in chapter 2 and modeled in chapter 3. To keep the focus clear, template figures include only the relevant segment being discussed, as you saw in chapter 5.

Additionally, this chapter prompts reflection on your willingness to engage with environmental issues and your school community's potential response. These are considerations only you can assess. As you work through this phase, think about how to adapt these ideas for your students, noting adjustments that align with their needs and your teaching approach.

Develop Your Thematic Question

When we look closely, it's clear that extreme weather connects us all. Hurricanes devastate coastal areas, but their impacts ripple far beyond, causing widespread flooding and agricultural disruptions that affect food supply chains and prices across the United States. Wildfires in the West degrade air quality for people thousands of miles away. Droughts in farming regions can lead to food shortages and higher costs. These interconnected effects demonstrate how extreme weather events in one place affect communities everywhere—economically, environmentally, and socially.

For this unit, we chose the thematic question, "How do extreme weather events connect our communities?" because it builds on the foundation laid by the question in the previous chapter: "How do landscapes shape us?" While the earlier thematic question focused on the physical and emotional connections young learners have with their surroundings, this thematic question expands the focus to include communities. It encourages students to think critically about how environmental changes, such as extreme weather events, flow through interconnected communities, fostering both challenges and opportunities for collaboration and resilience.

As always, if you feel inclined, you can adapt this process and create your own thematic question. Consider exploring big-picture questions such as, "How does extreme weather shape the way we live and work?" or "What can we learn from how communities respond to climate challenges?" You might ask, "What role do we play in building resilience and solutions for the future?" These types of questions allow you to look closely into the chapter's themes while tailoring the inquiry to your students' unique needs and frames of reference. The template is a starting point. Your insights and creativity can guide the development of a question. Consider teacher Helen's process as she developed her thematic question (figure 6.1).

Now that you have explored and chosen a thematic question, we support your thinking by providing commentaries designed as starting points for deeper reflection and planning.

Name: Helen (twelve years of teaching experience)

Grade level: Fourth grade

School context: Urban

PHASE 1: ENGAGE

Develop Your Thematic Question

Here are some guiding questions to consider as you develop your thematic question. Reflect on these prompts to clarify your focus.

1. Brainstorm

- What issue that could lead to a big idea about the environment are you most passionate about exploring with your students?

  I am most passionate about exploring with my students extreme weather events and how they affect our lives. I want them to understand how storms, rain, and other types of weather can change the places we live and the way we live. I wonder, too, if these extreme weather events might be a way for communities to connect to each other.

- What current events or real-world examples resonate with you and can help bring environmental issues to life for your students?

  One current issue that really stands out to me is that some of my students are new to our area because they had to leave their homes after the hurricanes. These big storms can cause so much damage, and families sometimes have to move to find a safer place to live. I think it's important for my students to understand how the environment and extreme weather can affect people's lives and the places they call home.

  I also see that some of my students are worried about how the weather changes—lots of snow, wildfires, and floods.

2. Prioritize

You might have more than one environmental issue you'd like to explore with your students. Now, think about which one will create the most meaningful conversations and learning.

  My students are curious but still learning about how weather affects their lives and the environment. I might need to take into consideration their emotions and feelings. Our school community is open to lessons that connect to our local area, and I think my administration would support a thematic question that focuses on something familiar, like extreme weather and its impact on our communities.

Figure 6.1: Completed "develop your thematic question" segment of the Green Literacy Thematic Unit Planning Template.

Continued ▶

> *While climate change is a tough topic and one my administrators would be supportive of learning, I want to make sure that I don't "doom and gloom." I'm very willing to engage with this issue because it helps my students connect to the environment in a meaningful way, especially if I can show how weather can connect our communities.*
>
> Through this brainstorming and prioritization process, write your thematic question. Some stems that might be useful are:
>
> - How can/do . . . ?
> - What might . . . ?
>
> Write your thematic question here.
>
> **How do extreme weather events connect our communities?**
>
> *See page 38 in the book for more information on creating thematic questions.*

Foster Your Thinking Through Commentary

We share commentaries to ignite curiosity and deepen critical thinking about the impact of extreme weather. These commentaries offer foundational knowledge and context to support you as you explore the impact of extreme weather on communities and their interconnections. Like all commentaries in this handbook, they are starting places.

As you engage with this step, actively brainstorm how to implement these ideas in your teaching. Consider how your students might interact with the complexities of extreme weather and the ways communities respond.

The following sections look at the topic through these lenses.

- **Explore the impact of extreme weather:** Extreme weather shifts our narrative as it disrupts learning and causes economic loss through school closures, infrastructure damage, and increased insurance costs, straining our community.

- **Navigate climate anxiety in the classroom:** Many young people suffer from anxiety due to extreme weather, especially young people who become climate refugees.

- **Teach resilience and create collaborative courage:** You can teach resilience to extreme weather by considering the seven Rs of resilience, teaching collaborative courage, and empowering students to work together for sustainable actions.

Explore the Impact of Extreme Weather

Extreme weather events are reshaping classrooms, communities, and the lives of students. These disruptions bring instability, loss, and uncertainty, affecting students' ability to learn and connect. While the media often amplifies destruction, it rarely captures the resilience and solidarity that emerge in the aftermath.

Each year, 175 million children worldwide are affected by natural disasters (Lai & La Greca, 2020). Wildfires have devastated towns like Paradise, California, and vast regions of

Australia and Greece. Hurricanes have battered the Gulf Coast, while catastrophic floods in Pakistan and extreme tornadoes in the United States have displaced thousands. Globally, events like Cyclone Idai in Mozambique and severe European heat waves highlight the far-reaching consequences of climate change. From 2010 to 2019, the United States alone experienced 119 separate billion-dollar natural disasters (Climate Central, 2020).

These disasters force families to relocate, making them climate refugees—people displaced due to extreme weather conditions (McLeman & Gemenne, 2018). Schools across the United States welcome students who have lost homes and stability. After Hurricane Katrina, four hundred thousand students had to relocate due to the destruction of 110 out of 126 public schools in New Orleans (Oblack, 2019). Behind each statistic is a young person navigating an uncertain future.

In times of crisis, communities unite—opening shelters, providing meals, and offering support. These acts of care become living lessons in environmental literacy, demonstrating the power of collective action. Schools play a key role in fostering resilience, empathy, and problem solving to help students understand and respond to climate challenges.

Recognizing the interdependence among people, animals, and ecosystems helps students see the wider impact of climate change.

- Extreme weather destroys crops, leading to food shortages and economic instability.

- Wildlife faces habitat loss—sea turtles abandon breeding areas, migratory birds struggle to complete journeys, and elephants cross borders searching for water.

- Rising temperatures intensify storms, floods, and droughts, reshaping landscapes and forcing communities to adapt (Intergovernmental Panel on Climate Change, 2019).

We at Green Literacy acknowledge that extreme weather events are linked to climate change. We also acknowledge that climate change can be a tricky topic to teach because it's sometimes seen as controversial. Some families or communities may have strong opinions and differing perspectives about it, which can create resistance when it comes up in class. To handle this, we suggest framing discussions by shared values like responsibility, care for others, and stewardship to make the topic more accessible and less divisive (Moser, 2007). This approach can help bring people together instead of causing division. We acknowledge that teaching climate change in grades K–5 requires careful thought to ensure it is age-appropriate and meaningful for young learners. At this age, students are starting to explore the natural world and build the critical thinking skills needed to understand complex issues. Introducing climate change through relatable examples, like how floods or heat waves impact their community, can make the topic easier to grasp. Focusing on solutions, like planting trees or conserving water, helps students feel hopeful and empowered rather than overwhelmed (Ojala, 2012). Using stories, hands-on activities, and real-life connections lets students engage with the topic in a way that feels relevant and positive.

As you think about the planning and teaching of this unit, consider how you and your students have been affected by extreme weather, which will depend on the geographic

Pause and Consider: How can you help your students build understanding of climate issues while fostering empathy, collaboration, and a sense of responsibility for their world? How can you use different viewpoints to help students explore the impact of extreme weather?

location of your school. Consider whether you or your students have been affected personally and if you know of students who have relocated because of extreme weather events. Both extreme weather and relocations can be impactful for students, so these experiences could be worthwhile topics to bring into your classroom. We often urge teachers to consider when privacy is at stake. We encourage teachers to have conversations about privacy and when it's appropriate and safe to share personal stories. Our hope is that as students have discussions about privacy, they may realize that sharing personal stories can create trust among themselves and their classmates.

Navigate Climate Anxiety in the Classroom

Young people today face the burden of an uncertain future, witnessing biodiversity loss, environmental degradation, and the increasing frequency of extreme weather events. Seeing images of climate disasters can profoundly affect students, often stirring fear, sadness, or helplessness in them. Younger students may feel overwhelmed, while older students begin asking urgent questions—"Why is this happening?" "What can we do?" Without the right tools, these emotions can lead to climate anxiety, a growing stress response to environmental collapse and the uncertainty of the future (Clayton, Manning, Krygsman, & Speiser, 2017). This reality takes an emotional toll—leading to anxiety, grief, and frustration. Supporting students through this means equipping them with knowledge, fostering resilience, and creating opportunities for action to help them develop personal and meaningful connections to the natural world.

The EPA (2025a) notes that children exposed to natural disasters and extreme weather may suffer from anxiety, depression, sleep disturbances, and post-traumatic stress. Their ability to cope depends on environmental stability and support systems, and their concerns often extend beyond personal experience to worries about the planet's future. Many of us in classrooms today have witnessed students suffering from climate anxiety. Consider these possible examples of young people's climate anxiety.

- Lily from Miami worries about rising sea levels and fears that her family may need to relocate.

- Diego from Fresno experiences poor air quality from wildfires, forcing him to wear a mask at school and stay indoors.

- Omar from London has seen severe flooding damage his neighborhood, making him wonder how climate change is increasing these events.

- Ava from Toronto faces unpredictable winters; she worries about how extreme ice storms will impact her daily life.

- Emma from Houston fears hurricanes and flooding and is concerned about potential evacuations and damage to her home.

These stories highlight how climate anxiety affects young minds. For students to develop emotional resilience, they need classroom spaces that acknowledge their concerns, resources that explore climate issues, and opportunities to take meaningful action. Providing books, digital media, and environmental projects like the ones found in *The Green Literacy Handbook* can help students productively process these fears (Hickman et al., 2021).

Our role as educators is vital in balancing tough environmental realities with empowerment and action. Research emphasizes the importance of emotional connections to nature, which build resilience and environmental stewardship (Judson, 2015; Keith, Brasier, & North, 2022). Engaging students in hands-on projects, discussions, and activism allows them to channel their concerns into meaningful change.

Gratefully, more educators are recognizing the need to integrate emotional support into environmental learning. Thought leaders like David W. Orr (2004) and Fritjof Capra (1996) advocate for teaching sustainability through hope, active engagement, and student empowerment. As Orr (2011) reminds us, "Hope is a verb with its sleeves rolled up" (p. 324).

As you think about the planning and teaching of this unit, consider how you and your students become anxious around the uncertainty of extreme weather. Dialoguing about such happenings in our lives can be helpful for emotional maturity. As before, the experiences brought forth in the discussion are likely to be dependent on the weather in your geographic location.

Teach Resilience and Create Collaborative Courage

Given the emotional impact that climate change can have on young people, a proactive approach for addressing that impact is beneficial. Kenneth R. Ginsburg, a pediatrician, professor, and author of several books on resilience, has developed a model that offers a framework for understanding resilience. He calls it the *seven Cs*: (1) competence, (2) confidence, (3) connection, (4) character, (5) contribution, (6) coping, and (7) control. These components are designed to empower individuals, particularly children and adolescents, to navigate life's challenges effectively (Ginsburg, 2011). Ginsburg's holistic approach emphasizes the development of skills and attributes that foster a robust and resilient personality.

The seven Cs he refers to are broken down as follows.

1. *Competence* involves mastering skills and knowledge.

2. *Confidence* is about believing in one's abilities.

3. *Connection* relates to establishing strong, supportive relationships.

4. *Character* involves developing a sense of right and wrong.

5. *Contribution* focuses on the importance of giving back to society.

6. *Coping* highlights the ability to manage stress and adversity.

7. *Control* underscores the belief in one's influence over life events.

At Green Literacy, we have adapted Ginsburg's seven Cs of resilience (see table 6.1, page 140) to help facilitate meaningful discussions about extreme weather events and climate change so students are well informed and equipped to resiliently engage with these global challenges.

Pause and Consider: How might integrating emotional support into your teaching help students balance climate realities with a hopeful and proactive outlook?

Table 6.1: Ginsburg's (2011) Seven Cs of Resilience, Adapted for Green Literacy Discussions About Extreme Weather

Competence	Teachers can provide students with knowledge and skills related to extreme weather events, the science behind these phenomena, emergency preparedness, and the importance of environmental conservation. Role-playing scenarios and problem-solving exercises can enhance students' competence in managing such situations.
Confidence	Encouraging students to participate in class discussions, share their thoughts on climate resilience, and engage in projects that contribute to environmental solutions can boost their confidence. Recognizing and celebrating their achievements and contributions builds their belief in their ability to make a difference.
	Encourage students to express their ideas and solutions for climate change, reinforcing their confidence in their ability to contribute to meaningful conversations and actions regarding environmental issues.
Connection	Foster a classroom environment that emphasizes teamwork on climate-related projects, such as community cleanups or sustainability initiatives. This highlights the importance of connection by showing students how collective efforts can make an impact.
	Facilitating group discussions on environmental sustainability or community service related to disaster preparedness fosters a sense of connection among students. Encouraging empathy and support within the classroom creates a supportive environment where students feel they belong and are understood.
Character	Engage students in ethical discussions about the responsibility of individuals, communities, and nations toward the environment.
	Discussing ethical considerations and the social impact of extreme weather events can help develop students' character.
	Debates and discussions on topics like environmental justice, sustainability, and the responsibility of individuals and communities promote moral reasoning and integrity.
Contribution	Organize activities that allow students to contribute to their community's environmental health, such as planting trees or creating educational materials on recycling for the community.
	Providing opportunities for students to contribute to their community's resilience, such as through tree planting, cleanup initiatives, or educational outreach, emphasizes the value of their input.
Coping	Teach coping strategies for eco-anxiety, a common response to learning about the impacts of climate change. Techniques like mindfulness, actionable steps, and solution-oriented discussions can help students manage their concerns constructively.
	Teaching students to express emotions through art or writing helps them deal with the anxiety or fear that may come with learning about extreme weather events. Creating a safe space for students to share their feelings and fears is central.
Control	Empower students by highlighting how their actions can influence environmental outcomes. Discussions and projects that focus on personal and collective actions for sustainability, such as reducing waste or advocating for renewable energy, can demonstrate the control they have over making a positive impact on the planet.
	Empowering students to take actionable steps toward climate resilience, like reducing waste, promoting recycling, or engaging in advocacy, helps them realize their control over their environment and future. Classroom discussions can focus on how individual actions contribute to larger environmental outcomes.

Young people learn resilience when they hear about individuals and communities that, faced with devastation, come together to rebuild and often create something stronger and more united than before. They learn courage by seeing people confront challenges head-on, make tough decisions, and take bold steps to secure a safer future. These stories nurture hope, showing that, despite loss and destruction, growth and rebuilding are possible.

Often, it's us, the teachers, who become powerful role models by sharing our own experiences of resilience in the face of environmental upheavals. Our ability to navigate loss caused by extreme weather events demonstrates that embracing these challenges can lead to growth and adaptation. This approach extends beyond emotional well-being, preparing students for the inevitable impacts of climate change in their lives. As students learn to lean into loss within the context of extreme weather events, they develop basic life skills and cultivate a deep understanding of the need for collective action in addressing environmental issues. Leaning into loss becomes a transformative force that shapes the next generation's emotional intelligence and environmental consciousness.

As you think about the planning and teaching of this unit, consider how you can bolster your students' competence and confidence around extreme weather events in their lives through role play and expression of their ideas. You can have ethical discussions where each student may express different ideas and make unique contributions as well as cope by taking actions that make sense to them.

Our idea for bringing communities together is to act with what we call collaborative courage in the face of environmental challenges. We define *collaborative courage* as when young people come together with shared bravery and resilience to address environmental and climate change issues in their schools and communities.

Collaborative courage uses empathy, cooperation, and shared efforts. When young people demonstrate collaborative courage, they combine their skills, knowledge, and resources to accomplish something they couldn't do as effectively on their own. Their collaborative courage is driven by a mutual understanding of the urgency and magnitude of environmental threats and a shared commitment to sustainable practices and solutions—reached collectively for all to benefit.

We draw inspiration from the work of Wangari Maathai (2006), Dian Fossey (1983), Jamie Margolin (2020), and Winona LaDuke (1999), who have all shown collaborative courage in their unique ways and taken a stand for environmental and social justice. Their stories, along with those that young people will share about themselves and their communities, can be nurtured so that all will be uplifted through them.

As you think about the planning and teaching of this unit, consider your students' experiences working with a teacher or with other students on a project where they thought they made a difference. (These experiences may relate to areas other than environmental issues.) You can explore with your students how these experiences impacted them.

Pause and Consider: How might you share your personal experiences of resilience to help your students navigate challenges? How can these elements equip young people with the mental, emotional, and social tools to build resilience, face challenges, recover from setbacks, and thrive in a rapidly changing world?

Green Literacy's Stance on Including Social-Emotional Learning When Teaching About Extreme Weather's Connection to Climate Change

The stark picture of a hungry polar bear stranded on melting ice was once the emblematic image of climate change. This past climate change messaging, often grim and frightening in its urgency, may have been off-putting. However, with time and a deeper understanding of climate change, teachers have grown in their appreciation for the roles that emotion and storytelling play in education. Green Literacy recognizes that to effectively teach about climate change, we need to engage with stories that resonate emotionally, inspiring both concern and hope for action aligned with sensitivity to our young people's social and emotional health.

Using social-emotional learning (SEL) when discussing extreme weather events with young people is essential because it helps them process their emotions and develop resilience. SEL provides tools to manage stress, foster empathy, and build supportive relationships, which are crucial in coping with the anxiety and trauma associated with extreme weather events (Jones & Doolittle, 2017).

Integrating SEL into climate change discussions helps students connect emotionally with the topic. SEL provides for a supportive environment where both teachers and students can explore their emotions, which makes it easier for them to understand complex environmental challenges. It equips students with coping skills to manage intense feelings like fear, anxiety, and hopelessness while fostering self-awareness and self-regulation. Through SEL, students learn the impact of climate change and are inspired to advocate for vulnerable communities and ecosystems. Students also develop enhanced collaboration and communication skills, which enable effective teamwork and innovative solutions.

Through building resilience, SEL prepares students to face environmental crises with adaptability and perseverance. Moreover, SEL supports critical thinking and informed decision making, empowering students to evaluate the credibility of information and recognize the urgency of taking action. It cultivates a sense of agency and responsibility, motivating students to make positive changes in their communities and beyond (Weissberg, 2019).

Consider how Helen explored ways to foster her thinking through commentary (figure 6.2). What areas might you be interested in diving deeper into?

Now that you've explored the commentary for this chapter, you're ready to use these insights to support your students. As you move on to phase 2, empower, keep in mind the ideas you've learned. You can build on them as you continue your learning and develop your thematic unit.

PHASE 2: EMPOWER

In this section, you will:

- Cultivate a list of Green Reads and Views
- Select Green Literacy strategies

Foster Your Thinking Through Commentary

First, review the following questions and respond to a few or all of them. Use a list or brainstorm freely to capture your ideas.

- Whose voices or stories do you need to hear to understand this issue, and why are they important to you?

    I'm interested in stories of people who have experienced extreme weather events.

    I'd like to find information on how young people cope with extreme weather events emotionally.

    I want to explore how extreme weather is connected to climate change.

- What unfair systems or problems do you want your students to think about when learning about this issue, and how can you help them ask questions and find ways to make things better?

    I want my students to think about unfair systems that make it harder for some people to recover from extreme weather events. For example, not everyone has the same access to resources like food, clean water, or safe shelter when a storm or flood happens. I can help my students ask questions like, "Why do some neighborhoods take longer to rebuild?" or "How can we make sure everyone gets the help they need?"

- Whose experiences or ideas are sometimes left out when this issue is talked about, and how can you share those voices in your classroom to help everyone learn more?

    I would like to explore how people are affected by extreme weather and how animals are impacted, too.

From your responses, begin to find springboards that will help you develop commentary that deepens your thematic exploration.

Springboards to Support Commentary

- Springboard 1: *Lai & La Greca, 2020*
    - Title or source: *Impact of extreme weather*
    - Key insights: *Facts about extreme weather and its impacts on people, animals, and land*
- Springboard 2
    - Title or source: *Climate anxiety search*
    - Key insights: *Young people worry about the Earth's future and climate change—their emotional health matters.*
- Springboard 3: *Resilience and collaborative courage*
    - Title or source: *Seven Cs of resilience (Ginsburg, 2011)*
    - Key insights: *How to understand resilience in young people*

See page 40 in the book for more information on developing springboards for commentary.

Figure 6.2: Completed "foster your thinking through commentary" segment of the Green Literacy Thematic Unit Planning Template.

The focus now shifts to the choices you make as a teacher to empower your students and amplify their environmental awareness of how extreme weather events connect communities. Your next steps are to curate your Green Reads and Views and select strategies to use.

As you move through empower, consider:

- How Green Reads and Views can foster environmental awareness by exposing students to diverse perspectives

- How strategies can inspire creativity, collaboration, and critical thinking

- How planning can balance structure with flexibility to meet your students where they are

- What stories or examples from students' lives you could use to make the learning more meaningful

Our House Is on Fire: Greta Thunberg's Call to Save the Planet
by Jeanette Winter
(2020)

This phase empowers you to create your own thematic unit tailored to your students' needs. We recommend designing your unit to last between two and four weeks. However, you may choose to extend or shorten this time frame depending on the needs of your students and the dynamics of your school.

Cultivate a List of Green Reads and Views

It's time to curate your Green Reads and Views. This chapter's thematic question, "How do extreme weather events connect our communities?," has the potential to include many areas. Because of this, we have placed the suggested books for this chapter into six categories: (1) extreme weather events impacting our communities, (2) animals in extreme weather events, (3) climate change, (4) experiences of extreme weather, (5) relationships with plants and animals, and (6) refugee experiences. A full list of resources for this chapter is available at **go.SolutionTree.com/literacy**. The books featured on the leaves throughout the chapter are our top picks, and some also appear in the planning template. If you want to use books or digital media not on the list, revisit chapter 2 (page 31) for guiding questions to help with your selections.

In figure 6.3, take note of the choices Helen made. How do they compare to yours?

Select Green Literacy Strategies

The strategies outlined in this section support critical thinking and empower students to make meaningful connections among their lives, the texts they read, and the larger world. At the same time, we encourage you to incorporate any of your own tried-and-true methods that have proven effective. As the teacher, you are in the process of curating strategies to align with your thematic unit, ensuring they resonate with your students' needs and your classroom's goals. Here, you are not merely observing a suggested classroom unit; you are encouraged to actively adapt and implement these ideas in the unique context of

PHASE 2: EMPOWER

Cultivate a List of Green Reads and Views

Consider the three cycles of comprehension as you choose your strategies: simple comprehension (retell and summarize), criteria comprehension (support thinking), and perspective comprehension (investigate explicit and implicit perspectives and move to systems thinking).

Select texts and digital media that flow from your thematic question and your commentary research. If you need help finding texts or digital media, consult **go.SolutionTree.com/literacy**, our companion website (www.greenliteracy.org), or your school or local librarian.

What types of texts or stories (fiction, nonfiction, poetry, or multimedia) can you use to help your students connect emotionally and critically to this environmental issue? What is the author's message?

After looking at the lists and talking with my teacher friend, I think these five books are perfect for my class.

Green Reads
Title: <u>Our House Is on Fire: Greta Thunberg's Call to Save the Planet</u> by Jeanette Winter (2020) Author's message: Students' activism on extreme weather
Title: <u>Mario and the Hole in the Sky: How a Chemist Saved Our Planet</u> by Elizabeth Rusch (2019b) Author's message: When we work together across nations, we make positive change.
Title: <u>The Day War Came</u> by Nicola Davies (2018) Author's message: How war impacts a young girl, who becomes a refugee
Title: <u>Lauren's Story: An American Dog in Paris</u> by Kay Pfaltz (2002) Author's message: More about being a newcomer
Title: <u>A Mama for Owen</u> by Marion Dane Bauer (2007) Author's message: Finding connection after extreme weather events

Figure 6.3: Completed "cultivate a list of Green Reads and Views" segment of the Green Literacy Thematic Unit Planning Template.

your classroom. As you move through this section, ask yourself, "How could this look in my classroom? What changes would make this approach most effective for my students?"

We present the following strategies for you to explore, many of which are paired with a Green Read to illustrate their applications.

- **Turn-and-Talk Conversation Cards:** These cards frame a prereading and postreading discussion strategy.

Mario and the Hole in the Sky: How a Chemist Saved Our Planet
by Elizabeth Rusch (2019b)

- **Immersive strategies:** Immersive strategies fully engage students by sparking curiosity and creativity through hands-on experiences.

  - *Human Knot*—Students form a "knot" by holding hands in a circle and work together to untangle themselves without letting go. Concluding dialogue concerns how this entanglement relates to ideas about our interconnectedness in light of extreme weather events.

  - *Web of Life*—Students take on roles as different organisms within an ecosystem, using string to make connections based on their relationships. Then dialogue focuses on what happens when one part of the web is disrupted.

- **Strategies toward the three cycles of comprehension:** These strategies focus on an author's ideas about how extreme weather events connect our communities and how young people can support their ideas through personal connection, text-to-text connection, and text-to-world connection.

  - *Intra-Act*—After reading a selected text, the teacher and students discuss the ideas in that reading selection. Then students discuss what they think of the author's ideas in small groups, react by themselves to value statements related to the selection, predict what they think the other group members' reactions might be, and then tell one another if they guessed correctly. The whole class then reflects on why consideration of classmates' values could be important when it comes to such complex issues as how severe weather impacts our communities.

  - *Visual Mapping*—By creating visual representations of characters' relationships in a story, or mapping them, students examine how the characters come together around such actions as protecting their homes, supporting each other during extreme weather events, and rebuilding afterward.

  - *Compare and Contrast Authors' Messages*—Students compare and contrast themes within texts chosen for the teaching unit.

The Day War Came
by Nicola Davies (2018)

As you choose your Green Literacy strategies, remember that chapter 3 (page 57) offers a model thematic unit created during a Green Literacy professional development experience. Chapter 4 (page 79) offers tips for developing a unit. Please refer to either chapter if needed as you use this ready-made unit, customize it, or develop your own new unit.

Next, we provide descriptions and examples for each strategy to model how you can implement them in your context.

Turn-and-Talk Conversation Cards

As with the thematic unit focused on how landscapes shape us, here, too, we recommend starting with the Turn-and-Talk Conversation Cards, as shown in figure 6.4. These cards are a great way to spark excitement among your students for the upcoming thematic unit. You can revisit them throughout the unit to see how your students' ideas have evolved and use them to reflect after the unit is complete. You can approach these questions with your whole group, have students discuss them with an elbow partner in a turn-and-talk, or use them as journal prompts. Additionally, you can guide students into perspective comprehension by discussing how the characters in the books or media you're focusing on might answer these questions. This approach helps deepen their understanding and encourages critical thinking.

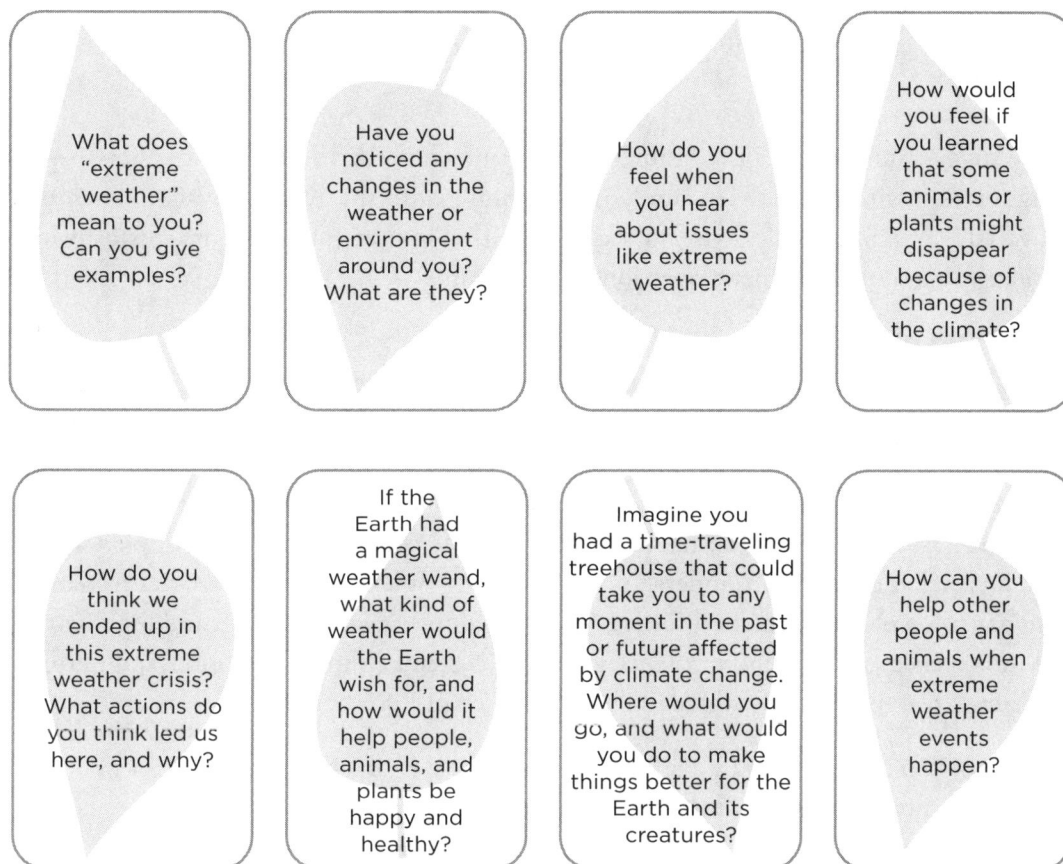

What does "extreme weather" mean to you? Can you give examples?	Have you noticed any changes in the weather or environment around you? What are they?	How do you feel when you hear about issues like extreme weather?	How would you feel if you learned that some animals or plants might disappear because of changes in the climate?
How do you think we ended up in this extreme weather crisis? What actions do you think led us here, and why?	If the Earth had a magical weather wand, what kind of weather would the Earth wish for, and how would it help people, animals, and plants be happy and healthy?	Imagine you had a time-traveling treehouse that could take you to any moment in the past or future affected by climate change. Where would you go, and what would you do to make things better for the Earth and its creatures?	How can you help other people and animals when extreme weather events happen?

Figure 6.4: Turn-and-Talk Conversation Cards.
*Visit **go.SolutionTree.com/literacy** for a free reproducible version of this figure.*

Human Knot

Adapted from common team-building practices used in educational and group-dynamics contexts, the Human Knot is a tried-and-true activity with a new spin that connects teamwork to real-world challenges like extreme weather events. In this version, students form a knot by holding hands in a circle and work together to untangle themselves without letting go. Do the Human Knot strategy by following these steps.

1. Divide students into groups of six to ten. Each group stands in a tight circle, shoulder to shoulder. Students reach into the circle with their right hand and grab someone else's hand—not the hand of someone standing next to them. They do the

same with their left hand, creating a knot. The challenge is for the group members to untangle themselves back into a full circle without letting go of each other's hands. The group requires careful communication, teamwork, and problem solving to succeed.

2. After the activity, facilitate a discussion about what happened. What strategies helped untangle the knot? What happened when someone let go? Use this reflection to explore how the act of tangling and untangling as a group relates to extreme weather events—what might it mean if one community received help while another didn't?

We suggest starting with the Human Knot. And we invite you to consider how beginning the unit with this activity, similar to beginning with the Wonder Walk in chapter 5 (page 107), might provide a visceral experience that ignites your students' curiosity and excitement about the thematic question for this unit.

Web of Life

The Web of Life strategy is an interactive and immersive game to help your students understand the interconnectedness of ecosystems—in the case of this unit, ecosystems affected by extreme weather events. In this activity, your students take on the perspectives of different organisms within an ecosystem, using string to make connections based on their relationships. As they explore what happens when one part of the web is disrupted, they'll gain a visual and hands-on understanding of the complex interdependencies in nature. This game is a powerful method for teaching environmental stewardship and highlighting the importance of maintaining balance within ecosystems (Illinois Extension, n.d.; Project Learning Tree, n.d.). Follow these steps for the Web of Life strategy.

I Am the Storm
by Jane Yolen
and Heidi E. Y.
Stemple (2020)

1. To set up the game, draw a large circle in the center of a big piece of paper or poster board to represent the Earth. Surround this central circle with smaller circles representing different natural elements (for example, an insect, a cloud, sunlight, a frog, a pond, a wilted plant and a healthy plant [with the implication that the plants are in different contexts], and so on), and put representative pictures inside each smaller circle.

2. Cut yarn or string into various lengths.

3. Have players take turns selecting an element on the paper or poster board and explaining its connection to another (for example, plants need sunlight for photosynthesis). Connect the chosen element to its related element with yarn, using tape to attach each end in the right spot.

4. Continue until all elements are interconnected, forming a weblike pattern.

We suggest you have this interactive learning experience toward the end of the thematic unit so that students can act on the information and knowledge they've learned from the books and media, the comprehension questions, and the extended learning activities encountered in the unit. In the following list, we offer examples of extreme weather events influenced by climate change, as well as a community action connected to climate change, and we share their connections to changes in our lives and world.

- **Drought:** Connect a withering plant to dry, cracked earth to show how a lack of water affects plants and crops.

  - *How it connects*—Droughts, caused by climate change, make it hard for plants to grow, which can lead to less food for people and animals.

- **Extreme weather:** Connect a storm cloud to a house to show how storms can damage homes and communities.

  - *How it connects*—Big storms, like hurricanes or floods, can destroy homes and make life harder for people in those areas.

- **Rising temperatures:** Connect melting glaciers to a polar bear habitat to show how warmer weather affects Arctic animals.

  - *How they connect*—As the planet gets warmer, ice melts and animals like polar bears lose their homes. This causes sea levels to rise.

- **Pollution:** Connect a factory releasing smoke to a nearby river to show how pollution affects water and the animals that live there.

  - *How it connects*—Pollution adds harmful gases to the air, which makes climate change worse, and it hurts rivers, lakes, and the creatures that depend on them.

- **Migration patterns:** Connect a bird on a migration route to changing weather to show how animals are affected by climate shifts.

  - *How they connect*—When weather changes, animals have trouble following their usual routes, which can make it harder for them to survive.

- **Community resilience:** Connect wind turbines or solar panels to a community to show how people are working to fight climate change.

  - *How it connects*—Communities are finding ways to use clean energy like wind and solar power to protect the planet and prepare for extreme weather.

Lauren's Story: An American Dog in Paris by Kay Pfaltz (2002)

After your students have played the Web of Life game, take a moment to guide them in reflecting on what they've learned. Emphasize that the game illustrates the interconnectedness of all living things within an ecosystem and how small disruptions can have a large impact. Encourage your students to think about how these connections relate to real-world environmental challenges and what actions they can take to maintain and protect these vital relationships in nature. Remind your students that, like in the game, their choices and actions play a vital role in keeping the planet healthy and balanced. How might emphasizing this connection inspire them to take more thoughtful actions for the environment?

Intra-Act

The Intra-Act strategy (Hoffman, 1979) involves recognizing the dynamic interaction between internal and external factors that influence learning. As a teacher, you can use it by observing students' behaviors, motivations, and responses, then adjusting your teaching methods and environment accordingly to optimize their learning experience. This approach emphasizes the importance of engaging with students and creating a supportive learning environment tailored to their individual needs and characteristics.

Pivotal to the Intra-Act strategy in this unit is that students engage in a process of valuing as they reflect on ideas in the text *Our House Is on Fire: Greta Thunberg's Call to Save the Planet* by Jeanette Winter (2020). According to Martin L. Hoffman (1979), students are more likely to engage in critical reading when they are involved in a valuing process. This approach allows them to interact with the text on a deep level, both intellectually and emotionally, through structured activities divided into four phases. The activities begin and end with a whole class or large group (phase 1 and phase 4) and move to small groups in between (phase 2 and phase 3). This method enhances students' critical reading skills and encourages collaborative learning and personal connection to the material (Etim, 2005).

A Mama for Owen
by Marion
Dane Bauer
(2007)

Phase 1: Simple Comprehension

Follow these steps for phase 1 of Intra-Act.

1. Show the class the cover of the book *Our House Is on Fire: Greta Thunberg's Call to Save the Planet.*

2. Ask students if they know of Greta Thunberg. If so, what do they know about her? Ask them what they think of the expression on Thunberg's face in the picture, as well as the many signs held up by children.

3. Read the book aloud or have students read the book on their own.

4. Discuss what occurs in the book as a whole group, making sure comprehension has occurred.

Phase 2: Relating

Follow these steps for phase 2 of Intra-Act.

1. Form small groups of four to six members.

2. Choose a leader for each group. The leader is responsible for shifting the discussion from the important ideas in the book to group members' personal reactions and values related to the ideas. The shift is likely to occur naturally. Some questions to consider may be:

   - How does the character's decision in the story relate to a decision you've had to make?

   - What lessons can you learn from the character's experiences and apply to your own life?

   - Do you share any traits or beliefs with the main character? How does this affect your understanding of the story?

Phase 3: Valuation

In this phase, the teacher distributes the reproducible "Game Sheet for the Intra-Act Valuation Phase," available at **go.SolutionTree.com/literacy**. Notice that the game sheet contains four declarative statements. Use the following steps in tandem with the game sheet.

1. On the sheet, each student first indicates their reaction to each of the four value statements by circling *A* (*agree*) or *D* (*disagree*).

2. Based on the previous phase's discussion, the students now predict how other members of the group responded (what they circled), so they are predicting what the other group members value.

Phase 4: Reflection

Begin the reflection phase of Intra-Act by scoring the game sheet. Group members take turns revealing how they each responded to the four statements. As each member says how they responded, the other members check whether their predictions agree with that member's actual responses. During this phase, the teacher acts as a facilitator, noting how students refrain from imposing points of view on others. The teacher encourages students to reflect on what they have learned.

Finally, the teacher leads a debriefing of the whole-group discussion using questions such as, "What did you learn from our participation in Intra-Act? Why is it important for each person in the group to participate? How did you contribute to your group's success? Was everyone in the group able to share their ideas and opinions? Why or why not? What could have been done differently to make the group work more effectively?" This discussion will make students sensitive to the problem-solving purpose of the Intra-Act procedure and the role of the reader in analysis by having them examine their ideas in comparison to classmates'.

Visual Mapping

Using the children's book *Flood* by Alvaro F. Villa (2013), students can create visual representations, such as concept maps, diagrams, or illustrations, to explore how extreme weather events like floods connect communities. For example, they might examine how the characters in the story come together to protect their homes, support each other during the flood, and rebuild afterward. By mapping out these connections, students can link the book's events to their own experiences or global issues, such as how communities worldwide respond to hurricanes, floods, or other disasters. This activity helps students see the shared impact of extreme weather and how collaboration strengthens resilience (Novak & Cañas, 2008).

Flood
by Alvaro F.
Villa (2013)

Compare and Contrast Authors' Messages

As you lead your students to compare and contrast authors' messages, we'd like to offer some strategies to help you explore the theme of how extreme weather events connect our communities.

One strategy is to have students write a comparative paragraph on different community responses to similar weather events in stories, such as the floods in *Lauren's Story: An*

American Dog in Paris by Kay Pfaltz (2002) and *The Storm in the Barn* by Matt Phelan (2009). These activities encourage students to think critically about the role of community in times of crisis.

You could have students compare and contrast author messages beginning with Jeanette Winter's (2020) *Our House Is on Fire: Greta Thunberg's Call to Save the Planet* and Elizabeth Rusch's (2019b) *Mario and the Hole in the Sky: How a Chemist Saved Our Planet*. We suggest that the theme of *Our House Is on Fire* is the importance of finding a way to speak out on the crucial issue of climate change as well as finding a way forward in the face of this reality. The theme of *Mario and the Hole in the Sky* may include how humanity saved the planet once and can do it again.

Comparing and contrasting author messages deepens students' understanding of the unit's central thematic question. This kind of exploration enriches the learning experience, enabling students to see the broad patterns and complexities woven into the fabric of literature. However, make sure to introduce comparing and contrasting messages after your students have engaged with at least one or two texts so they have a solid foundation to draw from.

Here are other ideas for bringing texts together to consider how extreme weather events connect our communities.

When the Storm Comes
by Linda Ashman (2020)

- Compare and contrast how different books convey the impact of extreme weather on communities and the environment. What can students learn about resilience and the importance of working together from how the books' characters respond?

- Ask students to identify and discuss the main themes in the books, focusing on how they address the effects of extreme weather events. Explore themes like survival and cooperation.

- Challenge your students to compare how different books explore the connections between extreme weather events and characters' lives. How might examining the causes and consequences of these events, as well as their influences on the plot and characters' decisions, deepen your students' understanding of the issues?

- Encourage students to investigate how different authors approach the topic of extreme weather events. Have them explore how cultural contexts influence the portrayal of these events and how characters from different backgrounds navigate similar challenges. Discuss how these stories can help students understand the broader implications of climate change and extreme weather.

Grades K–2 Consideration

The three Rs method—read, respond, and role play—engages early elementary students by having them read a text, respond to it through discussion or writing, and then role-play to further explore its themes (Robinson & Aronica, 2018). It nurtures a love for reading, strengthens comprehension skills, and fosters social and emotional development in K–2. It encourages creativity, promotes language development, and fosters empathy—all qualities that young people need to engage in real-world solutions around how extreme weather events connect our communities.

1. **Read:** Reading includes decoding words, images, or illustrations; grasping their meanings; and extracting information from written materials.

2. **Respond:** Responding involves expressing thoughts, opinions, and ideas about the material; asking questions; making connections; and reflecting. Responding encourages students to think critically, articulate their understanding, and participate in the learning process.

3. **Role play:** Role playing involves taking on different roles or characters to explore concepts, scenarios, or stories. This interactive approach fosters creativity, empathy, and deeper understanding by allowing students to immerse themselves in the content and view it from various vantage points.

The book we pair with this strategy for grades K–2 is Nicola Davies's (2018) *The Day War Came*, which acknowledges that war in different forms, as well as economic conditions, is a common trigger for people to move from their place of birth. Climate change and extreme weather events often play a role in war or exacerbate it. For teachers of older students, we offer role-playing ideas at our website (www.greenliteracy.org) and at **go.SolutionTree.com/literacy** as the reproducible "Role Play for Grades 3–5 and Beyond."

Brothers in Hope: The Story of the Lost Boys of Sudan by Mary Williams (2005)

Consider how Helen selected strategies and paired them with Green Reads and Views for this unit. Notice in figure 6.5 how her choices reflect the thematic question.

Select Green Literacy Strategies

What reading, writing, and drama strategies will encourage your students to express their thoughts, analyze the issue, and explore solutions?	How can you support all your students—no matter their reading level or background—to engage deeply with the issue and build their understanding?
Reading, Writing, and Drama Strategies:	Immersive Strategies:
Free-write	Web of Life
Intra-Act	
Role play	
Compare and Contrast Authors' Message	

See page 45 in the book for more information on selecting Green Literacy strategies.

See page 16 in the book for more information on the three cycles of comprehension.

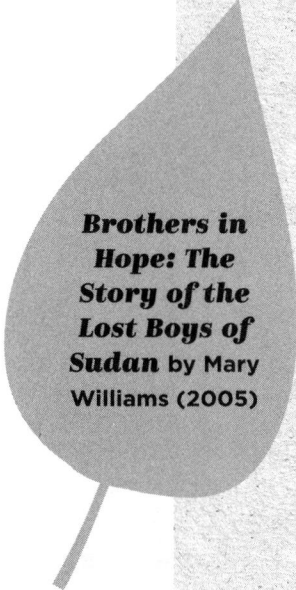

Figure 6.5: Completed "select Green Literacy strategies" segment of the Green Literacy Thematic Unit Planning Template.

You've put a lot of time and effort into planning and teaching your thematic unit, and you've likely seen areas of growth and spots where there's room to improve. Before wrapping up this section, you might revisit chapters 3 and 4 if you need additional guidance.

PHASE 3: SHIFT

In this section, you will:

- Develop Green Literacy ideals

This section invites you and your students to dive deeper into environmental themes by working together to create Green Literacy ideals. Through thoughtful discussions, students can share their ideas, find areas of agreement, and build a vision rooted in consensus. Unlike parts of this unit where you encourage individual thinking, this step is all about what you and your students agree on together. While we offer a few suggestions to guide you, this is also your opportunity to create something authentic and uniquely reflective of your classroom's shared goals and collective voice.

Develop Green Literacy Ideals

Just Help! How to Build a Better World
by Sonia Sotomayor (2022)

Now is the time for your students to pause and reflect on the learning journey. Encourage your students to look back at their experiences and insights to see how extreme weather events connect their communities. This reflection is about more than reviewing what they've learned—it's about shifting their perspectives and recognizing the subtle ways extreme weather influences their world. Working with your class on Green Literacy ideals will likely lead to meaningful discussions about personal connections to weather events, how to treat refugees, ways to build community when a destructive storm happens, anxiety around climate change, and much, much more. You may see your students reach shared understandings and agreements reflecting their deep engagement with how extreme weather events connect our communities. It is through the depth of critical thinking, the consensus-building process, and the shared ownership of Green Literacy ideals that students can ensure their learning endures and continues to inspire.

Green Literacy ideals generated by your class will be influenced by the books and media you choose, the themes you discuss, and whether you involve your students in the suggested immersive activities—in this case, Human Knot and Web of Life. For example, if you decide to engage your students with the books *Our House Is on Fire: Greta Thunberg's Call to Save the Planet* and *Mario and the Hole in the Sky: How a Chemist Saved Our Planet*, the Green Literacy ideals your class creates might be similar to the following.

- Young people have the right to speak their minds and make their voices heard on the difficult issue of what to do about climate change.

- We are all connected, and throughout history, we have come together to solve global challenges.

In figure 6.6, see how Helen and her students reflected on learning about how extreme weather connects our communities and created Green Literacy ideals. What reflections have you made?

PHASE 3: SHIFT

Develop Green Literacy Ideals

As you work with your students to create their Green Literacy ideals, remember this is something that happens naturally during your teaching. You can plan all the other steps ahead of time, but for this last part, you'll need to pause and observe how your students respond.

Reflection 1

As you plan how to guide your students in creating their Green Literacy ideals, take a moment to think about the lessons you've already taught. How did your students respond during these activities? What really stood out to you? Write down some notes or free-write about what you noticed happening in your classroom.

> When we explored how communities rebuild after extreme weather, students were curious about the role of helpers like firefighters, volunteers, and organizations. They asked thoughtful questions about how people can prepare for and recover from these events.
>
> While discussing extreme weather in other parts of the world, students showed empathy for those affected, with one commenting, "I didn't know it could be that bad." They began to see how global issues connect to local ones.

Reflection 2

In your free-writing, think about what stood out to you during class discussions about the books. What were some interesting things your students said about using the reading and writing strategies?

> A few students recognized how heavy rains in our area sometimes lead to flooded streets or homes. They reflected on how neighbors help one another by sharing resources or offering shelter during these times when we talked about Nicola Davies's (2018) picture book <u>The Day War Came</u>. Students created images of floods, tornadoes, and community support in a drawing activity about extreme weather. They explained their artwork, emphasizing teamwork and helping others.

See page 47 in the book for more information on how to facilitate the Green Literacy ideals discussion.

Figure 6.6: Completed "develop Green Literacy ideals" segment of the Green Literacy Thematic Unit Planning Template.

Consider referring to chapter 2 for more guidance on creating Green Literacy ideals and to chapter 3 for how teachers and their students created them. Please refer to chapter 4 for more insights.

Little Mole Finds Hope
by Glenys Nellist
(2020)

CONCLUSION

In this chapter, you explored how extreme weather events, driven by climate change, affect communities and the systems we depend on. Through examples, you saw how fostering critical thinking, resilience, and collective action can help students navigate these challenges. You were introduced to tools like Green Reads and Views, along with strategies to support your teaching. You may find that these resources help your students understand the impacts of climate change and address emotional responses like climate anxiety. They empower you and your students to develop Green Literacy ideals and engage in meaningful conversations connected to local environments, emphasizing resilience and the strength of working together.

Now, consider how this chapter has impacted your learning as a teacher. We offer a dedicated space for you to do so in the following "Teacher's Corner" reproducible tool (also available at **go.SolutionTree.com/literacy**). Whether you're working on your own, with a teaching partner, or within a schoolwide learning network, after exploring chapter 6, we encourage you to reflect on what you've learned.

Teacher's Corner

Here are some questions to support your reflection.

- How have you observed the impact of extreme weather events on your local community, and in what ways has it shaped the daily lives of students and families? Reflect on a specific instance where you witnessed the impact of extreme weather events on a student or family.

- How might you address the social and emotional aspects of extreme weather events in your teaching, considering the potential anxieties or concerns students may have about the changes in their environment?

Here are prompts for journaling.

- How can you integrate extreme weather event discussions into your curriculum in a meaningful and age-appropriate way? What resources or teaching strategies might enhance student engagement?

- Reflect on potential social and emotional challenges students may face in dealing with climate-related concerns. How can your teaching approach support their emotional well-being?

Here are discussion guidelines.

- Share your observations about this chapter with a colleague, and discuss potential ways these impacts might influence classroom discussions or activities aimed at building awareness around extreme weather events.

- Share your ideas with a fellow teacher, and discuss potential cross-disciplinary connections that can be explored to create a more comprehensive understanding of extreme weather events for students.

CHAPTER 7

How Systems Thinking Changes Our World

The scarcest resource is not oil, metals, clean air, capital, labour,, or technology. It is our willingness to listen to each other and learn from each other and to seek the truth rather than seek to be right.

—DONELLA H. MEADOWS

In this chapter, we offer ideas on how systems thinking can change our world by helping students grasp their interconnectedness with nature. By looking at mass consumption from a global to a local level, you and your students will explore how systems thinking helps them perceive this interconnectedness and its influence on their lives and thinking. We guide you through the individual steps that compose the larger Green Literacy actions of engage, empower, and shift. We offer a completed Green Literacy Thematic Unit Planning Template through the lens of a composite teacher to support and inspire you. In this chapter, you can follow along and customize the blank template, considering your teaching context.

PHASE 1: ENGAGE

In this section, you will:

- Develop your thematic question
- Foster your thinking through commentary

The engage section in this chapter explores systems thinking and its power to deepen understanding of environmental challenges. Systems thinking reveals

Chapter Snapshot—What You'll Explore

In this chapter, we share with you how to:

- Discover systems thinking's potential to affect how people create suitable solutions

- Organize a unit

- Pick Green Reads and Views and Green Literacy strategies, including K–2 consideration

- Navigate critical thinking, reading, speaking, and writing to create Green Literacy ideals

connections among people, places, and the environment, helping students recognize patterns, consider multiple perspectives, and take action.

In our completed example sections of the Green Literacy Thematic Unit Planning Template, we have provided a composite example as a guide, framed from the perspective of a fifth-grade teacher in a suburban setting, whom we call Wanda. As always, you can directly use this unit, modify it, or create your own approach, as outlined in chapter 2 and modeled in chapter 3.

As you plan, reflect on your willingness to engage, your school community's response, and the support available to you.

Develop Your Thematic Question

When we look closely, it's clear that systems thinking changes the way people view the world. For example, considering a community's effort to reduce food waste from a systemic perspective recognizes that the effort addresses local landfill issues, reduces greenhouse gas emissions, supports food-insecure populations, *and* promotes sustainable agricultural practices. Similarly, planting trees in urban areas improves air quality, mitigates the urban heat island effect, *and* creates gathering spaces that strengthen community bonds. These examples reveal how a systems-thinking approach allows us to see the interconnectedness of environmental, social, and economic factors; this interconnectedness offers opportunities for collaboration and meaningful change.

For the unit explored in this final chapter, we chose the thematic question, "How does systems thinking change our world?" because it builds on the foundation laid in the previous chapters. It expands on the themes of how landscapes shape us and how extreme weather connects our communities to more fully examine how environmental changes ripple through interconnected communities, fostering both challenges and opportunities for resilience and collaboration. Taking this next step encourages students to think broadly because exploring how systems thinking can change the world helps them see themselves within a larger, interconnected network and recognize their ability to shape and improve these systems. The thematic question guides students to understand the science and mechanics behind systems thinking, its impact on communities, and their role as agents of change. It challenges them to create solutions and build resilience for the future.

Feel free to adapt the process and develop your own thematic question for this unit if you like. Consider exploring big-picture questions such as, "How does understanding systems help us solve environmental problems?" or "What can we learn from communities that thrive by working together within systems?" You might ask, "What role do we play in shaping the systems around us for a better future?" Using the planning template is the starting point for customizing the unit.

Notice how teacher Wanda reflected on what she wanted her students to consider (figure 7.1). How might your thinking lend itself to systems thinking?

Now that you have explored and chosen a thematic question, we support your thinking by providing commentaries designed as starting points for deeper reflection and planning.

Name: **Wanda (five years of teaching experience)**

Grade level: ~~Fifth grade~~

School context: **Suburban**

PHASE 1: ENGAGE

Develop Your Thematic Question

Here are some guiding questions to consider as you develop your thematic question. Reflect on these prompts to clarify your focus.

1. Brainstorm

   - What issue that could lead to a big idea about the environment are you most passionate about exploring with your students?

     I'm interested in helping my students understand the big picture of how everything in the environment is connected. Using systems thinking, we explore how choices—like reducing waste or conserving energy—impact entire ecosystems and even the planet's health.

   - What current events or real-world examples resonate with you and can help bring environmental issues to life for your students?

     Fast fashion resonates with me—it's a real-world example of how consumerism impacts waste, resources, and pollution, helping students see the environmental cost of everyday choices.

2. Prioritize

You might have more than one environmental issue you'd like to explore with your students. Now, think about which one will create the most meaningful conversations and learning.

I'm new to systems thinking, and it's definitely a lot to wrap my head around, but I'm trying to learn. My administration is supportive and interested in systems thinking, so I want to make sure my approach fits our school culture. My students already know a little about recycling and waste, so I'd shape my question around how our school can reduce waste together. Framing it as a collaborative challenge—like a "zero-waste lunch week"—could get everyone involved and make it easier to address any concerns. I'm willing to engage with this issue, but I know I'll need support and guidance as I go.

Through this brainstorming and prioritization process, write your thematic question. Some stems that might be useful are:

- How can/do . . . ?
- What might . . . ?

Write your thematic question here.

Maybe the best question might be, How does systems thinking change our world?

See page 38 in the book for more information on creating thematic questions.

Figure 7.1: Completed "develop your thematic question" segment of the Green Literacy Thematic Unit Planning Template.

Foster Your Thinking Through Commentary

In this section, we provide commentaries designed to serve as springboards, or seed ideas, to ignite your curiosity and spark critical thinking about how systems thinking can change the world. We offer commentary to help you consider the complexities of systems thinking and its potential to connect diverse elements of the world into a unified understanding.

The following sections focus on the following.

- **Explore core concepts of systems thinking:** Sustainability and interconnectedness are key ideas in systems thinking. They encourage students to look at the bigger picture and understand how different parts of a system work together over the long term.

- **Discover systems thinking through two stories:** We paraphrase and discuss the Native American folktale "The Story of the Windigo," as retold by Robin Wall Kimmerer (2015) in her book *Braiding Sweetgrass*, to exemplify positive feedback loops in systems thinking and a way to resist overconsumption and greed so we take "only what we need." Also, we discuss the adult science fiction novel *The Ministry for the Future* by Kim Stanley Robinson (2020) and how systems thinking is the framework through which interconnected global challenges—like climate change, economic inequality, and geopolitical power dynamics—are addressed in that book.

- **Teach systems thinking with simulation games:** Simulation games can help teach students systems thinking and trigger a mindset shift in them.

Explore Core Concepts of Systems Thinking

Teaching systems thinking begins with knowing your students. Encourage them to look for patterns and relationships across different scales. Give them space to explore concepts embodied in questions like these: "How can we see beyond the obvious? How do our choices impact the world?" Mindset questions like these help students recognize the interconnectedness of all things and the long-term effects of their actions. Thinking systemically means seeing the world as a web of relationships, where each part influences the whole. Encourage students to ask, "What factors shape this situation? How do these pieces connect? What might happen if we choose this path?" These questions move them beyond surface-level thinking and engage them in the broader, interconnected world.

Consider the following points when working with students on the core concepts of systems thinking.

- With systems thinking, students learn to perceive environmental issues as interconnected components of larger systems, such as ecosystems, societies, and economies. For example, when studying the life of Wangari Maathai and her work with deforestation (as in chapter 3, page 57, looking at the Green Belt Movement), students employing systems thinking would consider the direct impact on forests and wildlife and explore the broader implications for climate, water cycles, biodiversity, and human livelihoods. They would analyze the interconnected relationships among deforestation, climate change, loss of habitat, and socioeconomic factors, recognizing the cascading effects across multiple systems. The book *Seeds of Change* (Johnson, 2010) gives students the background to make those evaluations.

- Systems thinking helps students identify feedback loops and unexpected outcomes within environmental systems, enabling a deeper understanding of dynamic interactions (Pontius & McIntosh, 2020). For example, systems thinking can be used to explore how urban sprawl impacts natural habitats and contributes to habitat loss, fragmentation, and the lifestyle of us humans, which in turn affect species survival and ecosystem health (much like the insights gained from *The Story of Stuff*, Leonard, 2010). Understanding these loops helps students predict environmental intervention effects and develop holistic conservation strategies (King, Romero, Prince, & Swanson, 2020).

- Systems thinking fosters interdisciplinary thinking and collaboration. You and your students can learn to integrate knowledge from various disciplines, such as biology, ecology, economics, and sociology, to comprehensively understand environmental issues like climate change, loss of biodiversity, and consumerism. This holistic approach reveals the interconnectedness of various factors, moving beyond isolated viewpoints. When studying topics like climate change, loss of biodiversity, or the impacts of consumerism, the focus extends beyond the scientific aspects to include economic impacts on communities, social implications for different populations, and ecological effects on natural habitats.

- Systems thinking encourages collaboration across different fields, so you and your students engage with diverse perspectives—from scientists and economists to community leaders, artists, and policymakers. This approach leads to innovative solutions by bringing together expertise from various areas, which is essential for tackling complex challenges like climate change, biodiversity loss, and consumerism.

Sustainability in systems thinking is about building systems that last and keep working well over time. It involves thinking about how our choices and actions impact the environment, the economy, and society in the long run. Sustainable systems are designed to use resources wisely, reduce waste, and help keep nature balanced. For example, sustainable farming practices take care of the soil, save water, and support a variety of plants and animals, which ensures people can continue growing food for many years to come (Capra & Luisi, 2014; Meadows, Randers, & Meadows, 2004; Sterman, 2000). Sustainability in teaching systems thinking requires an understanding of core concepts and how they connect.

Most often, urgent environmental questions that necessitate systems thinking to find solutions can quickly become controversial, especially when they intersect with political and social values. These questions often spark debates that highlight the complex relationships among ecological, economic, and cultural interests. As educators, we must start conversations on these topics with balance and care. Helping students explore their values and interests within these issues allows them to better understand the challenges. Systems thinking offers a way to examine environmental questions from different perspectives, showing how interconnected factors shape both the problems and possible solutions.

Here, we include three example questions that address urgent environmental issues. Through systems thinking, these questions can inspire strong reactions in young people. Encouraging students to reflect on the balance between human needs and environmental sustainability can help them think critically and engage meaningfully with these pressing topics.

1. **Should we use special seeds called *GMOs* in farming?** Some people say they help farmers grow more food, but others worry they might not be safe.

2. **What do you think about using special rules to make companies pay money if they pollute?** Some people think keeping the environment clean is a good idea, but others worry it might increase costs.

3. **How do you feel about using fracking, a special method of extracting natural gas from the ground?** Some people think it's good for generating more energy, but others are concerned it might harm the environment.

It often takes a crisis to make people realize the value of something they've overlooked. For example, they might not think much about water until a drought or pollution makes it scarce. Then, suddenly, they start saving water and looking for ways to conserve it because they've realized how important it is. The same goes for housing. When housing becomes too expensive or hard to find, people begin exploring ideas like cohousing, where sharing spaces makes living more affordable and builds community. These crises force us to pause and appreciate what we once took for granted. While it's unfortunate that it often takes a crisis to open our eyes, these moments can spark creativity and push us toward solutions that are more sustainable and fairer. Wouldn't it be better if we could recognize the value of these things and act to protect them before a crisis forces us to?

As you think about the planning and teaching of this unit, consider the extent of your and your students' knowledge of interconnected systems. Some systems you and your students may be familiar with if you have been working with *The Green Literacy Handbook* might be deforestation, climate change, water cycles, and biodiversity. Seeing the interconnections among these ideas encourages systems thinking, which can lead to environmental solutions. If you engage your students in such a dialogue, you can explain to them that they are moving into systems thinking. Also, consider how your and your students' experiences revolve around interconnections in your lives. For example, in your community, is there an example of how pollution affects students' enjoyment of nature? Or is there some environmental issue that may impact their families' or other families' livelihoods?

Discover Systems Thinking Through Two Stories

As we have said many times (and by now, you may feel the same!), stories can be powerful tools for building understanding. Here, we want to share two stories that act as tools for understanding systems thinking and its applications to real-world challenges. First, Robin Wall Kimmerer's (2015) *Braiding Sweetgrass* retells the Native American folktale "The Story of the Windigo," a cautionary story about overconsumption and greed, as a vivid example

Pause and Consider:
How can meaningful conversations with those around them—like their peers, family, and teachers—deepen students' understanding of environmental issues and shape well-informed, thoughtful opinions? In what ways might you help your students see these connections and empower them to take meaningful action on these issues?

of positive feedback loops and the importance of taking only what we need to maintain balance. Second, Kim Stanley Robinson's (2020) adult science fiction novel *The Ministry for the Future* uses systems thinking to explore interconnected global challenges such as climate change, economic inequality, and geopolitical power.

Kimmerer (2015) is a scientist, writer, and enrolled member of the Citizen Potawatomi Nation who brings together Indigenous knowledge and scientific knowledge in service of an urgent need to restore balance between humans and the natural world. Kimmerer's work invites readers to consider how their interactions with nature can reflect respect, reciprocity, and a deep understanding of the interconnectedness of all life. For Green Literacy teachers, this means integrating Indigenous perspectives with scientific knowledge to help students build a holistic understanding of environmental stewardship and sustainable living.

For example, in her book *Braiding Sweetgrass*, Kimmerer (2015) retells the story of the Windigo, a legendary monster, to emphasize how focusing on lacking something can lead to unchecked greed and overconsumption—and thus, degradation of the environment—which is an important idea to consider amid a consumerism-driven culture. This monster, the Windigo, is said to lurk behind people, stalking them in the woods as an outsize man with frost-white hair, arms like tree trunks, and feet like snowshoes. It has yellow fangs, which hang from a mouth gone raw where it has chewed its lips from hunger, and its heart is made of ice. The Windigo is the creation of a human who had insatiable cravings and could not stop eating. As the Windigo consumes, its hunger intensifies, leading to more consumption. This ever-growing hunger illustrates how greed and exploitation can spiral out of control, leading to destruction (Kimmerer, 2015).

Windigo stories have been told to young children to scare them into safe behavior and keep them from moving into insatiable hunger. "Take what you need" is the message of these Windigo stories, highlighting the need to live in harmony with nature and ensure that enough is left for others and for future generations.

Kimmerer's telling of the story illustrates a *positive feedback loop*, a key concept in systems thinking that occurs when an initial change triggers a cycle that amplifies the effect, creating an ever-increasing momentum. In the case of the Windigo, this loop involves the destructive consequences of insatiable consumption, leading to imbalance and harm in systemic science. The Windigo's insatiable hunger represents a change in one part of the system, which then triggers a similar change in another part—the availability of food. The more the Windigo consumes, the hungrier it becomes, leading to more rampant consumption. This self-reinforcing cycle creates a destructive feedback loop where the behavior intensifies with each iteration and ultimately leads to the monster's complete downfall.

At the end of the Windigo retelling, Kimmerer invites readers to reflect on their own lives and the ways in which they might be contributing to the "Windigo mindset" of endless consumption and environmental degradation. Consider the following questions.

- What drives the Windigo mindset?
- How does this mindset affect our relationships?

- What are the consequences of living with a Windigo mindset?

- How can we resist the Windigo mindset?

The Windigo story offers us, as educators, a unique way to explore systems thinking and the consequences of unchecked behaviors like greed and overconsumption. This story can prompt us to reflect on how we, too, may be part of systems that either sustain or amplify certain behaviors. We can ask ourselves how small actions in our teaching—our choices, habits, and interactions—might create cycles that either support or undermine the values we want to promote. For example, do we reinforce behaviors that lead to greater environmental harm, or do we create opportunities to disrupt those patterns with more sustainable practices?

Turning to the second story, the adult novel *The Ministry for the Future* by Robinson (2020) vividly depicts a near future where humanity faces the consequences of missed climate targets. Robinson weaves hard science into the narrative, using experts to explain atmospheric and oceanic phenomena to bureaucrats in the Ministry. The novel also explores economic history, exposing the power dynamics that have shaped modern civilization and exploring how these dynamics might be reimagined. Readers witness the Ministry's efforts to work with—and challenge—the world's most powerful economic players to shift system dynamics and address the root causes of the climate crisis.

We chose *The Ministry for the Future* for its profound exploration of global challenges through science fiction. The novel shifts focus from blaming individuals to addressing the systems causing these issues, highlighting the potential for collective change and systemic solutions.

For us, this science fiction novel serves as a powerful example of how systems thinking can move beyond surface-level solutions to address the deeper, structural causes of global crises. It underscores the need to analyze feedback loops, power dynamics, and interdependencies to create meaningful change. In teaching systems thinking, we hope teachers are empowered to reimagine the systems they are part of and work toward a future where human-designed systems prioritize sustainability, equity, and resilience. *The Ministry for the Future* shows us what is possible when people dare to think and act systemically—and why this mindset is essential for shaping a better world.

As you think about the planning and teaching of this unit, consider you and your students' experiences of different projects that involve sharing and recycling, such as potlucks and neighborhood rummage sales in which people share resources. How do such projects lead to a mindset of abundance rather than of lack or scarcity? Can you and your students connect such a mindset to the interdependence of different systems such as food resources, economic resources, and recycling?

Teach Systems Thinking With Simulation Games

Game-based learning is an engaging educational approach that uses games to foster learning and problem solving. It allows students to actively participate in simulated environments where they explore complex issues, make decisions, and see the outcomes of their actions. This type of learning is particularly effective in environmental education,

Pause and Consider:
How do the commentaries of these two stories invite you to examine the systems we live within?

as it challenges students to think critically about global challenges and consider multiple perspectives. Through game-based learning, students can develop skills in collaboration, decision making, and creative problem solving—skills that are essential for addressing urgent environmental issues.

In the classroom of award-winning teacher John Hunter (2013), students fearlessly tackle global problems and discover surprising solutions by playing his groundbreaking *World Peace Game*. In the *World Peace Game*, students from fourth grade to high school, in schools both well funded and under resourced, take on the roles of politicians, tribal leaders, diplomats, bankers, and military commanders. Through battles and negotiations, standoffs and summits, they strive to resolve dozens of complex, seemingly intractable real-world challenges, from nuclear proliferation to tribal warfare, financial collapse, and climate change. To "win" the *World Peace Game*, a class needs to "solve" many crises. The most challenging crisis to solve is global warming; solving it requires an enormous financial commitment from each country, as well as a highly coordinated international effort. Hunter (2013) offers a blueprint for a world that bends toward cooperation rather than conflict. Collaboratively solving global issues in the game fosters critical thinking, empathy, and a deeper understanding of interdependence.

Such games are useful for Green Literacy learning, as they are dynamic, hands-on learning experiences that challenge students to address complex geopolitical, environmental, and economic issues. Through simulation, students learn how their actions and decisions can affect a global system. Simulation games foster lifelong environmental awareness; they empower students to see themselves as problem solvers in environmental challenges. As students experiment with different decisions and see the results, their critical thinking and problem-solving skills improve (Goore, n.d.; Turner, Lamb, & Mazur, 2018).

We have found that simulation games focused on environmental sustainability have an almost-instant positive effect on young people's interest and motivation to learn. These interactive, immersive games mimic real-world ecological challenges, allowing students to manage resources, understand the complexity of ecosystems, and make decisions that can lead to sustainable outcomes. With them, you can dive into the complex relationships within systems in an engaging and fun way.

Teachers can draw on Hunter's approach and adapt similar games to bring environmental issues into their classrooms in a tangible way. Simulation games work well as midunit reinforcements of systems thinking or as end-of-unit reviews; some teachers dedicate time on Fridays for these activities, but the timing is flexible.

The following sections highlight games that deepen systems thinking through topics like ecosystems, wind, and crop impact and make complex ideas engaging and accessible. While there are many viable options on the market, the following simulation games, which focus on environmental sustainability through systems thinking, are the ones that we know teachers can use with a whole group or assign to individual players. Many games are free online, while others require a subscription. Like any fast-moving technology, online games change or cease to function. We recommend trying them yourself first to become familiarized with them.

Habitats

Developed by the Smithsonian Science Education Center (n.d.), *Habitats* is a visually engaging and educational game designed for students aged 8–12. It allows players to explore diverse ecosystems such as deserts, coral reefs, jungles, and marshes. Students are tasked with matching animals to their correct habitats, which encourages them to learn about biodiversity and understand the delicate balance within ecosystems. This game is an excellent introduction to the concept of biomes and ecological relationships, making it a great tool for teaching environmental interdependence in upper elementary and lower middle school science classes.

Wind Simulator Game

Offered by Field Day Learning Games (2022), the *Wind Simulator Game* is an interactive online simulation best suited for students aged 10–14. The game demonstrates how high- and low-pressure systems influence wind patterns. Experimenting with different variables to observe how pressure systems shape wind directions and speeds enhances players' understanding of weather and climate dynamics. This game aligns well with lessons on meteorology and climate change, as it offers a hands-on way to explore atmospheric science concepts.

Cornucopia

A free STEM education game by the California Academy of Sciences (n.d.), *Cornucopia* allows players to manage a plot of land, plant crops, and earn technology upgrades to make their farm successful. Through trial and error, students aged 9–13 learn the importance of sustainable farming practices and how resource management impacts agricultural productivity. *Cornucopia* provides a valuable perspective on the environmental and economic aspects of agriculture, fostering a deeper appreciation for sustainability.

Ecosystem Simulator

Ecosystem Simulator (n.d.) is an online game in which players create and manage their own ecosystems. Students aged 10–14 must balance factors like predator–prey relationships, plant growth, and biodiversity to maintain a stable environment. The game offers a practical way to understand ecological interdependencies and systems thinking. It's a particularly valuable tool for introducing middle school students to concepts of ecological balance, the food web, and the importance of biodiversity in sustaining life.

Fish Banks

Fish Banks is a simulation game developed by Dennis Meadows (2001) and the Sustainability Institute that simulates the management of a fishery. Players must make decisions about fishing quotas, conservation measures, and economic development to maintain a sustainable fish population. This game is a great way to learn about the challenges of resource management and the importance of sustainable practices. While *Fish Banks* is a game for middle schoolers and above, it could easily be adapted for advanced fifth graders by pairing them with an older student or an adult so they can contribute ideas while getting support for more complex decision making.

SimCity

According to Electronic Arts (2013), players of *SimCity* (aged 10 and up) can manage urban development and sustainability. While not explicitly focused on environmental sustainability, this popular simulation game allows players to design and manage virtual cities. Players must balance factors such as population growth, infrastructure development, environmental impact, transportation, and energy sources. They can explore how their choices affect the environment and sustainability of their city.

As you think about the planning and teaching of this unit, consider your and your students' experiences with games, both family-centered game time and video games in which they engage. Do you think it would be worthwhile to extend their game experience with some of the described games? Consider how Wanda addressed commentary in her answers in figure 7.2 (page 170).

Now that you've explored the commentary on how systems thinking changes our world, you're ready to use these insights to support your students. As you move on to phase 2, empower, keep in mind the ideas you've learned. You can build on them as you continue your learning and develop your thematic unit.

PHASE 2: EMPOWER

In this section, you will:

- Cultivate a list of Green Reads and Views

- Select Green Literacy strategies

We've selected Green Reads and Views—books and multimedia resources—and paired them with strategies that align with the unit's theme. These selections serve as examples of how thoughtfully chosen texts and strategies work together.

As you move through empower, consider:

- How Green Reads and Views can foster environmental awareness by exposing students to diverse perspectives

- How strategies can inspire creativity, collaboration, and critical thinking

- How planning can balance structure with flexibility to meet your students where they are

This phase empowers you to create your own thematic unit tailored to your students' needs. We recommend designing your unit to last between two and four weeks. However, you may choose to extend or shorten this time frame depending on the needs of your students and the dynamics of your school.

Cultivate a List of Green Reads and Views

For this chapter, each suggested multimedia resource or book has a theme to support teachers in planning this thematic unit. We've grouped the resources into three categories:

Pause and Consider: How might adding simulation games to your classroom change how your students understand systems thinking? What might you need to do to get your classroom ready for these games?

Foster Your Thinking Through Commentary

First, review the following questions and respond to a few or all of them. Use a list or brainstorm freely to capture your ideas.

- Whose voices or stories do you need to hear to understand this issue, and why are they important to you?

  I'd like to explore more about what happens to all of the stuff we buy. Who handles it, and where does it go? How does it affect them?

- What unfair systems or problems do you want your students to think about when learning about this issue, and how can you help them ask questions and find ways to make things better?

  Many of my students are wealthy and often do not think about how money is spent or made or who might be getting less than what they deserve.

- Whose experiences or ideas are sometimes left out when this issue is talked about, and how can you share those voices in your classroom to help everyone learn more?

  I'd like to find the connections to people and situations and show my students how everything is connected.

From your responses, begin to find springboards that will help you develop commentary that deepens your thematic exploration.

Springboards to Support Commentary

- Springboard 1: *General research on systems thinking*
  - Title or source: *Google search*
  - Key insights: *I found a book and some websites.*
- Springboard 2: *Simulation games*
  - Title or source: *Free eco-simulation game*
  - Key insights: *I found a game about biodiversity my students can play online, which helps with systems thinking.*
- Springboard 3: *Fast fashion*
  - Title or source: *Annie Leonard's (2010) The Story of Stuff*
  - Key insights: *This free open source tells what happens with our stuff.*

See page 40 in the book for more information on developing springboards for commentary.

The Story of Stuff by Annie Leonard (2007)

Figure 7.2: Completed "foster your thinking through commentary" segment of the Green Literacy Thematic Unit Planning Template.

(1) stories of interconnectedness: systems thinking; (2) videos on interconnectedness: consumerist culture; and (3) stories of consequences of interconnectedness: pollution. We have done this to help you begin to think like a systems thinker, observing patterns and connections between stories. A full list of resources for this chapter is available at **go.SolutionTree .com/literacy**. Our top picks are featured on the leaves throughout the chapter, with some

also appearing in the planning template. If you want to use books or digital media not on the list, revisit chapter 2 (page 31) for guiding questions to help with your selections.

If you decide you would like to immerse your students in the nuts and bolts of systems thinking, you could involve them in the books in the category *stories of interconnectedness: systems thinking*. For example, you may decide to read and discuss *The Old Ladies Who Liked Cats* (Greene, 1991), inspired by Charles Darwin's observations of the interdependence between clover and cats. This tale leads readers to consider easily occurring unintended consequences of decisions made; the other selections in this category address other aspects of systems thinking. Or you may choose to lead your students with book selections from the category of *stories of consequences of interconnectedness: pollution*. In either case, you could use the strategies we outline or use strategies of your choosing.

We selected *The Story of Stuff* (Leonard, 2007) as a digital media resource for the category of *videos on interconnectedness: consumerist culture* to align with this chapter's strategies. This free, open-access resource effectively illustrates the environmental impact of consumption, making sustainability and interconnectedness accessible to all students. Its openness fosters awareness, inspires action, and strengthens community.

Open-source tools and resources are freely shared, meaning others are allowed to use, adapt, and improve them. In environmental education, for example, teachers may collaborate on climate change curricula, sharing lesson plans on plastic waste reduction, school gardens, and composting, among other topics. While contributors don't earn money, they gain the satisfaction of making a positive impact, fostering environmental education, and being part of a collective effort. This mirrors systems thinking, where interconnected contributions enhance the whole, much like how an ecosystem's diverse elements work together.

Now, consider Wanda's Green Reads and Views picks (figure 7.3, page 172). How will yours compare?

Select Green Literacy Strategies

The strategies outlined in this section support critical thinking and empower students to make meaningful connections among their lives, the texts they read, and the larger world. At the same time, we encourage you to incorporate any of your own tried-and-true methods that have proven effective. As the teacher, you are in the process of curating strategies to align with your thematic unit, ensuring they resonate with your students' needs and your classroom's goals. Here, you are not merely observing a suggested classroom unit; you are encouraged to actively adapt and implement these ideas in the unique context of your classroom. As you move through this section, ask yourself, "How could this look in my classroom? What changes would make this approach most effective for my students?"

We present the following strategies for you to explore, many of which are paired with a Green Read to illustrate their applications.

- **Turn-and-Talk Conversation Cards:** These cards frame a prereading and postreading discussion strategy.

If You Give a Mouse a Cookie
by Laura J. Numeroff
(1985)

PHASE 2: EMPOWER

Cultivate a List of Green Reads and Views

Consider the three cycles of comprehension as you choose your strategies: simple comprehension (retell and summarize), criteria comprehension (support thinking), and perspective comprehension (investigate explicit and implicit perspectives and move to systems thinking).

Select texts and digital media that flow from your thematic question and your commentary research. If you need help finding texts or digital media, consult **go.SolutionTree.com/literacy**, our companion website (www.greenliteracy.org), or your school or local librarian.

What types of texts or stories (fiction, nonfiction, poetry, or multimedia) can you use to help your students connect emotionally and critically to this environmental issue? What is the author's message?

Green Reads
Title: <u>The Story of Stuff</u> by Annie Leonard (2007)   Author's message: Everything is connected.
Title: <u>If You Give a Mouse a Cookie</u> by Laura J. Numeroff (1985)   Author's message: A thought experiment on feedback or causal loops (in this case, A causes B, B causes C, which eventually comes back to A)
Title: <u>Trying</u> by Kobi Yamada (2020)   Author's message: We can learn when we fail.
Title: <u>The Story of Change</u> by Annie Leonard (2012)   Author's message: Change must include consumer awareness and change in the economic system.
Title: <u>Malala's Magic Pencil</u> by Malala Yousafzai (2017)   Author's message: Systems thinking

Figure 7.3: Completed "cultivate a list of Green Reads and Views" segment of the Green Literacy Thematic Unit Planning Template.

Trying
by Kobi Yamada (2020)

- **Immersive strategies:** Immersive strategies fully engage students by sparking curiosity and creativity through hands-on experiences.
  - *Thumb-Wrestling Game*—In this fun, interactive activity, two players try to pin each other's thumbs down within a set time in a friendly challenge that promotes collaboration instead of competition.
- **Strategies toward the three cycles of comprehension:** These strategies focus on an author's ideas about how systems thinking changes our world and how young people can support their ideas through personal connection, text-to-text connection, and text-to-world connection.

- *PReP With Three Phases*—This prereading technique activates prior knowledge, encourages brainstorming, and guides students to refine their understanding as they engage with the text.

- *Adapted Guided Reading Procedure*—This structured approach has students carefully read and reread a text to help improve their comprehension when the author presents a lot of information. It involves recalling key details, organizing information, and discussing the material to deepen understanding and critical thinking skills.

- *Compare and Contrast Authors' Messages*—Students compare and contrast themes within texts chosen for the teaching unit.

As you choose your Green Literacy strategies, remember that chapter 3 (page 57) offers a model thematic unit created during a Green Literacy professional development experience. Chapter 4 (page 79) offers tips for developing a unit. Please refer to either chapter if needed as you use this ready-made unit, customize it, or develop your own new unit.

Next, we provide descriptions and examples for each strategy to model how you can implement them in your context.

Turn-and-Talk Conversation Cards

We recommend starting with the Turn-and-Talk Conversation Cards (figure 7.4, page 174). These cards are a great way to spark excitement among your students for the upcoming thematic unit. You can revisit them throughout the unit to see how your students' ideas have evolved and use them to reflect after the unit is complete. You can approach these questions with your whole group, have students discuss them with an elbow partner in a turn-and-talk, or use them as journal prompts. Additionally, you can guide students into perspective comprehension by discussing how the characters in the books or media you're focusing on might answer these questions. This approach helps deepen their understanding and encourages critical thinking.

Thumb-Wrestling Game

We suggest playing this interactive game before diving into any of the readings or viewings. It's a fun and engaging way to help your students understand the concept of interconnectedness. This modified thumb-wrestling activity is inspired by *The Climate Change Playbook* (Meadows, Sweeney, & Mehers, 2016). In the original version, students stop after the first round. We've added a second round where students collaborate to find a way for everyone to win, followed by a group discussion to deepen understanding. We've noticed that in the first round, students try to score as many points as they can individually, but the overall points remain low. In the second round, when students realize they need to work together to increase their scores, the points go much higher. This game serves as a powerful metaphor for how collaboration can lead to better resource management and environmental outcomes.

The Story of Change
by Annie Leonard (2012)

How do you think what happens in your local park affects the animals and plants living there?

Imagine if one part of an ecosystem, like the bees, disappeared. What changes do you think would happen to the other parts of the ecosystem?

If you were a raindrop, what journey do you think you would take through the environment, and how would you impact the places you travel?

Imagine a world where every piece of trash we throw away can talk. Pick one item from your trash bin and tell its story. Where does it go, and what happens to it after it leaves your house?

Think about the last meal you had. Can you trace the journey of one food item from where it started (like a farm or a tree) to your plate? Who might have helped it along its journey?

Think about the last time it rained. How does rain affect our schoolyard, the streets, and the nearby parks? What happens to the water when it goes down the drain?

How can our choices about what we buy and use every day make a difference to the Earth's health? Can you give an example of a choice that helps the environment?

If you could create a game that connects people and nature, what would the game be? How would it be played?

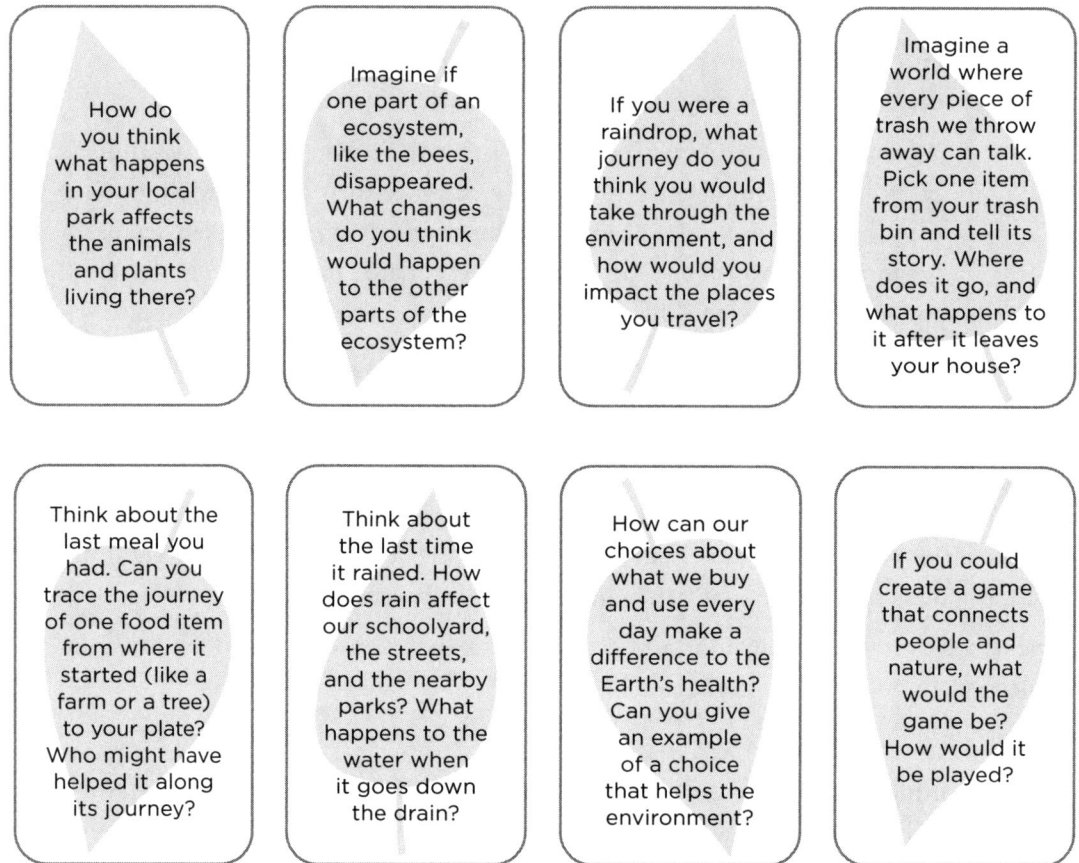

Figure 7.4: Turn-and-Talk Conversation Cards.

*Visit **go.SolutionTree.com/literacy** for a free reproducible version of this figure.*

The instructions for the Thumb-Wrestling Game, inspired by *The Climate Change Playbook* (Meadows et al., 2016), are as follows.

1. Explain to your students that they'll be doing a thumb-wrestling activity where the goal is to get the most points.

2. Have students pair up and thumb-wrestle the traditional way, trying to pin the other person's thumb as many times as possible.

3. After the round, discuss their experience. Ask questions like, "How did it feel to compete for points?" and "What was your strategy?"

4. Ask your students, "What if winning meant getting the most points together instead of pinning thumbs?" Allow them to brainstorm strategies.

5. Reorder the pairs and explain the new goal: working together to get as many points as possible.

6. Encourage students to take turns pinning each other's thumbs so both partners can score points.

7. After the second round, gather the students for a group discussion. Talk about how working together led to more points for everyone. Encourage students to share

how their strategies and thinking changed between the two rounds. Discuss how this shift from competition to cooperation can be applied to solving real-world problems, like environmental issues.

Following the game, you might ask students to reflect on how collaboration felt compared to competition, helping them connect the experience to the idea of interconnectedness in their own lives.

PReP With Three Phases

PReP (short for *Prereading Plan*; Langer, 1981) is a strategy designed to activate students' prior knowledge and scaffold their comprehension before they begin reading. The three-phase process involves brainstorming initial ideas, discussing and expanding on those ideas during reading, and refining understanding through reflection. This approach helps students build connections to the text and enhances their ability to engage critically with the material (Langer, 1981). We suggest this prereading strategy as a way for teachers to consider how much background information their students have going into a teaching unit.

We recommend using this strategy with the content in three fast-paced films by Annie Leonard: *The Story of Stuff* (Leonard, 2007), *The Story of Change* (Leonard, 2012), and *The Story of Solutions* (Leonard, 2013). In the films, Leonard talks about how the United States' consumerist system affects the Earth and how people can change it through working together, honing skills, and leading to unique, often local, solutions. Using PReP, a teacher is essentially asking students to brainstorm how the consumerist culture affects the natural world and assessing students' knowledge of how the consumerist culture affects the natural world, before watching and studying the films. This way, students will engage in systems thinking about how to begin changing the U.S. economic system, which presently has as its goal to make things faster, cheaper, and newer, into a system that makes their culture safer, healthier, and fairer.

A word of caution: These are fast-paced, information-packed films with ideas that may be new to students who presently think and live in a system that emphasizes and values faster, cheaper, newer products! If you choose to use these films in your classroom, we advise that you will probably benefit from having your class watch each of the films more than once. They are freely available on the internet, so you do not need to pay to access them.

Before beginning the PReP activity to teach these videos, you must watch the videos and decide if you want to use all three of them or to choose one or two to use with your class. The three phases of PReP as they relate to these films are as follows.

1. **Initial associations:** Say to your class, "Tell me what you think of when you hear, 'We have so much stuff and it affects the natural world.'" As the class brainstorms, write their ideas on a whiteboard.

2. **Reflections on initial associations:** Lead students to look back at each item in the brainstormed list, and ask them, "What made you think of _____?" for each item. In this way, students have a first opportunity to find associations between key concepts and their prior knowledge.

Malala's Magic Pencil
by Malala Yousafzai
(2017)

3. **Reformation of knowledge:** Ask your students, "Based on our discussion, before we watch the film (or films), do you have any new ideas about our having so much stuff and how it affects the natural world?" This phase allows students to verbalize and elaborate on connections that occurred through the discussion.

As the students brainstorm what they know about how the consumerist culture affects the natural world, listen to them to find out what knowledge each of them brings to the video *The Story of Stuff*. You can evaluate where students' responses land in three broad knowledge levels.

1. **Much prior knowledge:** Students can define and draw analogies, make conceptual links, and think categorically concerning how having so much stuff affects the natural world.

2. **Some prior knowledge:** Students can give examples and cite characteristics but may not be able to see relationships between ideas of how having so much stuff affects the natural world.

3. **Little prior knowledge:** Students respond to the PReP activity by making simple associations and misassociating ideas concerning how having so much stuff affects the natural world.

Mirror
by Jeannie
Baker (2010)

Adapted Guided Reading Procedure

We suggest that teachers also utilize an adapted version of the Guided Reading Procedure (Manzo, 1980) with Annie Leonard's films. We say *adapted* because instead of reading, students will be watching and listening to a video.

In this strategy, before having your class view *The Story of Stuff* (Leonard, 2007), direct them to watch to remember as much as they can and to take notes as they watch. Following the film, have students work in small groups to write down all that they remember from it. You can then help the whole class recognize that there is much they have not remembered or have represented incorrectly; students will usually have implicit inconsistencies that need to be corrected and further ideas that they need to consider to understand what Leonard is saying. For students to clarify these inconsistencies and gain further ideas, have the class get back into small groups and rewatch the film, starting and stopping it as needed so that they can create an outline of the ideas in *The Story of Stuff*. As they create an outline, each group may decide to develop a data chart, semantic map, or other graphic organizer. Groups then present their knowledge to the rest of the class, which leads to a class discussion of what they have learned about the U.S. economic system.

The main concepts Leonard discusses about the present economic system are the following: extraction, production, distribution, consumption, and disposal. She emphasizes the U.S. governing system of "by the people and for the people," as well as the role large corporations play in the economic system. She encourages Americans to consider how these aspects of the U.S. economy functioned fifty years ago, how they function today, and how they will function in the future.

As students watch *The Story of Stuff* a second time as a whole class, follow a similar procedure with *The Story of Change* (Leonard, 2012); that is, encourage the class to watch to remember as much as they can. Then, use the same process of having the class work in small groups to develop an outline of the content of the film.

The main idea Leonard shares in *The Story of Change* is that everyone could have less stuff and more fun with a different economic system in place. To change things, she says people first need to share a big idea for how things could be better for everyone, even if this means changing things that some people do not want to be changed. The idea is to change what the economy is prioritizing; that is, it could prioritize what is safer, healthier, and fairer. Second, people need to work together until the problem is solved. Third, they must each turn the big idea into action. Leonard asks viewers to think about what they like to do and in what ways they could contribute to the effort more personally: "How can you contribute as a changemaker?" As before, after the small groups have created outlines of the film *The Story of Change*, have the groups share their work with the whole class.

We suggest you follow a similar procedure for *The Story of Solutions* (Leonard, 2013): Before the class watches *The Story of Solutions*, tell them to remember as much as they can, and then, as before, move into small groups, with each group developing an outline of what Leonard says. Finally, each group shares its outline with the whole class, and the whole class discusses the ramifications of Leonard's ideas.

Leonard says in *The Story of Solutions* that Americans have thousands of problems to solve, and the stakes are high. She asks viewers to think about creating a new game or system where the goals are things like having better schools, better health, and more fun for everyone, rather than the current game or system, which is about having stuff that is faster, cheaper, and newer. Leonard emphasizes the importance of cooperating and sharing; she provides the acronym *GOAL* as a way to remember what viewers should want to achieve.

- *G* is for setting a *goal* that gives us power.
- *O* is for *opening* your eyes to see what is happening in the present system.
- *A* is for *accounting* for the present costs of how the system is functioning.
- *L* is for *lessening* the wealth gap.

Leonard says that if Americans use this as a guide, they can contribute to further such transformations, which are already happening all over the globe.

We set a goal of developing suggestions to support you in designing your thematic unit. The goal we set was to move your students into systems thinking, which we see as needed for a sustainable future. A way to do this is to support your students in learning from Leonard, who shares her films for anyone to use them. We hope after you immerse your students in systems thinking about what is happening in the U.S. economic system, they will reflect on the high stakes of continuing to live the same way, and they will think about how they can contribute to changing the present system.

One Turtle's Last Straw: The Real-Life Rescue That Sparked a Sea Change
by Elisa Boxer
(2022)

One Plastic Bag: Isatou Ceesay and the Recycling Women of the Gambia
by Miranda Paul
(2015)

Compare and Contrast Authors' Messages

As you dive into designing your own unit, we'd like to offer some strategies to help you explore the theme of how systems thinking changes our world and to have students compare and contrast authors' messages in texts—or in this case, digital media.

Drawing from the digital media in this unit, we have identified three related themes in the films we suggest.

1. *The Story of Stuff*: Our consumerist culture needs to change.

2. *The Story of Change*: Change must include consumer awareness *and* change in the economic system.

3. *The Story of Solutions*: Together, we can create meaningful change.

Here are other ideas for bringing texts together to consider how systems thinking changes our world.

- Encourage your students to think about how different systems—like infrastructure, natural resources, and social networks—are interconnected in the different books they read.

- Help your students identify connected ideas in the books that relate to systems thinking.

- Challenge your students to analyze how the stories they read reveal connections between consumerism, ocean pollution, and climate change. Use systems thinking to explore how these connections affect various aspects of life, such as food production, safety, and community health.

- Encourage your students to explore how different authors apply systems thinking in their stories.

Grades K–2 Consideration

The K–2 consideration we offer is a free YouTube video that is lesser known than the films in the *Story of Stuff* project. This video, "The Recycle Film," was created by Craig Matis (2023) and his preschool class in Northeast Ohio. To view the film, use the following video link: https://youtu.be/bpMsBLC_m1w.

To engage your young students, begin with a brainstorming session about what they already know about recycling and why it's important. Capture their ideas on a whiteboard. Next, have your students watch the film, and encourage them to pay close attention and remember as much as they can. After the film, ask them what they recall, and add their observations to the whiteboard.

Consider showing the video a second time, asking them to notice anything new. Finally, lead a discussion on why recycling is important and how they can contribute to this crucial effort. This strategy helps students connect what they know with what they've learned, reinforcing the importance of recycling through active participation.

Again, notice the choices Wanda made in the planning template (figure 7.5). What might you do?

Select Green Literacy Strategies

What reading, writing, and drama strategies will encourage your students to express their thoughts, analyze the issue, and explore solutions?	How can you support all your students—no matter their reading level or background—to engage deeply with the issue and build their understanding?
Reading, Writing, and Drama Strategies: Free-write PReP With Three Phases Journal	Immersive Strategies: Thumb-Wrestling Game Simulation games

See page 45 in the book for more information on selecting Green Literacy strategies.

See page 16 in the book for more information on the three cycles of comprehension.

Figure 7.5: Completed "select Green Literacy strategies" segment of the Green Literacy Thematic Unit Planning Template.

You've put a lot of time and effort into planning and teaching your thematic unit, and you've likely seen areas of growth and spots where there's room to improve. Before wrapping up this section, you might revisit chapters 3 and 4 if you need additional guidance.

PHASE 3: SHIFT

In this section, you will:

- Develop Green Literacy ideals

Now, as we transition to the final phase, you and your students will work together to develop Green Literacy ideals. This section invites you to guide students to create ideals that address the challenges and opportunities of interconnected systems, as seen in Leonard's *The Story of Stuff*. Working with your class on Green Literacy ideals will likely lead to meaningful discussions about how systems thinking changes our world. You may see your students shift their perspectives and reach shared understandings, reflecting their deep engagement with systems thinking. Through discussions, students can share ideas, find common ground, and build a shared vision.

Circle
by Jeannie
Baker
(2016)

Develop Green Literacy Ideals

Now is the time for your students to pause and reflect on the learning journey. Encourage your students to look back at their experiences and insights to see how systems thinking changes their world.

If you chose to show the films *The Story of Stuff*, *The Story of Change*, and *The Story of Solutions* and discuss them with your class, the class could come up with Green Literacy ideals such as the following.

- We need to be mindful of our connections with the living world, or else there may be unintended consequences.

- Our interconnectedness with the living world brings us joy.

- The stakes are high; we need to change our economic system.

- People, including many young people, are doing this work of changing our priorities in the economic system.

- We need to keep in mind a big goal of creating a world that is safer, healthier, and fairer.

- To do this, we need to cooperate with each other, share things as much as possible, and figure out how we can contribute to the change that is happening.

Green Literacy ideals generated by your class will be influenced by the books and media you choose, the themes you discuss, and whether you involve your students in the suggested immersive activities—in this case, the Thumb-Wrestling Game.

As we have noted, developing Green Literacy ideals is an intentional and impactful action step, one that is hard-earned and meaningful. Without this critical step, and without commitment to further or future action, the work risks losing its longevity. It is through the depth of critical thinking, the consensus-building process, and the shared ownership of Green Literacy ideals that students can ensure their learning endures and continues to inspire.

Wanda's reflections on her students and herself as they developed Green Literacy ideals appear in figure 7.6. How might you help your students reflect on their learning and create ideals?

Consider referring to chapter 2 for more guidance on creating Green Literacy ideals and to chapter 3 for how teachers and their students created them. Please refer to chapter 4 for more insights.

CONCLUSION

This chapter explored how systems thinking—rooted in interconnections and sustainability—can enrich your teaching. By engaging students in environmental complexities, you empower them to build a more sustainable world.

A Chair for My Mother
by Vera B. Williams (1982)

PHASE 3: SHIFT

Develop Green Literacy Ideals

As you work with your students to create their Green Literacy ideals, remember this is something that happens naturally during your teaching. You can plan all the other steps ahead of time, but for this last part, you'll need to pause and observe how your students respond.

Reflection 1

As you plan how to guide your students in creating their Green Literacy ideals, take a moment to think about the lessons you've already taught. How did your students respond during these activities? What really stood out to you? Write down some notes or free-write about what you noticed happening in your classroom.

> I'm still learning how to guide my students, but I've noticed they engage the most when they can make real-world connections. During a lesson on environmental impacts, they were eager to share examples from their own lives, like noticing litter in their neighborhood or changes in local parks. What stood out was their curiosity and willingness to collaborate when the topic felt relevant to them.

Reflection 2

In your free-writing, think about what stood out to you during class discussions about the books. What were some interesting things your students said about using the reading and writing strategies?

> When we watched Annie Leonard's <u>The Story of Stuff</u>, it really clicked for them—they started pointing out how the things they use every day, like water bottles or fast fashion, connect to bigger environmental impacts. What stood out was their curiosity and how they wanted to talk about solutions, like reusing items or buying less. It showed me that when the topic feels personal and relevant, they're eager to learn.

See page 47 in the book for more information on how to facilitate the Green Literacy ideals discussion.

Figure 7.6: Completed "develop Green Literacy ideals" segment of the Green Literacy Thematic Unit Planning Template.

We provided tools to design thematic units with Green Reads and Views, including immersive strategies and critical comprehension techniques to deepen systems thinking. You and your students can develop Green Literacy ideals through extended projects that connect to local landscapes and communities. Think of this chapter as an invitation to reimagine teaching, guiding students to see themselves as active participants in shaping a better future.

Now, consider how this chapter has impacted your learning as a teacher. We offer a dedicated space for you to do so in the following "Teacher's Corner" reproducible tool (also available at **go.SolutionTree.com/literacy**). Whether you're working on your own, with a teaching partner, or within a schoolwide learning network, after exploring chapter 7, we encourage you to reflect on what you've learned.

If You Plant a Seed
by Kadir Nelson
(2015)

Teacher's Corner

Here are some questions to support your reflection.

- Recall a time when you saw a student or group of students have an aha moment related to systems thinking in an environmental context. How did this impact you as an educator?

- In what ways have you observed systems thinking foster a deeper understanding of environmental issues among your students? Can you identify any changes in their behaviors or attitudes toward the environment?

Here are prompts for journaling.

- Write about a lesson or activity from this unit that engaged your students. How did it illustrate the principles of systems thinking?

- In what ways have you tailored the systems-thinking unit to address the unique needs and curiosities of your students, and what outcomes do you anticipate?

Here are discussion guidelines.

- How can your school community use systems thinking to identify and implement more sustainable practices within the school?

- How can teachers collectively continue to refine and deepen the systems-thinking unit, ensuring that it remains dynamic and responsive to evolving environmental challenges?

We Transform Futures Together

> Now let us begin. Now let us rededicate ourselves to the long and bitter, but beautiful, struggle for a new world.
>
> —MARTIN LUTHER KING JR.

Throughout *The Green Literacy Handbook*, we've guided you on a step-by-step journey to bring environmental awareness into your classroom through critical thinking, reading, and writing. Along the way, you've explored our model of teaching, learned how to integrate Green Literacy systems thinking into your teaching, and gained experience in thinking holistically, helping your students see the interconnectedness of people, nature, and the systems that shape our world. You've engaged with practical tips for Green Literacy teaching and explored content materials for teaching Green Literacy thematic units with ways to customize and design your own units. While *The Green Literacy Handbook* offers suggestions and choices for designing units and activities, it never prescribes one way forward. Instead, it provides ideas, trusting that you shape the journey to fit your own classroom and community.

At this point, you may ask, "What next?" Green Literacy centers on *meaningful* action. The reading, writing, speaking, and creating you engage in with your students represent powerful—and some might say transformative—acts of critical thinking and environmental awareness. These activities go beyond academic exercises; they lay the foundation for students to see themselves as active participants in the world around them. Developing this critical perspective is a vital step forward in a lifelong journey of understanding and advocating for the planet. We did not tie guidance for specific acts of environmental stewardship or advocacy to the chapters throughout the handbook. This was intentional. We believe that too often with teaching, there's a rush to "do something," a push toward action before laying the groundwork. While this urgency comes from a good place, it can sometimes lead to shallow efforts that don't create lasting change. We wanted to offer you and your students something deeper than rushed actions: the time and space to think critically, ask questions, and build a strong foundation together.

In your initial work with Green Literacy thematic units, you may have already noticed something powerful—conversations bring people together. Conversations give students opportunities to explore perspectives, share their ideas, and develop deeper understanding as a group. Whether through a quick think-pair-share or a class discussion, these moments create a dynamic, engaging space where learning thrives. By pausing to reflect and explore, your students can connect more authentically with environmental issues, sparking curiosity and thoughtful dialogue. Purposeful action grows from this process; in this way, the actions your students take in the future will have more relevance, impact, and sustainability than they might through a rush to act out superficial, disconnected projects.

We trust you to determine what works best for you, your students, and your school. Green Literacy offers flexibility, empowering you to reflect on your unique needs and priorities to foster authentic growth. This allows you to build on what you've started, expanding it into a lasting culture of environmental awareness and action within your community. We will say, however, the move from reflection and deepened thinking to transformative action begins with connection. You partner with environmentally aware colleagues who share your vision for a more sustainable and engaged learning environment, and you explore relevant professional development opportunities designed to equip you with practical tools, innovative strategies, and deeper insights to transform your teaching and collaboration with members of your community. The following sections offer some guidance on these modes of connection as ways forward with the work of Green Literacy.

WE TRANSFORM THE WAY FORWARD

When young people learn to think critically about environmental issues, they don't gain knowledge—they experience a transformation. This shift is both personal and systemic, reshaping how they see themselves and their place in the world. You, as their teacher, are part of this transformation, evolving alongside them as you guide them through the complexities of systems thinking and environmental awareness. It's a change that moves beyond the individual, sparking a deeper understanding of the interconnectedness of systems. The world is no longer a collection of isolated problems but a vast, dynamic network where every decision, action, and relationship holds the potential to ripple outward, influencing the whole (Gruenewald, 2004; Tilbury, 1995). This systems-change mindset empowers both you and your students to see how your choices matter and how you can all be agents of strategic, sustainable transformation.

Thomas L. Friedman (2008), an environmentalist writer and thought leader who influenced our thinking in developing Green Literacy professional development, discusses the complexity of changing people's behavior, particularly in relation to environmental issues. He argues that altering ingrained habits requires more than awareness of information; it demands a shift in attitudes, values, and societal norms. According to Friedman, studies suggest that for behavior to effectively change, people must feel a personal connection to the issue, recognize tangible benefits to their actions, and, often, be influenced by social pressures or incentives. Lasting change typically occurs when individuals understand the problem intellectually as well as feel emotionally and socially compelled to act (Friedman, 2008).

As a teacher, you've already done this important work alongside your students, guiding them toward critical thinking and environmental awareness. In the process, you may have changed as well. Perhaps your own perspective on environmental issues has deepened, or you've started to see yourself as part of the broader movement for sustainability. Recognizing and embracing your transformation are vital. Doing so underscores the power of your role as both an educator and a lifelong learner. Green Literacy has the ability to reshape how you teach, how you connect, and how you see the world.

WE TRANSFORM THROUGH COLLABORATION

While you can certainly use the handbook on your own, we believe the experience becomes much more powerful when you connect with other teachers and work as a team. Collaboration lays the groundwork for Green Literacy; it sustains and amplifies it. When you collaborate, you amplify the messages of Green Literacy by sharing ideas, solving problems, and sparking creativity. Teamwork provides a strong support network that helps you feel more confident as you navigate challenges and engage your students in meaningful environmental discussions and actions. We have found that diversity of opinions is helpful to the process and that the different opinions must be respectfully listened to and balanced in dialogues.

When teachers work in a Green Literacy team, their school administration is more likely to view their efforts favorably, recognizing both the initiative and the collective buy-in that collaboration fosters. Working together also strengthens connections and discussions with parents, expanding the reach of teachers' efforts beyond the classroom. Most importantly, a Green Literacy collaboration provides a network of support that helps you navigate the inevitable challenges that arise when addressing urgent and complex environmental issues as a teacher. As teachers work together, they have more possibility and opportunity and can more easily design initiatives that extend beyond individual classrooms, such as schoolwide sustainability projects, student-led environmental clubs, or interdisciplinary programs supported by Green Literacy. By leveraging each other's expertise and creativity, teachers build continuity in environmental education, ensuring that students engage with Green Literacy beyond a one-time lesson and toward an ongoing framework for action.

As we've emphasized throughout *The Green Literacy Handbook*, environmental topics can be met with resistance. When teachers collectively tackle these challenges in a team, they bring greater confidence, creativity, and resilience to the work, making Green Literacy efforts more impactful and sustainable. This teamwork also models for students the power of collective action, reinforcing the idea that environmental stewardship is not an individual task but a shared responsibility.

We want to help connect teachers who are using the handbook on their own. On our website, www.greenliteracy.org, we've developed resources, forums, and opportunities for educators to share their experiences, ask questions, and find encouragement as they work through *The Green Literacy Handbook*.

WE TRANSFORM THROUGH GREEN LITERACY PROFESSIONAL DEVELOPMENT

Together, through Green Literacy professional development, we can redefine what *professional development* means. This professional development aims to provide you with tools, strategies, and community support to create meaningful environmental learning experiences for your students and to spark future actions from these experiences. We strive to offer professional development that is authentic, engaging, and directly relevant to you and your school community. Whether virtual or in person, our professional development workshops and sessions provide hands-on strategies and meaningful discussions. Instead of following a generic, one-size-fits-all model, our professional development ensures that educators can connect Green Literacy principles to their unique teaching environments to foster real impact and sustainable change in classrooms and beyond. You can find Green Literacy professional development at our companion website (www.greenliteracy.org) and offerings at **go.SolutionTree.com/literacy**.

Green Literacy professional development should offer opportunities to do the following.

- **Reflect on your mindset:** This is fundamental to Green Literacy professional development. The chance to dive into your own environmental values and beliefs to align with Green Literacy principles is critical. As you reflect, you enhance your ability to model environmental stewardship and explore environmental issues with your students.

- **Develop advanced strategies:** Professional development participants gain actionable tools and techniques to guide students toward meaningful environmental actions. You learn how to design inquiry-based projects, foster critical thinking, and address real-world sustainability challenges and environmental issues.

- **Build connections with peers:** Join a network of educators to share ideas, celebrate successes, and collaborate on solutions to environmental challenges.

As you implement and refine what you learn in a Green Literacy–aligned professional development experience, you may witness profound results, like using systems thinking and Green Literacy in your daily teaching.

Teachers today face more challenges and pressures than ever before. Balancing the demands of your role with the need to create meaningful and engaging learning experiences requires thoughtful support and practical solutions. Our Green Literacy professional development, specifically, offers the fundamentals we noted as well as flexibility. We believe that Green Literacy professional development can occur in person or virtually, giving you the freedom to choose what works best. This flexibility ensures that all educators, regardless of location, have access to transformative learning opportunities.

In addition to flexibility, the best professional development offers rich learning in the moment and builds a foundation for future action. This kind of professional development builds relationships. Short-term Green Literacy professional development, lasting from a couple of hours to a couple of days or a couple of weeks of sessions, can be a great way to spark ideas and get things moving. Sometimes, it's all that the administration can offer, or all that you, as a busy teacher, have time for. Whether virtual or in person, short-term sessions can add immense value, providing focused opportunities to explore new concepts, connect with colleagues, and gain fresh insights. At Green Literacy, we recognize the importance of making the most of these sessions and ensuring they are meaningful and impactful. With short-term professional development, we prioritize follow-up and ongoing support to build relationships. As you've likely noticed in your teaching, Green Literacy is all about trust and the creation of connections. It's through these connections—among teachers, students, and the wider school community—that real change takes root and grows. How real change looks will depend on your local environment and school context.

Green Literacy professional development also leads to substantive change by serving as action research. In our professional development, we have drawn from the literature on collaborative action research, a process in which the school community (including teachers, administrators, or both) identifies a problem within the school or district, asks questions about it, collectively plans for gathering information and analyzing data, and implements the plan to address the problem (Bruce, Flynn, & Stagg-Peterson, 2011). The process is intended not to generalize findings but to solve the specific problem identified by the school community (Gordon, 2008). In the context of environmental awareness and activism, action research problems determined at the local level may include a lack of student engagement in sustainability initiatives, limited access to outdoor learning spaces, insufficient recycling and waste reduction efforts, or the need for more culturally relevant environmental education. For example, a school might identify the challenge of food waste in the cafeteria and develop a composting program, or recognize the absence of green spaces and initiate a student-led pollinator garden project. This kind of action research process typically unfolds over time, grounded in building strong partnerships between schools and educators and perhaps including universities.

Educators who join our professional development programs often come with a solid foundation in reading and writing instruction. They are skilled in fostering literacy skills, but many are new to the drama and immersive strategies and drama's potential as a teaching tool. As we collaborate with them, they discover how drama strategies can bring lessons to life, engage students in new ways, and make abstract concepts more tangible. These techniques enrich their teaching repertoire; they open doors to creativity, collaboration, and deeper student engagement. Through this process, both teachers and students benefit from a dynamic and holistic learning practice.

In sum, professional development is most transformative when it is authentic, responsive, and rooted in the needs of educators and their communities. Green Literacy reinforces this and ensures that learning remains meaningful, as it cultivates a mindset of adaptability and agency that equips educators to inspire engaged, resilient learners prepared to navigate an ever-changing world.

Collaborative Strategies to Build Green Literacy Teams Through School Professional Development Experiences

- **Green Literacy collaborative team:** Establish a collaborative team focused on integrating Green Literacy that works within the schoolwide professional learning community. Here, teachers share their experiences and strategies for incorporating Green Literacy into their teaching and fostering a culture of continuous learning, practice, and professional growth in the context of environmental sustainability. Effective professional development is critical for nurturing such communities, as it emphasizes collaborative learning sustained over time and grounded in practice (Darling-Hammond, Hyler, & Gardner, 2017).

- **Eco-friendly peer-mentoring programs:** Enhance peer-mentoring programs by pairing experienced teachers who are committed to Green Literacy with newer teachers or teachers who are seeking to infuse their teaching with Green Literacy. This mentorship can guide less experienced teachers in developing environmentally focused curricula and teaching strategies.

- **Interdisciplinary collaboration for environmental awareness:** Promote cross-grade and cross-subject collaboration emphasizing Green Literacy. This strategy encourages teachers from different grades and subjects to collaboratively create interdisciplinary learning experiences that highlight the importance of sustainability and environmental stewardship. These teachers share resources and insights to enrich the curriculum.

- **Project-based learning teams with an environmental focus:** Form project-based learning teams dedicated to designing and implementing projects that engage students in real-world environmental challenges. Through this collaboration, teachers pool their expertise to create engaging, impactful projects that educate students and instill a sense of environmental responsibility.

WE TRANSFORM THROUGH CONNECTIONS WITH COMMUNITY MEMBERS

To build strong connections for fostering Green Literacy and laying the groundwork for future actions, you must actively seek out opportunities and partnerships with members of your community, both near and far. Start by reaching out to subject-matter experts, as we discussed in chapter 4 (page 79), to deepen your knowledge and provide inspiration for your classroom. Either create a network of other educators within your school or join one of the Green Literacy communities we offer on our website. Collaborate with your school librarian, local libraries, and independent bookstores to explore programs or book clubs focused on environmental themes.

Look into local organizations in your city or town that focus on environmental awareness, such as conservation groups, botanical gardens, or environmental education centers. Parks and recreation departments, university extension programs, and sustainability-focused nonprofits often have workshops, guest speakers, or volunteer opportunities that align with your goals. Connecting with local chapters of environmental clubs, like the Sierra Club or National Audubon Society, can open doors to resources and partnerships.

For broader connections, consider joining national and global organizations dedicated to environmental education. Some great examples include the following.

- **The National Environmental Education Foundation:** Provides tools, webinars, and grants to support environmental literacy
- **EcoSchools U.S.:** Offers a program for K–12 schools to engage students in sustainability
- **The Green Schools National Network:** Focuses on transforming schools into models of sustainability and offers professional development
- **The Children & Nature Network:** Promotes initiatives to reconnect children with nature and offers tool kits and networks for educators
- **EarthDay.org:** Offers resources, tool kits, and a global network for environmental action and education
- **The Association for the Study of Literature and Environment:** Provides invaluable resources for integrating environmental themes into the humanities and offers conferences, webinars, and an extensive network of educators and scholars focused on the intersections of literature, culture, and the environment
- **The National Association for Multicultural Education:** Provides publications, professional development opportunities, and networking events as excellent resources for educators seeking to bring multicultural perspectives into classroom environmental and social justice discussions

In addition to those resources, consider online platforms to expand your network. Join groups like the National Council of Teachers of English, and participate in discussions related to incorporating environmental literacy into English curricula. Platforms like LinkedIn and Bluesky offer professional educator communities where you can use hashtags like #GreenLiteracy, #EnvironmentalEducation, or #ClimateEducation to find relevant conversations and connections.

Engaging with those communities can spark meaningful collaborations and inspire new classroom initiatives. For example, we know of a first-grade class in Illinois that connected with a second-grade class in Georgia to share nature journals, comparing the trees, animals, and weather they observed in their neighborhoods. This exchange encouraged young students to see how their local environment connects to a larger ecosystem.

We've also seen classrooms connect across countries, sharing in the joy and wonder of exploring their relationships with nature. A kindergarten class in the United States partnered with a school in Kenya to exchange drawings and stories about the plants and animals in their communities. While one class described squirrels and maple trees, the other shared stories of acacia trees and elephants. This helped students understand biodiversity through each other's eyes.

Local environmental projects can also provide powerful learning experiences. A fourth-grade class in North Carolina worked with a local conservation group to adopt a nearby creek; the class visited it regularly to observe wildlife, test water quality, and remove litter. Inspired by their work, the students wrote persuasive letters to the city council advocating for better protections for the waterway. This hands-on project reinforced science and literacy skills and also helped students see themselves as environmental advocates.

Now, imagine yourself as part of a Green Literacy community—one where educators support and inspire each other, where ideas flow freely, and where young learners develop a sense of wonder for the natural world. Picture your students participating in a virtual read-aloud with a class across the country, working on a shared recycling challenge, or exchanging letters about local conservation efforts.

These resources and ideas are a starting point. Like all the resources we offer, they are meant to head you in the right direction—*the direction you decide*. We encourage you to actively seek out what works best for you and your school community, tailoring these tools and connections to your unique needs and goals. If you're interested in joining a global network of Green Literacy educators, please contact us. We offer online training to help you get started and connect with others who share your passion for teaching environmental awareness. By building these connections and engaging with these resources, you can create a supportive community that empowers you to bring Green Literacy to life in your classroom and beyond.

FINAL THOUGHTS

As we bring this epilogue to a close, we invite you to hold fast to the truth that your role as an educator transcends sharing knowledge. It is about planting seeds of care and awakening in your students a profound and enduring love for this fragile, wondrous planet we call home. We believe with all our hearts that this work is about understanding the complexities of environmental issues and fostering a systems-thinking mindset. When we help students see the interconnectedness of people, communities, and ecosystems, we equip them to engage in challenges with empathy, creativity, and a holistic perspective. As the environmentalist Wangari Maathai once said, "You cannot protect the environment unless you empower people, you inform them, and you help them understand that these resources are their own, that they must protect them." In this spirit, may your teaching inspire and empower the next generation to care for and protect our shared home, embracing the beauty and complexity of our interconnected world.

Our hope is that *The Green Literacy Handbook* becomes a vibrant part of your teaching, fostering curiosity, inspiring critical thinking, and empowering your students to find their voices—voices that will advocate for a future that is both sustainable and just. Every green action you take matters. Each lesson you share on the environment holds the potential to spark change—change that can grow, thrive, and endure. As you explore the ideas within *The Green Literacy Handbook*, may you find fulfillment in knowing your work is an act of creation, shaping a brighter, greener world for all.

Green Literacy Thematic Unit Planning Template

This book is filled with ideas for how to use the thematic unit planning template, but as stated, we envision flexibility. You can follow along with our examples throughout the book and implement some or all of the model lessons, you can implement just the thematic questions from our model lessons and customize the template, or you can use the Green Literacy model and the planning template on page 194 to create entirely unique units to meet your students' needs. The template is meant to serve as a practical tool for whichever way you decide to use it, and it is *not* meant to bog you down with extra paperwork. It may help you streamline your process and energize you to focus on creating and teaching meaningful, engaging learning experiences.

Green Literacy Thematic Unit Planning Template

Name:

Grade level:

School context:

PHASE 1: ENGAGE

Develop Your Thematic Question

Here are some guiding questions to consider as you develop your thematic question. Reflect on these prompts to clarify your focus.

1. Brainstorm

- What issue that could lead to a big idea about the environment are you most passionate about exploring with your students?

- What current events or real-world examples resonate with you and can help bring environmental issues to life for your students?

2. Prioritize

You might have more than one environmental issue you'd like to explore with your students. Now, think about which one will create the most meaningful conversations and learning.

Through this brainstorming and prioritization process, write your thematic question. Some stems that might be useful are:

- How can/do . . . ?
- What might . . . ?

Write your thematic question here.

See page 38 in the book for more information on creating thematic questions.

Foster Your Thinking Through Commentary

First, review the following questions and respond to a few or all of them. Use a list or brainstorm freely to capture your ideas.

- Whose voices or stories do you need to hear to understand this issue, and why are they important to you?

- What unfair systems or problems do you want your students to think about when learning about this issue, and how can you help them ask questions and find ways to make things better?

- Whose experiences or ideas are sometimes left out when this issue is talked about, and how can you share those voices in your classroom to help everyone learn more?

From your responses, begin to find springboards that will help you develop commentary that deepens your thematic exploration.

Springboards to Support Commentary

- Springboard 1:
    - Title or source:
    - Key insights:

- Springboard 2:
    - Title or source:
    - Key insights:

- Springboard 3:
    - Title or source:
    - Key insights:

See page 40 in the book for more information on developing springboards for commentary.

PHASE 2: EMPOWER

Cultivate a List of Green Reads and Views

Consider the three cycles of comprehension as you choose your strategies: simple comprehension (retell and summarize), criteria comprehension (support thinking), and perspective comprehension (investigate explicit and implicit perspectives and move to systems thinking).

Select texts and digital media that flow from your thematic question and your commentary research. If you need help finding texts or digital media, consult **go.SolutionTree.com/literacy**, our companion website (www.greenliteracy.org), or your school or local librarian.

What types of texts or stories (fiction, nonfiction, poetry, or multimedia) can you use to help your students connect emotionally and critically to this environmental issue? What is the author's message?

Green Read Title:	Green Read Title:	Green Read Title:	Green Read Title:	Green Read Title:
Author's message:	Author's message:	Author's message:	Author's message:	Author's message:

Select Green Literacy Strategies

What reading, writing, and drama strategies will encourage your students to express their thoughts, analyze the issue, and explore solutions? Reading, Writing, and Drama Strategies:	How can you support all your students—no matter their reading level or background—to engage deeply with the issue and build their understanding? Immersive Strategies:

See page 45 in the book for more information on selecting Green Literacy strategies.

See page 16 in the book for more information on the three cycles of comprehension.

PHASE 3: SHIFT

Develop Green Literacy Ideals

As you work with your students to create their Green Literacy ideals, remember this is something that happens naturally during your teaching. You can plan all the other steps ahead of time, but for this last part, you'll need to pause and observe how your students respond.

Reflection 1

As you plan how to guide your students in creating their Green Literacy ideals, take a moment to think about the lessons you've already taught. How did your students respond during these activities? What really stood out to you? Write down some notes or free-write about what you noticed happening in your classroom.

Reflection 2

In your free-writing, think about what stood out to you during class discussions about the books. What were some interesting things your students said about using the reading and writing strategies?

See page 47 in the book for more information on how to facilitate the Green Literacy ideals discussion.

Choice Boards for Chapters 5–7

We created these choice boards to provide teachers with tangible examples of how to integrate environmental perspectives into student learning while honoring individuality and creativity. They are designed to inspire students to think critically, act responsibly, and connect their learning to real-world environmental challenges. They invite your students to engage profoundly with meaningful learning experiences while encouraging them to shift their perspective by exploring someone else's point of view. You can use these tools to foster empathy, critical thinking, and a richer understanding of the world around you and your students.

As you plan for implementation, consider how you might create rubrics or assessments that align with your school's culture and your unique classroom needs. Think about the ways you can adapt these tools to evaluate both the process and the outcome in a way that best supports your students' growth. Remember, there's no one-size-fits-all approach.

EXPLORING THE POWER OF LANDSCAPES: CHAPTER 5

Landscapes are more than places we see; they shape how we feel, think, and connect with the world around us. Chapter 5 (page 107) provides ideas to help your students explore how the natural world influences their lives and sparks creativity. The choice board in figure B.1 invites them to take on different roles, from an artist capturing beauty to an explorer making new discoveries. Through these creative projects and hands-on activities, your students will discover how landscapes can inspire stories, art, and a deeper understanding of the world.

Extended Learning Project	Perspective (Role)	Project Description
Picture Perfect	**Artist**	Draw a picture of your favorite landscape and write a short paragraph explaining how it makes you feel, like an artist sharing their feelings through their work.
Research Spree	**Nature detective**	Find out how landscapes make people feel, and share what you learn in a fun and creative way, like a detective solving a nature mystery.
Poetry Corner	**Poet**	Write a poem about a landscape that inspires you, focusing on the feelings it brings, like a poet turning feelings into words.
Map Quest	**Map maker**	Make up a pretend map of a new place with landmarks and explain how it might help people who live there, like a map maker building a world.
Storytelling Time	**Storyteller**	Write a short story about someone whose life is shaped by the land they live on, like a storyteller imagining adventures.
Comic Book	**Explorer**	Go for a nature walk, notice the world around you, and create a comic book about how the landscape makes you feel, like an explorer on a big adventure.
Transformative Art	**Earth helper**	Use art supplies to draw or paint how a landscape can change someone's feelings, like an Earth helper who inspires others to care about nature.
Compare and Contrast	**Global thinker**	Pick two landscapes and talk about how they are alike and different, like a big thinker who loves learning about the world.
Digital Collage	**Picture collector**	Make a digital collage of different landscapes and explain how each one makes people feel, like a collector gathering special memories.

Figure B.1: Choice board for chapter 5.

BRIDGING COMMUNITIES THROUGH EXTREME WEATHER: CHAPTER 6

Extreme weather events do more than impact our surroundings—they bring communities together in both challenges and solutions. Chapter 6 (page 133) helps your students explore the profound effects of these events by stepping into the shoes of individuals directly impacted by weather disasters. This choice board (figure B.2) offers engaging and creative activities, such as composing a song from the perspective of a climate refugee or writing a poem as an evacuee, allowing students to build empathy and explore diverse experiences. Designing maps of affected areas or creating a game to educate others invites your students to think critically about the causes of and responses to extreme weather events. These activities encourage creativity. They challenge students to analyze and address the complexities of climate change, empowering them to become thoughtful, solution-driven members of their communities.

Extended Learning Project	Perspective (Role)	Project Description
Create a Song	**Climate refugee**	Write and perform a song about how extreme weather has affected your community.
Write a Poem	**Evacuee of a natural disaster**	Write a poem that shows how extreme weather has impacted where you live.
Write a Letter	**Natural disaster relief worker**	Write a letter to a local leader asking them to help fight climate change.
Design a Map	**Climate refugee**	Make a map that shows which areas in your community have been affected.
Make a Brochure	**Community resilience meeting member**	Create a brochure to teach others about how extreme weather affects your neighborhood.
Design a Game	**Climate change scientist**	Invent a game to teach people about climate change and how it affects communities.

Figure B.2: Choice board for chapter 6.

MAKING CONNECTIONS WITH SYSTEMS THINKING: CHAPTER 7

Systems thinking helps us see how everything is connected and shapes the way we understand and interact with the world. Chapter 7 (page 159) helps students explore how these connections influence their lives and inspire creative thinking. The choice board (figure B.3) offers fun and engaging ways for students to step into different roles, like solving real-world problems or designing new ideas. Through these hands-on projects and activities, students will learn how systems thinking can spark creativity, solve challenges, and deepen their understanding of the world around them.

Extended Learning Project	Perspective (Role)	Project Description
Interconnections Poster	**Artist**	Make a colorful poster showing how people, animals, and plants are connected. Include examples of how actions like planting trees or using less water can help everything stay in balance.
Ecosystem Storytelling Challenge	**Storyteller**	Write or draw a story about how all living things depend on each other. For example, tell a story about a bee pollinating a flower or a tree providing shade for animals. Share your story with the class.
Sustainable Design Innovation	**Inventor**	Imagine and draw a new invention that could help take care of the Earth. It could be something to clean up trash, save energy, or protect animals. Write a short description of how it works.
Systems Explorer Journal	**Scientist**	Go outside and write down or draw what you see in nature. Look for connections—like how a bird uses a tree for its nest or how rain helps plants grow. Add labels to connect these relationships.
Community Habitat Plan	**Planner**	Plan a garden or park for your school or neighborhood. Draw a map showing where you'd put plants, flowers, and spaces for animals like birds or bees. Think about what those plants and animals need to survive.

Protect Habitats	Advocate	Make a poster, slideshow, or simple video to teach others why it's important to protect wildlife habitats. Include ideas like planting native flowers or recycling to help keep habitats clean and safe.
Circular Economy	Designer	Think of a product you use every day, like a juice box or toy, and come up with a way to reuse or recycle it so it doesn't become trash. Draw your idea and share how it helps nature.
Systems-Thinking Comic Strip	Visual storyteller	Create a comic strip about what happens when one part of nature changes—like when people cut down trees or build a park. In a fun and creative way, say how it affects animals, plants, and people.
Eco-Pledge Banner	Community leader	Work with your classmates to make a big banner filled with promises to help the Earth. For example, pledge to recycle, use less water, or plant trees. Hang it up for others to see and learn from.
Stuff Tracker Challenge	Consumer	Inspired by Annie Leonard's (2007) *The Story of Stuff*, track where something you use every day (like a backpack or a toy) comes from. Research or imagine its journey—how it was made, who made it, and where it might go after you're done using it. Draw a diagram to tell its "life story."
Trash-to-Treasure Challenge	Waste detective	Think about all the trash you see in a day. What could be reused, recycled, or turned into something new? Choose one type of trash (like a plastic bottle or an old T-shirt) and design a creative way to give it a new purpose. Write about how this helps reduce waste and saves resources.

Figure B.3: Choice board for chapter 7.

References and Resources

Albers, P., Harste, J. C., Vander Zanden, S., & Felderman, C. (2008). Using popular culture to promote critical literacy practices. In Y. Kim, V. Risko, D. L. Compton, D. K. Dickson, M. K. Hundley, R. T. Jimenez, et al. (Eds.), *57th yearbook of the National Reading Conference* (pp. 70–83). National Reading Conference.

Allen, M., & Phillips, M. (2022, January 24). *Using choice boards to boost student engagement.* Edutopia. Accessed at www.edutopia.org/article/using-choice-boards -boost-student-engagement on August 23, 2024.

Alvermann, D. E. (1991). The discussion web: A graphic aid for learning across the curriculum. *The Reading Teacher, 45*(2), 92–99.

Alvermann, D. E., & Moore, D. W. (1991). Secondary school reading. In R. Barr, M. L. Kamil, P. Mosenthal, & P. D. Pearson (Eds.), *Handbook of reading research* (Vol. 2, pp. 951–983). Erlbaum.

American Psychological Association. (2019, October 30). *Mindfulness meditation.* Accessed at www.apa.org/topics/mindfulness/meditation on March 24, 2025.

Anganuzzi, C. (2024). *The ocean gardener* (C. Anganuzzi, Illus.). Tiger Tales.

Applegate, K. (2020). *The one and only Bob* (P. Castelao, Illus.). Harper.

Archer, M. (2021). *Wonder walkers* (M. Archer, Illus.). Nancy Paulsen Books.

Arnold, M. D. (2000). *The bravest of us all* (B. Sneed, Illus.). Dial Books for Young Readers.

Ashman, L. (2020). *When the storm comes* (T. Yoo, Illus.). Nancy Paulsen Books.

Baker, J. (1987). *Where the forest meets the sea* (J. Baker, Illus.). Greenwillow Books.

Baker, J. (2010). *Mirror* (J. Baker, Illus.). Candlewick Press.

Baker, J. (2016). *Circle* (J. Baker, Illus.). Candlewick Press.

Bang, M. (1997). *Common ground: The water, earth, and air we share* (M. Bang, Illus.). Blue Sky Press.

Bash, B. (1989). *Tree of life: The world of the African baobab* (B. Bash, Illus.). Sierra Club Books.

Bauer, M. D. (2007). *A mama for Owen* (J. Butler, Illus.). Simon & Schuster Books for Young Readers.

Bauer, M. D. (2017). *Winter dance* (R. Jones, Illus.). Houghton Mifflin Harcourt.

Beaty, A. (2016). *Ada Twist, scientist* (D. Roberts, Illus.). Abrams Books for Young Readers.

Behar, R. (2017). *Lucky broken girl* (R. Behar, Illus.). Nancy Paulsen Books.

Berthold, P. (2001). *Bird migration: A general survey* (2nd ed.). Oxford University Press.

Bildner, P. (2015). *Marvelous Cornelius: Hurricane Katrina and the spirit of New Orleans* (J. Parra, Illus.). Chronicle Books.

Biswas-Diener, R. (2012). *The courage quotient: How science can make you braver.* Jossey-Bass.

Borovoy, A. E. (2012, April 6). *5-minute film festival: School gardens* [Blog post]. Accessed at www.edutopia.org/blog/film-festival-school-gardens on March 20, 2025.

Boxer, E. (2022). *One turtle's last straw: The real-life rescue that sparked a sea change* (M. Á. Miguéns, Illus.). Crown Books for Young Readers.

BrainPOP. (2024). *Biofuels.* Accessed at www.brainpop.com/science/energy/biofuels on July 22, 2024.

Breitrose, P. (2013). *Mousemobile* (S. Yue, Illus.). Disney-Hyperion Books.

Brown, M. (2007). *Butterflies on Carmen Street* (A. Ward, Illus.). Piñata Books.

Brown, P. (2009). *The curious garden* (P. Brown, Illus.). Little, Brown.

Bruce, C. D., Flynn, T., & Stagg-Peterson, S. (2011). Examining what we mean by collaboration in collaborative action research: A cross-case analysis. *Educational Action Research, 19*(4), 433–452.

Burnett, F. H. (1911). *The secret garden.* Lippincott.

Bush, E. (2020). *Our House Is on Fire: Greta Thunberg's Call to Save the Planet* by Jeanette Winter (review). *Bulletin of the Center for Children's Books, 73*(6), 282. https://doi.org/10.1353/bcc.2020.0146

California Academy of Sciences. (n.d.). *Cornucopia: A free environmental simulation game* [Simulation game]. PBS LearningMedia. Accessed at https://pbslearningmedia.org/resource/cornucopia/educational-games on March 24, 2025.

Calkins, L., Ehrenworth, M., & Lehman, C. (2012). *Pathways to the Common Core: Accelerating achievement.* Heinemann.

Cañas, D. (2022). *Memories of a birch tree* (B. Millán, Illus.). Cuento de Luz.

Capra, F. (1996). *The web of life: A new scientific understanding of living systems.* Anchor Books.

Capra, F., & Luisi, P. L. (2014). *The systems view of life: A unifying vision.* Cambridge University Press.

Carson, R. (1962). *Silent spring.* Houghton Mifflin.

Cazden, C. B. (2001). *Classroom discourse: The language of teaching and learning* (2nd ed.). Heinemann.

CBC News. (2023, August 14). *Youth win Montana climate lawsuit, hailed as a 'game-changer'* [Video file]. Accessed at www.youtube.com/watch?v=ZPXYkW_mNfE on March 20, 2025.

Cherry, L. (1990). *The great kapok tree: A tale of the Amazon rain forest* (L. Cherry, Illus.). Harcourt Brace Jovanovich.

Cherry, L. (1992). *A river ran wild: An environmental history* (L. Cherry, Illus.). Harcourt Brace Jovanovich.

Cherry, L. (2004). *The sea, the storm, and the mangrove tangle* (L. Cherry, Illus.). Farrar Straus Giroux.

Clayton, S., Manning, C., Krygsman, K., & Speiser, M. (2017, March). *Mental health and our changing climate: Impacts, implications, and guidance.* American Psychological Association & ecoAmerica. Accessed at www.apa.org/news/press/releases/2017/03 /mental-health-climate.pdf on August 23, 2024.

Climate Central. (2020, February 10). *Decades of disaster data: Local and national.* Accessed at www.climatecentral.org/climate-matters/decades-of-disaster-data on July 22, 2025.

Climate Interactive. (n.d.). *The C-ROADS Climate Change Policy Simulator.* Accessed at www.climateinteractive.org/c-roads on August 23, 2024.

Climate Interactive, MIT Sloan Sustainability Initiative, & UMass Lowell Climate Change Initiative. (n.d.). *World climate simulation.* Accessed at www.climateinteractive.org/world -climate-simulation on March 24, 2025.

Clinton, C. (2019). *Don't let them disappear: 12 endangered species across the globe* (G. Marino, Illus.). Philomel Books.

Cole, H. (2007). *On Meadowview Street* (H. Cole, Illus.). Greenwillow Books.

Cole, K. (2001). *No bad news.* Whitman.

Coleman, D., & Pimentel, S. (2012, April 12). *Revised publishers' criteria for the Common Core State Standards in English language arts and literacy, grades K–2.* National Governors Association, Council of Chief State School Officers, Achieve, Council of the Great City Schools, & National Association of State Boards of Education. Accessed at www.thecorestandards.org/wp-content/uploads/Publishers_Criteria_for_Literacy _for_Grades_K-2.pdf on August 22, 2024.

Conway, D. (2008). *Lila and the secret of rain* (J. Daly, Illus.). Frances Lincoln Children's Books.

Costa, A. L., & Kallick, B. (Eds.). (2008). *Learning and leading with habits of mind: 16 essential characteristics for success.* ASCD.

Cousteau, P., & Hopkinson, D. (2016). *Follow the moon home: A tale of one idea, twenty kids, and a hundred sea turtles* (M. So, Illus.). Chronicle Books.

Crafton, L. K., Brennan, M., & Silvers, P. (2007). Critical inquiry and multiliteracies in a first-grade classroom. *Language Arts, 84*(6), 510–518.

Crawford, A. (2023). *A wild promise: An illustrated celebration of the Endangered Species Act* (A. Crawford, Illus.). Tin House.

Daniels, H. (1994). *Literature circles: Voice and choice in book clubs and reading groups.* Stenhouse.

D'Aquino, A. (2022). *She heard the birds: The story of Florence Merriam Bailey* (A. D'Aquino, Illus.). Princeton Architectural Press.

Darling-Hammond, L. (2005). Teaching as a profession: Lessons in teacher preparation and professional development. *Phi Delta Kappan, 87*(3), 237–240.

Darling-Hammond, L., Hyler, M. E., & Gardner, M. (2017, June). *Effective teacher professional development.* Learning Policy Institute. Accessed at https://learning policyinstitute.org/media/476/download?inline&file=Effective_Teacher_Professional _Development_REPORT.pdf on August 26, 2024.

Davies, N. (2018). *The day war came* (R. Cobb, Illus.). Candlewick Press.

Davies, N. (2020). *Last: The story of a white rhino* (N. Davies, Illus.). Tiny Owl.

Dek, M. (2017). *A walk in the forest* (M. Dek, Illus.). Princeton Architectural Press.

Dennis, G., & Walter, E. (1995). The effects of repeated read-alouds on story comprehension as assessed through story retellings. *Reading Improvement, 32*(3), 140–153.

DiSalvo-Ryan, D. (1994). *City green* (D. DiSalvo-Ryan, Illus.). Morrow Junior Books.

Dorros, A. (1991). *Follow the water from brook to ocean* (A. Dorros, Illus.). HarperCollins.

Dosch, M., & Zidon, M. (2014). "The course fit us": Differentiated instruction in the college classroom. *International Journal of Teaching and Learning in Higher Education, 26*(3), 343–357.

Dr. Seuss. (1961). *The sneetches and other stories*. Random House Books for Young Readers.

Dr. Seuss. (1971). *The Lorax*. Random House.

Ecosystem Simulator. (n.d.). *Ecosystem simulator* [Simulation game]. Accessed at https://ecosimulator.netlify.app on August 23, 2024.

Eeds, M., & Wells, D. (1989). Grand conversations: An exploration of meaning construction in literature study groups. *Research in the Teaching of English, 23*(1), 4–29.

Electronic Arts. (2013). *SimCity* [Simulation game]. Maxis.

Elias, M. J., Zins, J. E., Weissberg, R. P., Frey, K. S., Greenberg, M. T., Haynes, N. M., et al. (1997). *Promoting social and emotional learning: Guidelines for educators*. ASCD.

Ellen MacArthur Foundation. (n.d.). *What is a circular economy?* Accessed at www.ellen macarthurfoundation.org/topics/circular-economy-introduction/overview on August 23, 2024.

Ellis, C. (2015). *Home* (C. Ellis, Illus.). Candlewick Press.

Epstein, T. (2019, August 27). *Creating choice boards to meet the needs of every student*. Accessed at https://achievethecore.org/peersandpedagogy/creating-choice-boards-mee -needs-every-student on August 23, 2024.

Etim, J. E. (2005). *Curriculum integration K–12: Theory and practice*. Bloomsbury Academic.

Facklam, M. (1990). *And then there was one: The mysteries of extinction* (P. Johnson, Illus.). Sierra Club Books.

Farrell, A. (2019). *The hike* (A. Farrell, Illus.). Chronicle Books.

Field Day Learning Games. (2022, January 17). *Wind simulator game* [Simulation game]. Oregon Climate Education. Accessed at https://oregonclimateeducation.org/external -resources/wind-simulator-game on March 24, 2025.

Fischetti, T. (2015). *Data analysis with R: Load, wrangle, and analyze your data using the world's most powerful statistical programming language*. Packt.

Fisher, D., & Frey, N. (2014). *Better learning through structured teaching: A framework for the gradual release of responsibility* (2nd ed.). ASCD.

Fisher, D., Frey, N., & Hattie, J. (2016). *Visible learning for literacy, grades K–12: Implementing the practices that work best to accelerate student learning*. Corwin Press.

Fleischman, P. (1997). *Seedfolks* (J. Pedersen, Illus.). HarperCollins.

Fleming, D. (1996). *Where once there was a wood* (D. Fleming, Illus.). Holt.

Flook, L., Smalley, S. L., Kitil, M. J., Galla, B. M., Kaiser-Greenland, S., Locke, J., et al. (2010). Effects of mindful awareness practices on executive functions in elementary school children. *Journal of Applied School Psychology, 26*(1), 70–95. https://doi.org /10.1080/15377900903379125

Fossey, D. (1983). *Gorillas in the mist*. Houghton Mifflin.

Freebody, P., & Luke, A. (1990). Literacies programs: Debates and demands in cultural context. *Prospect: An Australian Journal of TESOL, 5*(3), 7–16.

Freire, P. (1970). *Pedagogy of the oppressed* (M. B. Ramos, Trans.). Continuum.

Friedman, L. (2010). *Mallory goes green!* (J. Kalis, Illus.). Darby Creek.

Friedman, T. L. (2008). *Hot, flat, and crowded: Why we need a green revolution—and how it can renew America.* Farrar, Straus and Giroux.

Friends of Attention. (2019, August). *Twelve theses on attention.* Accessed at https://friends ofattention.net/sites/default/files/2020-05/TWELVE-THESES-ON-ATTENTION -2019.pdf on March 24, 2025.

Fuhrman, C. (2021, October 7). A poem to acknowledge that the land itself—along with the people whose language, culture, and religion were born of it—is rarely acknowledged. *Inlander.* Accessed at www.inlander.com/comment/a-poem-to -acknowledge-that-the-land-itself-along-with-the-people-whose-language-culture -and-religion-were-born-of-it-is-rarely-acknowledg-22469536 on July 16, 2024.

Fun World For Kids. (2021, July 30). *How to take care of the environment—Save environment (Learning videos for kids)* [Video file]. Accessed at www.youtube.com/watch?v=belXC _IoW4o on March 21, 2025.

Gall, C. (2013). *Awesome Dawson.* Little, Brown.

Garet, M. S., Porter, A. C., Desimone, L., Birman, B. F., & Yoon, K. S. (2001). What makes professional development effective? Results from a national sample of teachers. *American Educational Research Journal, 38*(4), 915–945.

Gee, J. P. (1996). *Social linguistics and literacies: Ideology in discourses* (2nd ed.). Taylor & Francis.

Geldard, R. (2023, October 5). *Here's how extreme weather is affecting animal migration.* Accessed at www.weforum.org/stories/2023/10/climate-crisis-impacting-animal -migration on March 21, 2025.

Gewertz, C. (2012, April 24). Common standards ignite debate over prereading. *Education Week.* Accessed at www.edweek.org/teaching-learning/common-standards -ignite-debate-over-prereading/2012/04 on August 26, 2024.

Ginsburg, K. R. (2011). *Building resilience in children and teens: Giving kids roots and wings* (2nd ed.). American Academy of Pediatrics.

Godsey, M. (2018). *Not for me, please! I choose to act green* (C. J. Kellner, Illus.). CreateSpace.

Goore, N. (n.d.). *Games to foster systems thinking.* Accessed at www.mkthink.com/post /gaming-systems-thinking-using-games-to-foster-systems-thinking on August 23, 2024.

Gordon, S. P. (Ed.). (2008). *Collaborative action research: Developing professional learning communities.* Teachers College Press.

Gove, M. K., & Kennedy-Calloway, C. (1992). Action research: Empowering teachers to work with at-risk students. *Journal of Reading, 35*(7), 526–535.

Green, J. (2019). *The magic & mystery of trees* (C. McElfatrick, Illus.). DK Children.

Green, M. (2012). Place, sustainability and literacy in environmental education: Frameworks for teaching and learning. *Review of International Geographical Education Online, 2*(3), 326–346.

Greenberg, M. T., & Harris, A. R. (2012). Nurturing mindfulness in children and youth: Current state of research. *Child Development Perspectives, 6*(2), 161–166. https://doi .org/10.1111/j.1750-8606.2011.00215.x

Greene, C. (1991). *The old ladies who liked cats* (L. Krupinski, Illus.). HarperCollins.

Gruenewald, D. A. (2003). The best of both worlds: A critical pedagogy of place. *Educational Researcher, 32*(4), 3–12. https://doi.org/10.3102/0013189X032004003

Gruenewald, D. A. (2004). A Foucauldian analysis of environmental education: Toward the socioecological challenge of the Earth Charter. *Curriculum Inquiry, 34*(1), 71–107.

Hamalainen, K. (2020). *Extreme weather and rising seas: Understanding climate change.* Scholastic.

Hannah, L., Midgley, G. F., & Millar, D. (2007). Climate change-integrated conservation strategies. *Global Ecology and Biogeography, 11*(6), 485–495. https://doi.org/10.1046/j.1466-822X.2002.00306.x

Hardin, G. (1968). The tragedy of the commons. *Science, 162*(3859), 1243–1248.

Harjo, J. (2023). *Remember* (M. Goade, Illus.). Random House.

Harper, J. (2006). *All the way to the ocean* (M. Spusta, Illus.). Freedom Three.

Harris, S. (2021). *Have you ever seen a flower?* (S. Harris, Illus.). Chronicle Books.

Heberlein, T. A. (2012). *Navigating environmental attitudes.* Oxford University Press.

Herrington, A., & Herrington, J. (Eds.). (2006). *Authentic learning environments in higher education.* Information Science.

Hest, A. (2007). *Remembering Mrs. Rossi* (H. Maione, Illus.). Candlewick Press.

Hickey, W. S. (2010). Meditation as medicine. A critique. *CrossCurrents, 60*(2), 168–184.

Hickman, C., Marks, E., Pihkala, P., Clayton, S., Lewandowski, R. E., Mayall, E. E., et al. (2021). Climate anxiety in children and young people and their beliefs about government responses to climate change: A global survey. *The Lancet Planetary Health, 5*(12), e863–e873. https://doi.org/10.1016/S2542-5196(21)00278-3

Hoffman, J. L. (2011). Coconstructing meaning: Interactive literacy discussions in kindergarten read-alouds. *The Reading Teacher, 65*(3), 183–194.

Hoffman, J. V., Roser, N. L., & Battle, J. (1993). Reading aloud in classrooms: From the modal toward a "model." *The Reading Teacher, 46*(6), 496–503.

Hoffman, M. L. (1979). Development of moral thought, feeling, and behavior. *American Psychologist, 34*(10), 958–966.

Honders, C. (2018). *Chasing extreme weather.* PowerKids Press.

hooks, b. (2009). *Belonging: A culture of place.* Routledge.

Hopkins, H. J. (2013). *The tree lady: The true story of how one tree-loving woman changed a city forever* (J. McElmurry, Illus.). Beach Lane Books.

Horst, M. T. (2021). *Palm trees at the North Pole: The hot truth about climate change* (W. Panders, Illus.). Greystone Kids.

Hunter, J. (2011, March). *Teaching with the World Peace Game* [Video file]. TED Conferences. Accessed at www.ted.com/talks/john_hunter_teaching_with_the_world_peace_game on August 23, 2024.

Hunter, J. (2013). *World peace and other 4th-grade achievements.* Houghton Mifflin Harcourt.

Husgafvel, V. (2016). On the Buddhist roots of contemporary non-religious mindfulness practice: Moving beyond sectarian and essentialist approaches. *Temenos: Nordic Journal of Comparative Religion, 52*(1), 87–126.

Illinois Extension. (n.d.). *Web of life.* Accessed at https://extension.illinois.edu/natural -resources/web-life on August 23, 2024.

Intergovernmental Panel on Climate Change. (2019). *Special report on the ocean and cryosphere in a changing climate.* Cambridge University Press.

JASON Project, National Geographic, Ewing Marion Kauffman Foundation, & Filament Games. (2009). *Energy City* [Simulation game]. Authors.

Jeffers, O. (2017). *Here we are: Notes for living on planet Earth* (O. Jeffers, Illus.). Philomel Books.

Jenkins, M. (2011). *Can we save the tiger?* (V. White, Illus.) Candlewick Press.

Jensen, E. (2001). *Arts with the brain in mind.* ASCD.

Johnson, J. C. (2010). *Seeds of change: Planting a path to peace* (S. L. Sadler, Illus.). Lee & Low Books.

Johnson, J. C. (2019). *The story of environmentalist Wangari Maatha*i (S. L. Sadler, Illus.). Lee & Low Books.

Jones, S. M., & Doolittle, E. J. (2017). Social and emotional learning: Introducing the issue. *The Future of Children, 27*(1), 3–11.

Judge, L. (2021). *The wisdom of trees: How trees work together to form a natural kingdom* (L. Judge, Illus.). Roaring Brook Press.

Judson, G. (2010). *A new approach to ecological education: Engaging students' imaginations in their world.* Peter Lang.

Judson, G. (2015). *Engaging imagination in ecological education: Practical strategies for teaching.* Pacific Educational Press.

Kabat-Zinn, J. (1994). *Wherever you go, there you are: Mindfulness meditation in everyday life.* Hyperion.

Kabat-Zinn, J. (2003). Mindfulness-based interventions in context: Past, present, and future. *Clinical Psychology: Science and Practice, 10*(2), 144–156. https://doi.org /10.1093/clipsy/bpg016

Kagan, S. (1990). The structural approach to cooperative learning. *Educational Leadership, 47*(4), 12–15.

Kamkwamba, W. (2007, June). *How I built a windmill* [Video file]. TED Conferences. Accessed at www.ted.com/talks/william_kamkwamba_how_i_built_a_windmill on March 20, 2025.

Kamkwamba, W. (2009, July). *How I harnessed the wind* [Video file]. TED Conferences. Accessed at www.ted.com/talks/william_kamkwamba_how_i_harnessed_the_wind on March 20, 2025.

Kamkwamba, W., & Mealer, B. (2009). *The boy who harnessed the wind: Creating currents of electricity and hope.* William Morrow.

Keene, E. O. (2008). *To understand: New horizons in reading comprehension.* Heinemann.

Keene, E. O., & Zimmermann, S. (2007). *Mosaic of thought: The power of comprehension strategy instruction* (2nd ed.). Heinemann.

Keith, S. E., Brasier, A. R., & North, A. J. (2022). Fostering environmental stewardship through emotional connections to nature. *Journal of Environmental Education, 53*(2), 123–135.

Kimmerer, R. W. (2015). *Braiding sweetgrass: Indigenous wisdom, scientific knowledge, and the teachings of plants*. Milkweed Editions.

King, H. T. (2021). *Saving American Beach: The biography of African American environmentalist MaVynee Betsch* (E. Holmes, Illus.). G. P. Putnam's Sons Books for Young Readers.

King, K., Romero, M., Prince, K., & Swanson, J. (2020). *Looking beneath the surface: The education changemaker's guidebook to systems thinking*. KnowledgeWorks. Accessed at https://knowledgeworks.org/resources/education-changemakers-guidebook-systems -thinking on August 23, 2024.

Kintsch, W. (1998). *Comprehension: A paradigm for cognition*. Cambridge University Press.

Knapp, M. S. (1995). *Teaching for meaning in high-poverty classrooms*. Teachers College Press.

Knauer, L. (Director). (2011). *Jane's journey* [Film]. Animal Planet; CC Medien; NEOS Film; Sphinx Media.

Kübler-Ross, E. (1969). *On death and dying*. Macmillan.

Kuntz, D., & Shrodes, A. (2017). *Lost and found cat: The true story of Kunkush's incredible journey* (S. Cornelison, Illus.). Crown Books for Young Readers.

LaDuke, W. (1999). *All our relations: Native struggles for land and life*. South End Press.

Lai, B. S., & La Greca, A. (2020, August). Understanding the impacts of natural disasters on children. *Society for Research in Child Development Child Evidence Brief, 8*, 1–2. Accessed at www.srcd.org/sites/default/files/resources/FINAL_SRCDCEB-NaturalDisasters_0.pdf on August 23, 2024.

Lakoff, G. (2005). *Don't think of an elephant! Know your values and frame the debate*. Chelsea Green.

Langer, J. A. (1981). From theory to practice: A prereading plan. *Journal of Reading, 25*(2), 152–156.

Langer, J. A. (1986). *Children reading and writing: Structures and strategies*. Ablex.

Lankshear, C., & Knobel, M. (2006). *New literacies: Everyday practices and classroom learning* (2nd ed.). Open University Press.

Larkin, S. (2019). *The thing about bees: A love letter* (S. Larkin, Illus.). Readers to Eaters.

Lawlor, L. (2012). *Rachel Carson and her book that changed the world* (L. Beingessner, Illus.). Holiday House.

Layne, S. L. (2015). *In defense of read-aloud: Sustaining best practice*. Stenhouse.

Le, K. (2018). *The lonely polar bear* (K. Le, Illus.). Happy Fox Books.

Learn Bright. (2020, October 28). *What is biofuel? Biomass and biofuels for kids* [Video file]. Accessed at www.youtube.com/watch?v=ZCFByeWEZzQ on March 21, 2025.

Lebeuf, D. (2019). *My forest is green* (A. Barron, Illus.). Kids Can Press.

Lennox, S. (2013). Interactive read-alouds—An avenue for enhancing children's language for thinking and understanding: A review of recent research. *Early Childhood Education Journal, 41*(5), 381–389.

Leonard, A. (2007, December). *The story of stuff* [Video file]. Free Range Studios. Accessed at www.storyofstuff.org/movies/story-of-stuff on August 23, 2024.

Leonard, A. (2010). *The story of stuff: How our obsession with stuff is trashing the planet, our communities, and our health—and a vision for change*. Free Press.

Leonard, A. (2011). *The story of stuff: The impact of overconsumption on the planet, our communities, and our health—and how we can make it better.* Free Press.

Leonard, A. (2012, July). *The story of change* [Video file]. Free Range Studios. Accessed at www.storyofstuff.org/movies/story-of-change on August 23, 2024.

Leonard, A. (2013, October). *The story of solutions* [Video file]. Free Range Studios. Accessed at www.storyofstuff.org/movies/the-story-of-solutions on August 23, 2024.

Lewis, G. (2011). *Wild wings* (Y. Onoda, Illus.). Atheneum Books for Young Readers.

Linden, J. (2022). *Scrap metal swan: A river clean-up story* (E. Caracol, Illus.). Barefoot Books.

Lindstrom, C. (2020). *We are water protectors* (M. Goade, Illus.). Roaring Brook Press.

Long, T. W., & Gove, M. K. (2004). How engagement strategies and literature circles promote critical response in a fourth-grade, urban classroom. *The Reading Teacher, 57*(4), 350–361.

Lord, M. (2020). *The mess that we made* (J. Blattman, Illus.). Flashlight Press.

Louv, R. (2005). *Last child in the woods: Saving our children from nature-deficit disorder.* Algonquin Books of Chapel Hill.

Louv, R. (2008). *Last child in the woods: Saving our children from nature-deficit disorder* (Updated and expanded ed.). Algonquin Books of Chapel Hill.

Luke, A., Comber, B., & O'Brien, J. (1996). Critical literacies and cultural studies. In G. Bull & M. Anstey (Eds.), *The literacy lexicon* (pp. 29–44). Prentice Hall.

Luyken, C. (2021). *The tree in me* (C. Luyken, Illus.). Dial Books for Young Readers.

Lyman, F. (1981). The responsive classroom discussion: The inclusion of all students. In A. S. Anderson (Ed.), *Mainstreaming digest: A collection of faculty and student papers* (pp. 109–113). University of Maryland Press.

Lyon, G. E. (2011). *All the water in the world* (K. Tillotson, Illus.). Atheneum Books for Young Readers.

Maathai, W. (2004a). *The Green Belt Movement: Sharing the approach and the experience* (Rev. ed.). Lantern Books.

Maathai, W. (2004b, December 10). *Wangari Maathai Nobel lecture* [Speech]. Accessed at www.nobelprize.org/prizes/peace/2004/maathai/lecture on August 22, 2024.

Maathai, W. (2006). *Unbowed: A memoir.* Knopf.

Mandela, N. (1990, June 23). *Speech at Madison Park High School, Boston* [Speech]. Nelson Mandela Foundation Archive. Accessed at https://archive.nelsonmandela.org /index.php/za-com-mr-s-1569 on March 20, 2025.

Mangal, M. (2021). *Jayden's impossible garden* (K. Daley, Illus.). Free Spirit.

Manzo, A. V. (1980). The Guided Reading Procedure. In N. B. Smith & H. A. Robinson (Eds.), *Reading instruction for today's children* (pp. 87–91). Prentice Hall.

Marcinkowski, T. J. (2010). Contemporary challenges and opportunities in environmental education: Where are we headed and what deserves our attention? *The Journal of Environmental Education, 41*(1), 34–54.

Margolin, J. (2020). *Youth to power: Your voice and how to use it.* Hachette Go.

Marino, G. (2012). *Meet me at the moon* (G. Marino, Illus.). Viking Books for Young Readers.

Mark, G. (2023). *Attention span: A groundbreaking way to restore balance, happiness and productivity*. Hanover Square Press.

Martin, J. B., & Lee, J. J. (2022). *Sandor Katz and the tiny wild* (J. Wilson, Illus.). Readers to Eaters.

Martinez, M., & Roser, N. (1985). Read it again: The value of repeated readings during storytime. *The Reading Teacher, 38*(8), 782–786.

Martinez-Neal, J. (2021). *Zonia's rain forest* (J. Martinez-Neal, Illus.). Candlewick Press.

Marzano, R. J. (2007). *The art and science of teaching: A comprehensive framework for effective instruction*. ASCD.

Matis, C. (2023, November 1). *The recycle film title 02 01* [Video file]. Accessed at www .youtube.com/watch?v=bpMsBLC_m1w on August 23, 2024.

Mayer, R. E. (2009). *Multimedia learning* (2nd ed.). Cambridge University Press.

McDonnell, P. (2011). *Me . . . Jane* (P. McDonnell, Illus.). Little, Brown Books for Young Readers.

McGee, L. M. (1995). Talking about books with young children. In N. L. Roser & M. G. Martinez (Eds.), *Book talk and beyond: Children and teachers respond to literature* (pp. 105–115). International Reading Association.

McGee, L. M., & Schickedanz, J. A. (2007). Repeated interactive read-alouds in preschool and kindergarten. *The Reading Teacher, 60*(8), 742–751.

McLeman, R., & Gemenne, F. (Eds.). (2018). *Routledge handbook of environmental displacement and migration*. Routledge.

McMillan, B. (2007). *How the ladies stopped the wind* (Gunnella, Illus.). Houghton Mifflin.

Meadows, D. (2001). *Fish Banks Ltd.* [Board game]. Interactive Learning Laboratory.

Meadows, D., Sterman, J., & King, A. (n.d.). *Fishbanks: A renewable resource management simulation* [Simulation game]. MIT Sloan School of Management. Accessed at https:// forio.com/simulate/mit/fishbanks/simulation/login.html on March 20, 2025.

Meadows, D., Sweeney, L. B., & Mehers, G. M. (2016). *The climate change playbook: 22 systems thinking games for more effective communication about climate change*. Chelsea Green.

Meadows, D. H. (2008). *Thinking in systems: A primer*. Chelsea Green.

Meadows, D. H., Randers, J., & Meadows, D. (1972). *The limits to growth*. Chelsea Green.

Meadows, D. H., Randers, J., & Meadows, D. (2004). *Limits to growth: The 30-year update*. Chelsea Green.

Meiklejohn, J., Phillips, C., Freedman, M. L., Griffin, M. L., Biegel, G., Roach, A., et al. (2012). Integrating mindfulness training into K–12 education: Fostering the resilience of teachers and students. *Mindfulness, 3*(4), 291–307. https://doi .org/10.1007/s12671-012-0094-5

Messner, K. (2017). *Over and under the pond* (C. S. Neal, Illus.). Chronicle Books.

Miller, C., & Saxton, J. (2004). *Into the story: Language in action through drama*. Heinemann.

Morales, Y. (2018). *Dreamers* (Y. Morales, Illus.). Neal Porter Books.

Moser, S. C. (2007). In the long shadows of inaction: The quiet building of a climate protection movement in the United States. *Global Environmental Politics, 7*(2), 124–144.

National Geographic Society. (2023, October 19). *The influence of climate change on extreme environmental events.* Accessed at https://education.nationalgeographic.org/resource/influence-climate-change-extreme-environmental-events on March 24, 2025.

Native Governance Center. (2019, October 22). *A guide to Indigenous land acknowledgment.* Accessed at https://nativegov.org/news/a-guide-to-indigenous-land-acknowledgment on August 23, 2024.

Neelands, J., & Goode, T. (2015). *Structuring drama work* (3rd ed.). Cambridge University Press.

Nellist, G. (2020). *Little Mole finds hope* (S. Garland, Illus.). Beaming Books.

Nelson, K. (2015). *If you plant a seed* (K. Nelson, Illus.). Balzer + Bray.

Nelson, S. (2022). *A park connects us* (E. Rooney, Illus.). Owlkids Books.

Nicol, D., Thomson, A., & Breslin, C. (2014). Rethinking feedback practices in higher education: A peer review perspective. *Assessment and Evaluation in Higher Education, 39*(1), 102–122.

Noble, T. H. (2006). *The legend of Michigan* (G. van Frankenhuyzen, Illus.). Sleeping Bear Press.

Novak, J. D., & Cañas, A. J. (2008). *The theory underlying concept maps and how to construct them.* Institute for Human and Machine Cognition. Accessed at http://cmap.ihmc.us/Publications/ResearchPapers/TheoryUnderlyingConceptMaps.pdf on March 24, 2025.

Numeroff, L. J. (1985). *If you give a mouse a cookie* (F. Bond, Illus.). Harper & Row.

Oblack, R. (2019, February 6). *Back-to-school after Hurricane Katrina.* Accessed at www.thoughtco.com/backv-to-school-after-hurricane-katrina-3443854 on August 23, 2024.

O'Garden, I. (2013). *Forest, what would you like?* (P. Schories, Illus.). Holiday House.

Ojala, M. (2012). Hope and climate change: The importance of hope for environmental engagement among young people. *Environmental Education Research, 18*(5), 625–642. https://doi.org/10.1080/13504622.2011.637157

Oliver, C. (2023). *Building an orchestra of hope: How Favio Chavez taught children to make music from trash* (L. Uribe, Illus.). Eerdmans Books for Young Readers.

Orr, D. W. (2004). *Earth in mind: On education, environment, and the human prospect* (10th anniversary ed.). Island Press.

Orr, D. W. (2011). *Hope is an imperative: The essential David Orr.* Island Press.

Ouchley, A. G. (2013). *Swamper: Letters from a Louisiana swamp rabbit.* Louisiana State University Press.

Owens, J. (2022). *One winter up north* (J. Owens, Illus.). University of Minnesota Press.

Pak, K. (2016). *Goodbye summer, hello autumn* (K. Pak, Illus.). Holt.

Parry, R. (2020). *A whale of the wild* (L. Moore, Illus.). Greenwillow Books.

Paul, M. (2015). *One plastic bag: Isatou Ceesay and the recycling women of the Gambia* (E. Zunon, Illus.). Millbrook Press.

Peet, B. (1970). *The wump world* (B. Peet, Illus.). Houghton Mifflin Harcourt.

Pfaltz, K. (2002). *Lauren's story: An American dog in Paris.* J. N. Townsend.

Pfost, M., Hattie, J., Dörfler, T., & Artelt, C. (2014). Individual differences in reading development: A review of 25 years of empirical research on Matthew effects in reading. *Review of Educational Research, 84*(2), 203–244.

Phelan, M. (2009). *The storm in the barn* (M. Phelan, Illus.). Candlewick Press.

Pontius, J., & McIntosh, A. (2020). *Critical skills for environmental professionals: Putting knowledge into practice.* Springer.

Population Education. (2014, September 12). *One for all: A natural resources game* [Simulation game]. Science Friday. Accessed at www.sciencefriday.com/educational -resources/one-for-all-a-natural-resources-game on March 24, 2025.

Pozas, M., & Schneider, C. (2019). Shedding light on the convoluted terrain of differentiated instruction (DI): Proposal of a DI taxonomy for the heterogeneous classroom. *Open Education Studies, 1*(1), 73–90.

Project Learning Tree. (n.d.). *Activity: Web of life.* Accessed at www.plt.org/learn-forests /web-of-life on August 23, 2024.

Purtill, S. (2021). *The wonder of thunder: Lessons from a thunderstorm* (T. Piper, Illus.). Dunhill Clare.

Rawls, W. (1961). *Where the red fern grows.* Doubleday.

Reilly, T. (2021). *Connecting personal experiences to global environmental awareness: A framework for environmental education.* University of Wisconsin–Stevens Point.

Robinson, K., & Aronica, L. (2018). *You, your child, and school: Navigate your way to the best education.* Viking.

Robinson, K. S. (2020). *The ministry for the future.* Orbit.

Rockwell, A. (2006). *Why are the ice caps melting? The dangers of global warming* (P. Meisel, Illus.). HarperCollins.

Rosenthal, A. K. (2009). *Duck! Rabbit!* (T. Lichtenheld, Illus.). Chronicle Books.

Roth, S. L., & Trumbore, C. (2011). *The mangrove tree: Planting trees to feed families* (S. L. Roth, Illus.). Lee & Low Books.

Rusch, E. (2019a). *Glacier on the move* (A. Brereton, Illus.). West Margin Press.

Rusch, E. (2019b). *Mario and the hole in the sky: How a chemist saved our planet* (T. Martínez, Illus.). Charlesbridge.

Santoro, L. E., Chard, D. J., Howard, L., & Baker, S. K. (2008). Making the *very* most of classroom read-alouds to promote comprehension and vocabulary. *The Reading Teacher, 61*(5), 396–408. https://doi.org/10.1598/RT.61.5.4

Sayre, A. P. (2015). *Raindrops roll.* Beach Lane Books.

Sayre, A. P. (2019). *Bloom boom!* Beach Lane Books.

Scanlon, L. G. (2018). *Kate, who tamed the wind* (L. White, Illus.). Schwartz & Wade Books.

Schlechty, P. C. (2011). *Engaging students: The next level of working on the work.* Jossey-Bass.

Sensoy, O., & DiAngelo, R. (2012). *Is everyone really equal? An introduction to key concepts in social justice education.* Teachers College Press.

Shannon, P. (1990). *The struggle to continue: Progressive reading instruction in the United States.* Heinemann.

Shannon, P. (1995). *Text, lies, and videotape: Stories about life, literacy, and learning.* Heinemann.

Shareefa, M., Moosa, V., Zin, R. M., Abdullah, N. Z. M., & Jawawi, R. (2019). Teachers' perceptions on differentiated instruction: Do experience, qualification and challenges matter? *International Journal of Learning, Teaching and Educational Research, 18*(8), 214–226.

Shor, I. (1992). *Empowering education: Critical teaching for social change.* University of Chicago Press.

Shor, I., & Freire, P. (1987). What is the "dialogical method" of teaching? *Journal of Education, 169*(3), 11–31.

Short, K. G., & Harste, J. C. (1996). *Creating classrooms for authors and inquirers* (2nd ed.). Heinemann.

Shotka, J. (1960). Critical thinking in the first grade. In A. J. Mazurkiewicz (Ed.), *New perspectives in reading instruction* (pp. 297–305). Pitman.

Siddals, M. M. (2014). *Compost stew: An A to Z recipe for the earth* (A. Wolff, Illus.). Dragonfly Books.

Sidman, J. (2011). *Swirl by swirl: Spirals in nature* (B. Krommes, Illus.). Houghton Mifflin Harcourt.

Silverstein, S. (1964). *The giving tree* (S. Silverstein, Illus.). Harper & Row.

Sipe, L. R. (1998). How picture books work: A semiotically framed theory of text-picture relationships. *Children's Literature in Education, 29*(2), 97–108. https://doi.org/10.1023/A:1022459009182

Sloley, C. (2023, October 31). *Schroders steps up thematic green push with pair of new funds.* Citywire. Accessed at https://citywire.com/wealth-manager/news/schroders-steps-up-thematic-green-push-with-pair-of-new-funds/a2429338 on March 24, 2025.

Smith, A. B. (2020, January 8). *2010–2019: A landmark decade of U.S. billion-dollar weather and climate disasters* [Blog post]. Accessed at www.climate.gov/news-features/blogs/beyond-data/2010-2019-landmark-decade-us-billion-dollar-weather-and-climate on March 24, 2025.

Smith, E. E., & Kosslyn, S. M. (2007). *Cognitive psychology: Mind and brain.* Pearson.

Smith, H. (2019). *The phone booth in Mr. Hirota's garden* (R. Wada, Illus.). Orca Book.

Smith, R. L., & Katz, R. W. (2013). U.S. billion-dollar weather and climate disasters: Data sources, trends, accuracy and biases. *Natural Hazards, 67,* 387–410.

Smithsonian Science Education Center. (n.d.). *Habitats* [Simulation game]. Accessed at https://ssec.si.edu/habitats on March 24, 2025.

Sobel, D. (1996). *Beyond ecophobia: Reclaiming the heart in nature education.* Orion Society.

Sobel, D. (2008). *Childhood and nature: Design principles for educators.* Stenhouse.

Sotomayor, S. (2022). *Just help! How to build a better world* (A. Dominguez, Illus.). Philomel Books.

Stanovich, K. E. (1986). Matthew effects in reading: Some consequences of individual differences in the acquisition of literacy. *Reading Research Quarterly, 21*(4), 360–407.

Sterling, S. (2001). *Sustainable education: Re-visioning learning and change.* Green Books.

Sterman, J. D. (2000). *Business dynamics: Systems thinking and modeling for a complex world.* Irwin/McGraw-Hill.

Stern, M. J., Powell, R. B., & Hill, D. (2014). Environmental education program evaluation in the new millennium: What do we measure and what have we learned? *Environmental Education Research, 20*(5), 581–611. https://doi.org/10.1080/13504622.2013.838749

Stewart, M. (2006). *A place for butterflies* (H. Bond, Illus.). Peachtree.

Strauss, R. (2007). *One well: The story of water on Earth* (R. Woods, Illus.). Kids Can Press.

Strobel, J., Wang, J., Weber, N. R., & Dyehouse, M. (2013). The role of authenticity in design-based learning environments: The case of engineering education. *Computers and Education, 64,* 143–152.

Strother School of Radical Attention. (n.d.). *About.* Accessed at www.schoolofattention.org/about-1 on January 6, 2025.

Sweeney, L. B. (2001). *When a butterfly sneezes: A guide for helping kids explore interconnections in our world through favorite stories.* Pegasus Communications.

Tarshis, L. (2011). *I survived Hurricane Katrina, 2005* (S. Dawson, Illus.). Scholastic.

Thunberg, G. (2021). *No one is too small to make a difference.* Penguin Books.

Tilbury, D. (1995). Environmental education for sustainability: Defining the new focus of environmental education in the 1990s. *Environmental Education Research, 1*(2), 195–212. https://doi.org/10.1080/1350462950010206

Tomlinson, C. A. (2001). *How to differentiate instruction in mixed-ability classrooms* (2nd ed.). ASCD.

Tomlinson, C. A. (2015). Teaching for excellence in academically diverse classrooms. *Society, 52*(3). https://doi.org/10.1007/s12115-015-9888-0

Tomlinson, C. A. (2017). *How to differentiate instruction in academically diverse classrooms* (3rd ed.). ASCD.

Tomlinson, C. A., & Moon, T. R. (2013). *Assessment and student success in a differentiated classroom.* ASCD.

Tornio, S., & Keffer, K. (2013). *The kids' outdoor adventure book: 448 great things to do in nature before you grow up* (R. Riordan, Illus.). Falcon Guides.

Trembath, C. A. (2022). *Pass the feather: Walking Lake Erie* (D. W. Craig, Illus.). Lakeside Publishing.

Tresselt, A. (1965). *Hide and seek fog* (R. Duvoisin, Illus.). Lothrop, Lee & Shepard.

Tuan, Y.-F. (1977). *Space and place: The perspective of experience.* University of Minnesota Press.

Tullis, J. G., & Goldstone, R. L. (2020). Why does peer instruction benefit student learning? *Cognitive Research: Principles and Implications, 5,* Article 15.

Turner, S., Lamb, R., & Mazur, A. (2018). Serious games to enrich the learning experience. *International Journal of Educational Technology in Higher Education.*

UNESCO. (1977, October). *Intergovernmental Conference on Environmental Education: Final report.* Accessed at https://unesdoc.unesco.org/ark:/48223/pf0000032763 on March 24, 2025.

UNICEF. (2014, April). *Early childhood development in emergencies: Integrated programme guide.* Accessed at www.unicef.org/documents/early-childhood-development-emergencies-integrated-programme-guide on July 21, 2025.

Urhahne, D., & Wijnia, L. (2023). Theories of motivation in education: An integrative framework. *Educational Psychology Review, 35*(2), Article 45.

U.S. Environmental Protection Agency. (2013, May 13). *Environmental justice-related terms as defined across the PSC agencies.* Accessed at www.epa.gov/sites/default/files/2015-02 /documents/team-ej-lexicon.pdf on March 24, 2025.

U.S. Environmental Protection Agency. (2025a, March 25). *Climate change and children's health.* Accessed at www.epa.gov/climateimpacts/climate-change-and-childrens -health on April 30, 2025.

U.S. Environmental Protection Agency. (2025b, March 3). *Climate change impacts on health.* Accessed at www.epa.gov/climateimpacts/climate-change-impacts-health on August 24, 2024.

Vacca, J. L., Vacca, R. T., Gove, M. K., Burkey, L., Lenhart, L. A., & McKeon, C. A. (2003). *Reading and learning to read* (5th ed.). Allyn & Bacon.

Vacca, J. L., Vacca, R. T., Gove, M. K., Burkey, L., Lenhart, L. A., & McKeon, C. A. (2011). *Reading and learning to read* (8th ed.). Pearson.

Valencia, S. W., & Wixson, K. K. (2001). Inside English/language arts standards: What's in a grade? *Reading Research Quarterly, 36*(2), 202–217.

van den Broek, P., & Espin, C. A. (2012). Connecting cognitive theory and assessment: Measuring individual differences in reading comprehension. *School Psychology Review, 41*(3), 315–325.

Vasquez, V. (2010). *Getting beyond "I like the book": Creating spaces for critical literacy in K–6 classrooms* (2nd ed.). International Reading Association.

Vasquez, V., Tate, S. L., & Harste, J. C. (2013). *Negotiating critical literacies with teachers: Theoretical foundations and pedagogical resources for pre-service and in-service contexts.* Routledge.

Verde, S. (2016). *The water princess* (P. H. Reynolds, Illus.). G. P. Putnam's Sons Books for Young Readers.

Villa, A. F. (2013). *Flood* (A. F. Villa, Illus.). Picture Window Books.

Wallace, S. N. (2020). *Marjory saves the Everglades: The story of Marjory Stoneman Douglas* (R. Gibbon, Illus.). Simon & Schuster Books for Young Readers.

Wasik, B. A., & Bond, M. A. (2001). Beyond the pages of a book: Interactive book reading and language development in preschool classrooms. *Journal of Educational Psychology, 93*(2), 243–250.

Weissberg, R. P. (2019). Promoting the social and emotional learning of millions of school children. *Perspectives on Psychological Science, 14*(1), 65–69.

Wheatley, M. J. (2002). *Turning to one another: Simple conversations to restore hope to the future.* Berrett-Koehler.

Wiesner, D. (2008). *Hurricane* (D. Wiesner, Illus.). Clarion Books.

Williams, L. (2017). *If sharks disappeared* (L. Williams, Illus.). Roaring Brook Press.

Williams, L. (2018). *If polar bears disappeared* (L. Williams, Illus.). Roaring Brook Press.

Williams, L. (2021). *If bees disappeared* (L. Williams, Illus.). Roaring Brook Press.

Williams, M. (2005). *Brothers in hope: The story of the Lost Boys of Sudan* (R. G. Christie, Illus.). Lee & Low Books.

Williams, V. B. (1982). *A chair for my mother* (V. B. Williams, Illus.). HarperCollins.

Winter, J. (2008). *Wangari's trees of peace: A true story from Africa* (J. Winter, Illus.). Harcourt.

Winter, J. (2020). *Our house is on fire: Greta Thunberg's call to save the planet* (J. Winter, Illus.). Beach Lane Books.

Wolfson, J. (2006). *Home, and other big, fat lies.* Holt.

Wong, H. K., & Wong, R. T. (2009). *The first days of school: How to be an effective teacher.* Wong.

World Wildlife Fund. (2015, Fall). Animals affected by climate change. *World Wildlife Magazine.* Accessed at www.worldwildlife.org/magazine/issues/fall-2015/articles/animals-affected-by-climate-change on August 23, 2024.

Yamada, K. (2016). *What do you do with a problem?* (M. Besom, Illus.). Compendium.

Yamada, K. (2020). *Trying* (E. Hurst, Illus.). Compendium.

Yolen, J. (1992). *Letting Swift River go* (B. Cooney, Illus.). Little, Brown.

Yolen, J., & Stemple, H. E. Y. (2020). *I am the storm* (K. Howdeshell & K. Howdeshell, Illus.). Rise x Penguin Workshop.

Young, E. (2016). *The cat from Hunger Mountain* (E. Young, Illus.). Philomel Books.

Young, K. R. (2022). *Antarctica: The melting continent* (A. Hsieh, Illus.). What on Earth Books.

Yousafzai, M. (2017). *Malala's magic pencil* (Kerascoët, Illus.). Little, Brown.

Zenner, C., Herrnleben-Kurz, S., & Walach, H. (2014). Mindfulness-based interventions in schools: A systematic review and meta-analysis. *Frontiers in Psychology, 5,* Article 603. https://doi.org/10.3389/fpsyg.2014.00603

Index

Place-Based Learning
Micki Evans, Charity Marcella Moran, and Erin Sanchez
Understand the impact a sense of place has on education, culture, and community. The authors share seven place-based learning design principles and how to smoothly implement place-based learning projects using their project-planning tool, community asset map, and other resources.
BKG106

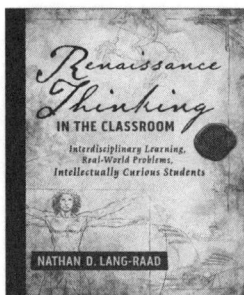

Renaissance Thinking in the Classroom
Nathan D. Lang-Raad
In this book, Nathan D. Lang-Raad details nine specific habits of thinking and a challenge-based framework that educators should systematically integrate to promote students' academic knowledge and lifelong learning. Using this guide, teachers can design lessons that foster necessary behaviors.
BKG127

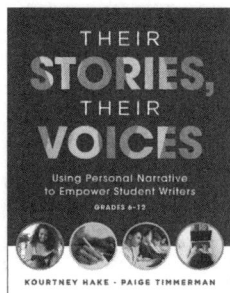

Their Stories, Their Voices
Kourtney Hake and Paige Timmerman
Kourtney Hake and Paige Timmerman share a step-by-step, build-your-own framework that helps students excel in writing and life, showing how personal narrative harnesses students' natural urge to tell stories.
BKG173

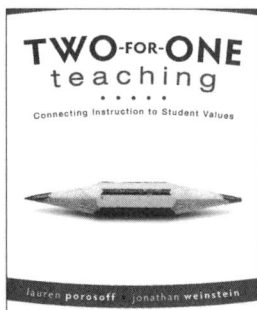

Two-for-One Teaching
Lauren Porosoff and Jonathan Weinstein
Embed student-centered, equity-driven social-emotional learning into every stage of an academic unit. *Two-for-One Teaching* offers 30 protocols that transform lessons, assignments, and assessments into opportunities for students to explore and enact the values they want to bring to their work, relationships, and lives.
BKF923

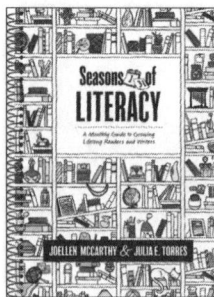

Seasons of Literacy
JoEllen McCarthy and Julia E. Torres
This monthly planning guide equips teachers, principals, instructional coaches, librarians, and district leaders with impactful classroom and individual literacy activities. Featuring themes like belonging, curiosity, and renewal, it offers tools to improve and inspire practice and long-lasting engagement.
BKG227

Solution Tree | Press   a division of ▲ Solution Tree

Visit **SolutionTree.com** or call 800.733.6786 to order.